PENGUIN CLASSICS

A VINDICATION OF THE
RIGHTS OF WOMAN

MARY WOLLSTONECRAFT (1759–97) was an educationalist and miscellaneous writer. She worked at a school at Newington with her sister, and as a governess with Lord Kingsborough. Then she made her living by writing, as a translator, and as a reader for Johnson, a London publisher. She was a member of a group of Radicals which included William Godwin, Tom Paine, Joseph Priestley and Henry Fuseli, the painter. Godwin lived with her following her attempted suicide at Putney Bridge, after she had been deserted by her lover. He married her shortly before the birth (which proved fatal) of her daughter, the Mary Wollstonecraft Godwin who became Shelley's second wife and wrote *Frankenstein*.

MIRIAM BRODY was educated at the University of Pennsylvania and Cornell University. Her research and writing have been about gender and language, most notably in *Manly Writing: Rhetoric, Gender, and the Rise of Composition* (1993), a historical study of advice to writers. Her contribution to Wollstonecraft scholarship has included studies of Wollstonecraft's attitudes towards romantic love and analysis of the rhetorical strategy of *A Vindication of the Rights of Woman*. Miriam Brody has written biographies of Mary Wollstonecraft and the nineteenth-century American reformer Victoria Woodhull (2000 and 2003). She lives in Ithaca, New York.

MARY WOLLSTONECRAFT

A Vindication of the Rights of Woman

REVISED EDITION

Edited with an Introduction and Notes by
MIRIAM BRODY

PENGUIN BOOKS

PENGUIN BOOKS

Published by the Penguin Group
Penguin Books Ltd, 80 Strand, London WC2R 0RL, England
Penguin Group (USA) Inc., 375 Hudson Street, New York, New York 10014, USA
Penguin Books Australia Ltd, 250 Camberwell Road, Camberwell, Victoria 3124, Australia
Penguin Books Canada Ltd, 10 Alcorn Avenue, Toronto, Ontario, Canada M4V 3B2
Penguin Books India (P) Ltd, 11 Community Centre, Panchsheel Park, New Delhi – 110 017, India
Penguin Group (NZ), cnr Airborne and Rosedale Roads, Albany, Auckland 1310, New Zealand
Penguin Books (South Africa) (Pty) Ltd, 24 Sturdee Avenue, Rosebank 2196, South Africa

Penguin Books Ltd, Registered Offices: 80 Strand, London WC2R 0RL, England

www.penguin.com

First published 1792
Published in Pelican Books 1975
Reprinted in the Penguin English Library 1982
Reprinted in Penguin Classics 1985
Reprinted with a revised introduction 1992
Reprinted with new notes 1992
Revised edition 2004

19 21 23 25 24 22 20

Introduction and notes copyright © Miriam Brody, 1992, 2004
All rights reserved

ISBN-13: 978-0-141-44125-2
Set in Sabon

Except in the United States of America, this book is sold subject to the condition
that it shall not, by way of trade or otherwise, be lent, resold, hired out, or otherwise
circulated without the publisher's prior consent in any form of binding or cover other
than that in which it is published and without a similar condition including
this condition being imposed on the subsequent purchaser.

The scanning, uploading, and distribution of this book via the Internet or via any other means
without the permission of the publisher is illegal and punishable by law. Please purchase only
authorized electronic editions and do not participate in or encourage electronic piracy
of copyrightable materials. Your support of the author's rights is appreciated.

ALWAYS LEARNING   PEARSON

Contents

Chronology

1759 27 April   Born in the silk-weaving London neighbourhood of Spitalsfield to Edward and Elizabeth Dickson Wollstonecraft, their second child and first daughter

1768 After unsuccessful efforts at gentleman farming in Epping and Barking, Edward Wollstonecraft moves his family to Beverley in Yorkshire, which Mary will regard nostalgically as her childhood home

1775 Family moves to Hoxton near London where Mary meets Fanny Blood, her important girlhood friend, with whom she corresponds

1776 Family moves to Laugharne, a small town in Wales by the sea

1777 Family returns to London; resumes friendship with Fanny Blood

1778 Moves to Bath as companion to Mrs Dawson

1780 Returns to London to nurse her mother, ill with dropsy

1782 Mother dies; family breaks apart; Mary lives with Fanny Blood's family, whom she helps to support with needlework

1784 Helps unhappy sister Eliza Wollstonecraft Bishop escape from marriage; with Eliza, their sister Everina and Fanny Blood establishes school at Newington Green, a centre of intellectual, dissenting community of writers and reformers in London; meets Dr Richard Price, Dissenting minister and reformer

1785 Travels to Lisbon, Portugal, to attend to Fanny Blood Skeys in childbirth; Fanny dies; Mary returns to London and breaks up her school, which had been losing students

1786 Meets liberal publisher and bookseller Joseph Johnson who encourages her to write; writes *Thoughts on the Education of Daughters* (published 1787); takes up residence in Ireland as governess to elder daughters of Lord Kingsborough

1787 Travels to Dublin with Kingsborough family; dismissed by the Kingsboroughs, returns to London to earn her living by writing; writes *Mary, A Fiction* (1788); writes but does not complete novel 'The Cave of Fancy'; writes 'Original Stories from Real Life'

1788 Writes reviews and translations for Joseph Johnson's journal, *Analytical Review*

1790 *A Vindication of the Rights of Men*, one of the earliest published responses to Edmund Burke's *Reflections on the Revolution in France*

1792 *A Vindication of the Rights of Woman*; begins residence in Paris

1793 Meets American author and speculator Gilbert Imlay; leaves Paris for suburb of Neuilly for safety during Terror; registers as Imlay's wife at American embassy for protection of American citizenship after hostilities break out between France and England

1794 *An Historical and Moral View of the Origin and Progress of the French Revolution*; May gives birth to Fanny Imlay in Le Havre; Imlay leaves for Paris, then London, to pursue business interests; Wollstonecraft resides briefly in Paris with Fanny

1795 Returns to London with Fanny; travels to Scandinavia with Fanny and nursemaid as business representative for Imlay; after discovering Imlay's infidelities, attempts suicide by leaping from Putney bridge into the Thames

1796 *Letters Written During a Short Residence in Sweden, Norway, and Denmark*; meets anarchist philosopher William Godwin; begins writing but does not complete *Maria – The Wrongs of Woman*

1797 29 March Marries William Godwin in London; 30 August gives birth to Mary Godwin (later Mary Shelley, author of *Frankenstein*); 10 September dies from infection contracted during childbirth

1798 *Posthumous Works*

Introduction

THE LIBERATION OF MARY
WOLLSTONECRAFT – LIFE
AND WRITINGS

Mary Wollstonecraft was the first major feminist, and *A Vindication of the Rights of Woman*, written in the western tradition when the issue of the rights of man was bringing revolution to the United States, to France, and threatening even to shake the venerable English Parliament, is the feminist declaration of independence. Wollstonecraft dared to take the liberal doctrine of inalienable human rights, a doctrine which was inflaming patriots on both sides of the Atlantic, and assume these rights for her own sex. No women's revolt followed the publication of the *Vindication*. Indeed, if one had, *A Vindication of the Rights of Woman* would belong only to the historians. Instead, Mary Wollstonecraft's argument has a freshness and immediacy of attitude as if the author herself had only now entered the contemporary debate on women's rights.

Wollstonecraft brought no women to the barricades, but she inspired passion in all her readers. No one who read her work when it was written, or reads it in our own time, could remain indifferent to its argument, or incurious about its author. Wollstonecraft inspired enthusiasm, outrage, admiration, hostility, eulogies and barely printable insults. Her own contemporaries called her a shameless wanton, a 'hyena in petticoats', a 'philosophizing serpent', or wrote jibing epigrams in the *Anti-Jacobin Review*, like

> For Mary verily would wear the breeches
> God help poor silly men from such usurping b—s.[1]

Early-twentieth-century readers have called her an archetypal castrating female. 'God's angry woman', a man-hater whose feminist crusade was caused by penis-envy or, perhaps, an erotic love for her own mother, whose need for rescue Wollstonecraft projected onto the whole of her sex.

In the nineteenth century and through much of the twentieth, some of her natural constituency, feminists themselves, shrank from association with their notorious progenitor. The name 'Wollstonecraft', once considered synonymous with the destruction of all sacred virtues, disowned by the feminist movement as it marched for votes or pressed for admission to universities, became an obscure reference indeed. Today Mary Wollstonecraft is being read all over again. The Fawcett Society saw fit to lay a wreath on her grave at St Pancras Old Church for the bicentenary anniversary of her birth in 1959 and academic symposia were convened in her honour for the bicentenary of the publication of the *Vindication* in 1992.

A Vindication of the Rights of Woman speaks as much to the problems of women in the twenty-first century as it did to those of the contemporaries of Mary Wollstonecraft in 1792. She has triumphed finally over her more virulent detractors, who recommended, like one commentator at her death, that her life and works be read

> with disgust by every female who has any pretensions to delicacy; with detestation by every one attached to the interests of religion and morality, and with indignation by anyone who might feel any regard for the unhappy woman, whose frailties should have been buried in oblivion.[2]

Mary Wollstonecraft's experience in childhood and as a young woman, in a class-bound and male-dominated society, influenced and shaped the ideas she would later develop into a feminist argument. The argument and the passion Wollstonecraft brings to her defence of feminism is, therefore, not only more poignant but more comprehensible with awareness of the trial and anguish of her struggle for a full life – for personal liberation, economic independence and for a release from the emotional insecurity imposed on her by her refusing the traditional safeguard of early marriage. If this introduction dwells at some length on the life of Mary Wollstonecraft, it is because the life she endeavoured to lead, her experiences and friendships, are directly relevant to the subject, mood and arguments of the *Vindication*.

The childhood Mary Wollstonecraft would recall in later years was one characterized by disappointment, petty cruelties and, happily for her, fresh air. In 1759, while Edward Wollstonecraft was working as a clerk for his father, who had prospered in the silk-weaving trade, Mary, his second child and oldest daughter, was born in London. The family would eventually include six children, three sons and three daughters, all of whom were moved about from farm to farm in England and Wales, while Edward Wollstonecraft unsuccessfully attempted to recast himself as a gentleman farmer. Her father, not made more tractable by the steady erosion of his inheritance, frequently broke into a violent rage, and Mary often tried to defend her mother by throwing herself between them. Unfortunately, if she remembers her father as tyrannical, her mother, she recalls, was too willingly his victim.

Mary Wollstonecraft may have been recalling her own childhood when her narrator in *Maria – The Wrongs of Woman* says that her mother was a vague and uncertain figure. She seemed only to dote on her oldest son, 'a boy', Mary Wollstonecraft wrote later, 'and the darling of my mother, he did not fail to act like an heir-apparent'.[3]

Yet in spite of the fighting, and the financial losses, Mary Wollstonecraft felt she had been spared in her childhood the more long-lasting dangers of a conventional female upbringing – the kind of atmosphere most middle-class girls were subjected to and which Wollstonecraft believed resulted in physical, if not mental, infirmity in later life. When her family moved to a farm in Yorkshire in 1768, she was left to play with her brothers in the countryside, instead of being confined to a stuffy drawing-room learning useless 'accomplishments', and the experience seems to have left her with an abiding confidence in the restorative qualities of simple fresh air. As for her education, it was predictably meagre. There were day-schools around Beverley in Yorkshire, but like most of the educated women of her time, she was self-taught. Intellectual curiosity developed in a girlhood correspondence with a friend, Fanny Blood, but was fed with great effort. Not only was the Wollstonecraft family unsympathetic to her request for privacy; they were unlikely to have provided her with the well-equipped library which had been the traditional informal schoolroom for such learned women as Lady Mary Wortley Montague and Catherine Macaulay.

But once Wollstonecraft began seriously to work at improving her writing it became an avocation she never put down, and finally, it became her vocation. In 1778, after waging a long struggle with her parents, who were reluctant to see her go, she left their household and began a long quest for financial independence. Eventually, until she became a journalist, Mary Wollstonecraft worked in all of the traditional genteel female employments, all rather limited in scope and none particularly rewarding. The first of these, in 1778, was as companion to an elderly widow at Bath, a lonely and unhappy experience, she wrote later, but one she stuck at nonetheless until her mother's illness called her home. The large, peripatetic Wollstonecraft family finally separated in 1782 after the death of Mrs Wollstonecraft. Ironically, in spite of the bitterness, the jealousy and the resentment, it was Mary, not the eldest son (who was established by then in a profession in London), who assumed most of the responsibility for looking after her irascible father. As she began to earn money herself, she became virtually his sole support, and eventually she financed the education of her younger brothers and sisters as well – found them employment when she could, and kept spare beds in her own limited rooms in case they needed a temporary home. She even stage-managed the flight of one sister from an unhappy marriage.

By 1784, however, she had chosen the means by which she would be self-sufficient. Gathering together her sisters and Fanny Blood, hopeful that, 'With economy we can live on a guinea a week, and that we can with ease earn', Wollstonecraft established a school at Newington Green which, in London, at the end of the eighteenth century, provided an informal education for these novice teachers as well. Newington Green was an attractive suburban community of affluent Dissenters, who were for the most part liberal intellectuals and ministers, like James Burgh, the advocator of parliamentary reform who had kept a school there. Another neighbour who preached at Newington Green Meeting House, was Dr Richard Price, parliamentary reform-advocate who would become an enthusiastic supporter of the French and American Revolutions. Considering the liberal dispensations of the surrounding communities, the atmosphere at Newington was not one in which conventional attitudes dismissive towards women flourished. Dissenting ministers would have encouraged Wollstonecraft's desire for financial independence, because, to these sympathetic and learned neighbours, the young teachers were exercising the virtues of purposeful hard work while they struggled to keep their school alive. In her turn Mary Wollstonecraft conceived a respect for the elderly Dr Price which was warm and long-lasting. What had begun as a youthful rebellion against parental authority became slowly, under the influence of the liberal philosophers of Newington Green, a condemnation of all arbitrary power. Her native drive for independence was reinforced with a conviction that moral character is developed with hard work. Later, in the pages of the *Vindication*, she borrows an application to feminism from the moral theology of Dr Price, denying on the basis of her own personal apprehension of Divine virtue the attribution of inferiority to all women by Divine ordinance.

During these years of intellectual growth, Wollstonecraft was continually confronted with personal crisis and economic instability. The death of her close friend, Fanny Blood, and the failure of the school at Newington followed each other in close succession. Although in her personal correspondence she gave voice to loneliness and pessimism, she met each crisis with energy and confidence. One of her Newington neighbours, the bookseller and publisher Joseph Johnson, suggested she write and publish to meet heavy personal debts, and, without pausing to consider the unwomanliness of such an occupation, Wollstonecraft assembled her opinions on a subject she knew well. *Thoughts on the Education of Daughters* (1787) made little stir, and was not particularly original, but it was a beginning. Like the better-known works published earlier by Dr James Fordyce and Dr John Gregory with which Wollstonecraft would argue continually in the *Vindication*, her first book did not challenge the traditional Christian attitude about the proper domestic sphere of women as much as it regretted the vanity and frivolousness to which her fellow creatures seemed disposed. As Wollstonecraft developed confidence in her own prospects and capacity, she became less enamoured of the traditional restraints on her sex and more convinced that women's shortcomings were the result of a flawed environment.

In spite of her own indebtedness, Wollstonecraft gave the ten guineas she received from *Thoughts on the Education of Daughters* to the Blood family so that they could resettle in Ireland, and accepted for herself a loan from personal friends and an introduction to a prospective employer. Though in 1786 she was compelled by necessity to accept what she considered was demeaning employment as a governess, this experience would contribute significantly to her understanding of the privileged, moneyed class of women – women who need never undergo the rugged character-building brought about by hard work. Wollstonecraft accepted employment with the Kingsborough family, landed gentry in Ireland, her first close encounter with a leisured, frivolous style of life, against which she would soon take up arms.

She had even seen close at hand the privileged young élite at Eton, where she stopped with friends on the way to Ireland. The hierarchical structure of public school life, the fagging, the vanity, the substitution of artificial authority for rational authority, disturbed her. Some of these objections to boarding-school life appear in the *Vindication* in the discussion of an ideal education for young children. There were also vanity and abuse of authority in the Dublin household of her employers. Considering the indolent, luxurious life of Lady Kingsborough, and recalling the submissiveness of her own mother, Wollstonecraft had now a very vivid model of all a woman should not be, but all too frequently was. 'You cannot conceive,' she wrote to her sisters, 'the dissipated lives the women of quality lead. Five hours do many, I assure you, spend in dressing – without making preparations for bed, washing with Milk of Roses, etc. etc.' And their conversation was only of 'matrimony and dress'.[4] What use could these ladies be? They were indifferent to the intellectual and moral development of their own children; they cared little for administering to the needs of the suffering poor who existed in appalling conditions around them. Their self-indulgence, their insipid interests were for Wollstonecraft examples to flee from, and then, later, to correct.

Happily, her tenure as a governess was not an extended one. A year later, not surprisingly, Lady Kingsborough seems to have become uncomfortable with her sharp-eyed, and probably sharp-tongued, employee. And Wollstonecraft had been busy with her own plans. She had been corresponding with Johnson, who had published *Thoughts on the Education of Daughters*, a man of liberal politics and a generous disposition, the patron of many aspiring and hungry young writers, one of whom was William Blake. Johnson promised to publish Wollstonecraft's first novel, *Mary, A Fiction* (1788), and with a promise of more work for her, he encouraged her to move back to London.

Mary is a sentimental novel, an outpouring of the trials of these years of uncertainty and hardship. But much in the novel dramatizes as well the awakening consciousness of a young woman to degrading and inhibiting social forces. 'Mary' is a high-spirited, rebellious heroine, one rather like the authoress herself. Running away from an unhappy marriage which had been arranged for her by her father, she announces that she will not be 'thrown away', or 'given in with an estate'.[5] She wanders about instead administering benevolently to the sick and poor until finally she dies, uttering with her last breath that she hopes to enter a country where 'there is neither marrying, nor giving in marriage'.[6] The keen-eyed observations in *Mary*, particularly the descriptions of abject poverty and moral degeneration, point to themes which Wollstonecraft develops in all her important writings. In *Mary* the youthful heroine tries to overcome the evils of her environment by selflessly doing good wherever she can. These individual acts of benevolence will later be developed in the *Vindication* into a universal call for reform of the whole of society.

In London once again in 1787, Wollstonecraft found she had substituted the gossip and vanity of the Kingsborough drawing-room for an impressive circle of liberal and radical intellectuals who gathered from time to time in Johnson's rooms above his bookshop. Wollstonecraft became a member of a cosmopolitan London-based group which included Henry Fuseli, the Swiss painter, Joseph Priestley, the famous chemist and radical in politics and theology, William Godwin, the political philosopher, the poet William Blake and Thomas Paine, the international patriot. Living alone in the city, supporting herself, Wollstonecraft writes that she is 'the first of a new genus',[7] a woman who is a professional writer. She began but did not finish an oriental tale called 'The Cave of Fancy', and produced a collection of narratives for the instruction of children called 'Original Stories from Real Life', in the tradition of Thomas Day's classic *Sandford and Merton*.

Moral and didactic children's literature was among the few literary genres cultural convention permitted to women authors. Their representation of rational mothers and governesses suggests the late Enlightenment reinterpretation of motherhood in which Wollstonecraft's *Vindication* would play so large a part. Holding girls accountable to the same mature ideals as boys, such stern mentors as Wollstonecraft's Miss Mason represented powerful alternatives to the childlike, helpless female, more conventionally idealized. As Mitzi Myers has argued, these moral and rational care-takers 'never speak of women's rights, but they make large strategic claims for female nature and capacities and for woman's ability to make a difference in her social world'.[8] Wollstonecraft's early works included the anthology *The Female Reader* for which she wrote a preface and four prayers. She may have been the first woman writer to lay claim to this new textbook literature for girl students, a literature in which she would 'imprint some useful lessons on the mind' with a selection of writings taken largely from the

Bible and Shakespeare. The theme that an 'expanding mind' is 'the surest foundation of virtue' was common parlance among Wollstonecraft's reform-minded Dissenter friends at Newington Green, a theme that Wollstonecraft herself enlarged later in the *Vindication*.[9] Now twenty-eight years old, she shed the schoolmistress role and vowed she would live by the work of her pen.

The picture left to us of Wollstonecraft during these years is of a singularly active and purposeful young woman, but one in whom the contemplative and romantic was always just beneath the surface. John Opie's portrait, done later in her life, shows a remarkably pretty face, rather dreamy-eyed and compassionate in expression – while all her polemical writings and her achievements in the face of great odds speak of grit and fire. All she needed to set to work was challenge. Once when she complained of difficulty with a writing project, Johnson sympathetically offered to withdraw the commitment. Shocked at such capitulation, she rushed home and finished with no trouble. She was not particularly careful about her appearance. In fact Fuseli, whom she admired, dismayed at her long black worsted stockings and dishevelled hair, called her a 'philosophical sloven'. Her living quarters were kept sparsely furnished and when Talleyrand visited her in London she offered him tea in cracked cups. Money, not easily earned, was not spent frivolously: Mary Wollstonecraft aspired to be something quite different from the elegant Lady Kingsborough.

Her apprenticeship as a literary hack, translating and writing reviews for Johnson's journal, *Analytical Review*, was for Wollstonecraft a period of developing self-confidence in her own social, political and aesthetic observations. The range of books and pamphlets passing her desk inevitably stimulated and enlivened her own interests. Catherine Macaulay's *Letters on Education*, which she reviewed for the *Analytical Review*, laid some of the groundwork for *A Vindication of the Rights of Woman*, as did Price's sermon 'On the Love of Country', delivered in 1789, a speech which set off the great political debate which produced both Edmund Burke's *Reflections on the Revolution in France* and Thomas Paine's *The Rights of Man*. But for

Wollstonecraft the tumult that followed Dr Price's sermon constituted a literary *rite de passage* in which the journalistic hack
and the composer of polite works on the education of daughters
and small children emerged a thinker and writer of substance,
speaking her own mind.

Dr Price had begun that night by merely congratulating the
French National Assembly and rejoicing in the prospects of civil
and religious liberty for France. In 1789 the initial euphoria
generated by the assault on the Bastille had not been dispelled
by any of the excesses of the Reign of Terror. The Bourbon
monarchs, Louis XVI and Marie Antoinette, were under guard,
but very much alive. Still, for English conservatives like Burke,
the sudden upheaval of traditional authority, the bold substitution of the rights of man for the divine right of kings, was a
change laden with sinister portent: the lid was off Pandora's
box and the disease was infectious. Price had fed these fears; for
while he had always advocated parliamentary reform, by now
a familiar refrain, there was a subtle change that night in his
speech which Burke felt indicated something more subversive.
Price talked about one's being a citizen of the world, about
universal benevolence and the doctrine of perfectibility which
justified one's tampering with the social order as if it were a
series of cogs and wheels which could be put right with the skills
of a mechanic.

Burke's answer to Price's speech, the *Reflections*, appeared in
November 1790, a careful denial of the doctrine of perfectibility
and the rights of man, prophesying terror and chaos for France.
Many began to write answers to Burke. One of the earliest
published was Wollstonecraft's *A Vindication of the Rights of
Men* (1790) – a vigorous and angry rebuttal in which she
defended those principles dear to the hearts of London's liberal
reformers, a loose-knit group of parliamentary reformers and
apostles of the Enlightenment in which she now enthusiastically
included herself. Wollstonecraft championed the new philosophy. Civil and religious liberties were part of one's birthright.
Only ignorance could corrupt an individual and despotism prevent one from assuming a God-given prerogative. Burke spoke
of the dangerous assault on the aristocracy by the radical Jaco-

bins of France. Wollstonecraft answered, labelling the aristocracy who do not work 'profligates of rank, emasculated by
hereditary effeminacy'.[10] Burke had said that chivalry soothed
and civilized power. Had it not died in France a thousand hands
would have drawn swords to defend the fair form of the French
Queen against her enemies. To Wollstonecraft, however, Marie
Antoinette was only another decadent aristocrat – another, more
dissipated, Lady Kingsborough. Burke's notion of chivalry,
objected Wollstonecraft, was hypocritically selective. He pitied
a few rich and titled women, and ignored the thousands of
women who suffered.

> Misery, to reach your heart, I perceive, must have its cap and
> bells; your tears are reserved, very naturally considering your
> character, for the declamation of the theatre, or for the downfall
> of queens, whose rank alters the nature of folly, and throws a
> graceful veil over vices that degrade humanity; whilst the distress
> of many industrious mothers, whose helpmates have been torn
> from them, and the hungry cry of helpless babes, were vulgar
> sorrows that could not move your commiseration, though they
> might extort an alms.[11]

The seeds of *A Vindication of the Rights of Woman* are sown
in this answer to Burke, as surely as the rights of man must
imply the rights of women.

A Vindication of the Rights of Woman was written in 1791
and published by Joseph Johnson in 1792. A second edition, on
which most subsequent editions are based, was prepared by
Wollstonecraft and published later the same year. It was the first
sustained argument for female emancipation based on a cogent
ethical system. Predictably the argument found its friends and
enemies, depending on how enthusiastically or suspiciously the
reader viewed the great social changes being undertaken in
France. Typical of the response the *Vindication* met within the
community of revolutionary sympathizers was that of Thomas
Cooper, a radical Manchester cotton manufacturer who later
became President of the University of South Carolina: 'Let the
defenders of male despotism, answer (if they can) the *Rights of*

Woman.[12] But the conservative reaction in London was vitri-
olic. Wollstonecraft was called a 'hyena in petticoats'[13] by
Horace Walpole, and Hannah More wrote that there was something so ridiculous in the very title that she had no intention of
reading the book. Not one of Wollstonecraft's critics thought it
necessary to answer her arguments. She was one of the 'impious
amazons of Republican France' whose proposals were self-
evidently wicked. As Wollstonecraft's personal life became more
publicly unconventional, her proposals were taken even less
seriously. Her bohemianism was proof enough of the inherent
evils of feminism.

The reaction in Paris, undergoing revolution, was quite different. Wollstonecraft crossed the Channel late in 1792, to improve
her French, she wrote to her sisters. But more compelling was
the desire to see the Revolution close at hand. Her reputation
as the new champion of her sex had travelled to Paris before her,
where the *Vindication* had already been published in French.
She was welcomed into an international group of literary and
political writers which included Helen Maria Williams, the
English poet, Joel Barlow, an American patriot and political
writer, the exiled Paine whom she had met earlier in London,
and the moderate French revolutionary leader Brissot, who, to
her horror, would be guillotined during the Terror. So much a
part of the French community did Wollstonecraft feel that she
had dedicated the *Vindication* to Talleyrand, hoping, in vain,
to influence legislation before the French Assembly on women's
education. William Godwin wrote later that her enthusiasm for
the French Revolution extinguished finally any respect Wollstonecraft may have held over from her youth for establishments. But the course the Revolution was to take, even while
she lived in Paris, dampened this enthusiasm and considerably
modified her optimism about the ease with which human civilizations could undergo important changes.

She was at first disappointed and then deeply disturbed that
the French people, newly released from tyranny, failed to emerge
virtuous. Writing to Johnson in London, shocked that so many
men and women had been guillotined merely because they were,
in name, noble, Wollstonecraft worried about human perfecti-

bility being vulnerable to human viciousness. Later, as an Eng-
lishwoman in Paris, in some personal danger herself because
of the war that had broken out between the two countries,
Wollstonecraft had to be restrained by a passer-by from being
too visibly horrified and angry when she passed the guillotine
fresh with blood. But as she wrote *An Historical and Moral
View of the Origin and Progress of the French Revolution*,
published in London later in 1794, Wollstonecraft came gradually to terms with her disenchantment and was able to write
with qualified optimism. 'Yet I feel confident of being able to
prove that the people are essentially good . . . Out of this chaotic
mass a fairer government is rising than has ever shed the sweets
of social life on the world. But things must have time to find
their level.'[14]

Even while she was reaffirming her faith in the innate goodness
of man, Wollstonecraft met in Paris an American, Gilbert Imlay,
who seems to have been destined to try that faith. He was a
patriot, and an author of a sentimental novel, who had travelled
to Paris to interest the French government in a land speculation
scheme in the territory of Kentucky. A record of Imlay's relationship with Mary Wollstonecraft survives in an exchange of letters
published originally by Johnson in *Posthumous Works* (1798)
– a record of painful, almost tragic incompatibility. Although
her attitude to marriage, and to swearing obedience, had not
substantially changed since she wrote so disparagingly about it
in *Mary*, Wollstonecraft had formed a profound tie with Imlay
and intended their union to be a permanent one. Although not
married – indeed marriage at this time of political upheaval in
France would have been difficult – Wollstonecraft was called
'Mrs Imlay' in Paris and later in London, by many who preferred
to assume there had been a marriage. Still, long after it must have
been apparent to their friends, certainly to the reader of the letters,
that the wandering Imlay had lost all interest in her, Wollstonecraft clung tenaciously to whatever hopes he intermittently gave
her. The two seem to have shared very few happy interludes in
a stormy relationship which endured three years.

They were together when their daughter, Fanny Imlay, was
born in May 1794 in Le Havre, and Wollstonecraft wrote

humorously, 'My little Girl begins to suck so *manfully* that her father reckons saucily on her writing the second part of the R–ts of Woman.'[15] But within weeks, Imlay's business ventures separated them and kept them almost constantly apart. With her baby and one nursemaid, Wollstonecraft followed after him, travelling from Paris to Le Havre, back to Paris, even to London, although in 1795 while England was in the midst of an intense period of conservative political reaction, Wollstonecraft was loath to return. Anguished and confused by Imlay's fortune-hunting, writing to him that she for one did not mind if they must 'struggle cheerfully together – drawn closer by the pinching blasts of poverty', Wollstonecraft reproached Imlay constantly about his 'money-getting face', or his being only 'stupidly useful to the stupid'.[16] Had Imlay sought, as did Wollstonecraft, a permanent union, or been as contemptuous as she of material possessions, it is doubtful that his waning affections would have been restored by her anger. As for Wollstonecraft, the stable and harmonious vision of domestic life she wrote about in *A Vindication of the Rights of Woman*, indeed that she felt was necessary for proper childrearing, was as remote to her experience with Gilbert Imlay as Lady Kingsborough in Dublin had been to her model of the virtuous woman. Wollstonecraft delighted in watching her little daughter develop, chronicled happily each new accomplishment, but she would have preferred to share the happiness with the child's father. When in one letter she confessed to Imlay that she sometimes feared developing the mind of her own young daughter, Wollstonecraft is painfully aware of the loneliness and vulnerability of her own independence.

In summer 1795 Mary Wollstonecraft travelled again, accompanied not by Imlay but by their small daughter and one nursemaid, to Scandinavia, where Wollstonecraft played the unlikely role of Imlay's business agent. The travel journal she styled as letters to an absent lover Johnson published months later as *Letters Written During a Short Residence in Sweden, Norway, and Denmark* (1796). On the eve of the greatest personal crisis in her life, the *Letters* are striking in their serenity. While her earlier works, essays and fictions were disputatious and heated, this travelogue of a thoughtful though obviously deeply troubled woman pleased even her most outspoken critics. One even suggested that perhaps marriage and motherhood had softened her.[17] In the *Letters* from Scandinavia she is poetic and critical, blending lyrical and pleasing description of natural beauty with her always keen eye for local manners. Her consciousness of the corrupting influence of power on morality has never been sharper. Tyranny is everywhere in evidence. Denmark tyrannizes over its weaker neighbours, men over women, and at the root of all tyranny is the ownership of property. 'Still harping on the same subject, you will exclaim – How can I avoid it?'[18] Her contempt for the aristocracy, her conviction that the rich can glitter only if the poor suffer, is as evident in this, her last published work, as it was in her frankly more political works. Passing near convicts at work on a road one day, she observes caustically that the stars and gold keys on a nobleman disgrace him more than fetters do prisoners. In fact, she argues, the same injustice which bestows the gold bar and key on the aristocrat produces the fetters on the other. 'I am more and more convinced,' she writes, 'that the same energy of character which renders a man a daring villain, would have rendered him useful to society, had that society been well organized.'[19]

The interlude in Scandinavia only postponed an inevitable denouement with Imlay. In London once again in 1795, Wollstonecraft could no longer delude herself about him, for Imlay was living openly with another woman. Wollstonecraft had met the various crises in her struggle for economic independence with characteristic resilience and determination, but Imlay's infidelity and all it implied of her misplaced trust left her desperate. Finally, too, travel weary, with no appetite to begin again, she was as far as she had ever been from her fantasies of a harmonious and stable home. Her response to all of this was suicide. She left instructions for the care of her child and walked out at night to look for a secluded spot along the Thames where, making sure her clothes were heavy with water, and assuming she was unobserved, she at last leapt from a bridge. But in spite of her precautions she had been noticed and was pulled unconscious from the water by a passer-by. Later she told

William Godwin that the pain associated with the attempt on her own life was so great she was resolved never to try again. Perhaps the suicide attempt exhausted the worst of her despair for after a few embarrassing meetings with him she was able at long last to resolve to forget Gilbert Imlay, and began to make plans for her own and her daughter's future, moving about within her London circle of reassuring friends.

One of these friends, although not of long standing, was William Godwin, who was, in 1796, at the peak of his career. In his *Enquiry Concerning Political Justice* (1793) he had condemned government and urged men to cultivate sincerity, to be their own and each other's guardians in an anarchistic society. Godwin and Wollstonecraft had met years before at Joseph Johnson's, but neither had been much pleased with the other. Godwin complained that he had gone to dine at Johnson's to hear Thomas Paine, who was to be one of the company, while instead he and Wollstonecraft, who disagreed on every subject raised, monopolized the evening. But since then he had read her *Letters* from Scandinavia and said of them, 'if ever a book calculated to make a man in love with its author, this appears to me to be the book'.[20] They were introduced by a mutual friend and when they became neighbours in Somerstown they renewed the acquaintanceship with interest. The little notes that passed between the two make pleasurable reading after the tortured correspondence with Imlay. Godwin and Wollstonecraft gossip about friends, plan to meet for dinner and maintain a steadily increasing affectionate banter. The ménage Wollstonecraft and Godwin finally established was a singular one. They eventually did marry in March 1797 when Wollstonecraft discovered she was pregnant, but submitting to the ceremony was embarrassing for both of them. Godwin had spoken and written energetically in *Political Justice* about the evils of cohabitation. Both of them thought the marriage contract was an artificial bond which two virtuous individuals did not need. Godwin argued further that two individual personalities could not harmoniously exist under one roof.

While she lived, the marriage was a happy one. 'A husband is a convenient part of the furniture of a house', Wollstonecraft wrote cheerfully to Godwin.[21] And he assured his friends that they did not entirely cohabit, inasmuch as he maintained a separate residence up the street where he worked privately for some hours during the day. They were both careful not to intrude on one another's friendships, satisfying another principle about individuality within marriage. But philosophy appeased, the two seem to have enjoyed each other. While she awaited the birth of her second child, Wollstonecraft was busy working on another novel, *Maria – The Wrongs of Woman*, and preparing a work on infant and child management (published in *Posthumous Works*).

Wollstonecraft's happiness was destined to be short-lived. Mary Wollstonecraft died after complications in childbirth in September 1797. Her infant daughter, Mary, survived the birth and lived to marry the poet Shelley and write the Gothic novel *Frankenstein*, a work that some argue investigates the trauma of her own conception causing her mother's death.[22] At the age of thirty-eight, a mother of modern feminism was dead of one of the oldest scourges of women. Her long struggle for liberation and a 'useful' life was ended. To those other ancient scourges, economic exploitation and restriction by prejudice and harassment of a full emotional and intellectual life, Wollstonecraft had thrown down her gauntlet.

'BLISS WAS IT IN THAT DAWN . . .' – THE POLITICAL SETTING OF *A VINDICATION OF THE RIGHTS OF WOMAN*

When Hannah More, one of Wollstonecraft's more conservative contemporaries, remarked that there was something fantastic and absurd in the very title of *A Vindication of the Rights of Woman*, she was trying to ignore that, ridiculous as it may have seemed to some, its moment had arrived. Wollstonecraft's work was written during a period of great social and political upheaval.

In France the Revolution was proclaiming the rights of man, and in England radicals were bringing fear to the aristocracy and defenders of it like Edmund Burke. Political agitation had been part of the community in which Wollstonecraft matured. She had come of age intellectually the friend of men like Dr Richard Price and part of a group of artists and intellectuals which included men such as Thomas Paine, author of *The Rights of Man* (1791). It was an age in England that seemed to usher in a new era of freedom, when the young Wordsworth wrote:

> Bliss was it in that dawn to be alive.
> But to be young was very heaven!

All about her the conversation was about reform – reform in France, reform of the English Parliament and reform of the English electorate. *A Vindication of the Rights of Woman* was written by a woman and a radical who took the egalitarian reform principles of her age and applied them, for the first time in the long annals of literature about women, to her own sex. The *Vindication* is at once a product of this period of radicalism and a pioneer in its new application. It could only have been written when all social and political values were under fundamental challenge. But since this challenge had its roots in four decades of agitation, some sense of the radical fervour of late-eighteenth-century England is essential in order to understand Wollstonecraft's feminist challenge to English conservatism.

The intellectual core of English radicalism in the late eighteenth century was as old as Locke's *Second Treatise* (1689) and as recent as Rousseau's *Social Contract* (1762). The argument was simple. Sovereign power did not dwell in the monarchy or in any aristocracy or oligarchy. A political community derived legal authority only from the consent of each individual governed by it, a consent which could be withdrawn by each individual as freely as it had been given. Careful readers of both Locke and Rousseau could conclude, then, that the constitution and the institutions to which it gave power should be changed by the people governed, if these institutions abused the authority lent to them. The individuals in the community would exercise their sovereign power by virtue of the capacity to reason intelligently with which they were born, a capacity strengthened by proper education.

The response of the traditionalists emphasized an hierarchical order within society. Respect for rank and special privileges was necessary to maintain liberty. For Montesquieu, Blackstone and Burke the English Constitution in the eighteenth century ensured that this important balance of power and privilege would be passed on to generations of Englishmen as their birthright. The nobility would protect the Crown and the people if they, the nobility, were allowed special privileges in exchange. As for Parliament, so far from being at the disposal of the electorate, traditional theorists reasoned, Lords and Commons were autonomous, their power safely beyond the reach of the King or the people.

The question was not then how Parliament should be reformed, but more particularly, who should reform it? Edmund Burke had no faith in the innate rationality of the people. He gave voice to an older, more traditional scepticism about man's capacity to reason. Parliament did not need the approval of its electorate; its legitimacy grew out of its longevity, out of generations of Englishmen expressing their collective will across the centuries, so that Parliament now existed in its own right, invulnerable to restless demands for change in this age or that. Burke could be roused to a jealous protection of Parliamentary rights whenever he felt they were threatened either by monarch or people.

In the last half of the eighteenth century Burke felt that the threat came from both, and finally most threateningly from the people – especially Dissenters – demanding Parliamentary reform. The House of Lords was comprised of Lords who inherited their seats: the House of Commons represented a minuscule fraction of the English population. It was possible for 15,000 voters (½ per cent of the adult male population) to choose a majority. In addition certain powerful Lords had numerous seats in the Commons at their disposal. It was estimated that 144 powerful individuals could in fact return a majority of the House. The commercial middle classes of newly industrialized England were unrepresented. No town had received borough rights or rights to representation since 1678, leaving the new industrial centres of Manchester, Leeds and Birmingham disenfranchised. Parliament thus sat with little representation of England's influential dissenting population, all of whom were also proscribed by the Test and Corporation Acts from holding any Crown appointment in civil government, or belonging to any municipal corporation in a borough, or holding Oxford or Cambridge University degrees. Until these laws were repealed, the dissenting community of Presbyterians, Baptists and Independents were segregated from the civil life of the community. For the most part, Dissenters were solidly middle-class patriots, who established their own prestigious Dissenting Academies in the industrial communities. These vocal centres continually sent petitions of repeal to Parliament and argued for the establishment of a secular state, on the model of the American government, which would give equal protection to all churches and confer an equal status on all citizens.

To proposals for reform of Parliament and repeal of the Test and Corporation Acts, conservatives like Burke answered that the House of Commons represented all of England, because the men sitting there were interested in the prosperity of the whole, regardless of which small section of the country had given them a seat. As for the Dissenters, since they eschewed the established religion, the Church of England must be protected from them.

The advocates of reform and the upholders of the traditional constitution fought many battles in the last half of the eighteenth century. The first was the great *cause célèbre* of the 1760s, the case of John Wilkes, the popular London hero barred by Parliament from taking the seat to which he was duly elected. In the 1770s the great debate on reform centred on attitudes towards the American Revolution. In the 1780s Christopher Wyvil and the gentry of Yorkshire launched the Associational Movement in an unsuccessful effort to reform the House of Commons by adding county seats. All these decades of reform, of protest, of agitation, came to a head in the early years of the French Revolution – years of optimism and of a search for social justice which could produce *A Vindication of the Rights of Woman*. In the 1790s the reform movement acquired a base of popular support broader than merely that of dissenting ministers like the good Rev. Price and Joseph Priestley. Popular democratic movements such as Thomas Hardy's London Corresponding Society, formed in 1792, were made up of tradesmen, mechanics and shopkeepers – Hardy himself was a master shoemaker with his own shop. They were willing to reprint and distribute pamphlets like Thomas Paine's *The Rights of Man*, of which some 200,000 copies were sold by 1793, as compared to only 30,000 of Burke's *Reflections*. Some of their meetings in London's Chalk Farm attracted over 100,000 people. The Society's members were hard-working men who called each other 'citizen', and many of them were more likely to send rifles to the French soldiers than to take up arms against them. Their immediate goal was the reform of Parliament, which the more wealthy middle-class reformers had failed to achieve. The London Corresponding Society was in constant contact with other radical associations in Sheffield, Norwich, Leeds, Birmingham and Manchester, and there was talk of calling a national constitutional convention. This self-conscious reference to French models became all the more suspect when war with France was declared in 1793. Now it seemed to many, especially to Pitt's government, to be talk of revolution. Pitt's government struck back.

In 1794 Thomas Hardy, Horne Tooke and John Thelwall, all leaders of the London Corresponding Society, were indicted with nine other radicals as traitors. They were acquitted, but Pitt's repression was irresistible. The Treasonable Practices Act broadened the definition of treason, the Seditious Meetings Act made it illegal to gather for a lecture without a law officer present, and in 1798 Habeas Corpus was suspended. The movement for Parliamentary reform in England was effectively incapacitated by this counter-attack and most of the reform goals had to wait until the Great Reform Bill of 1832. Reactions set in, and the Napoleonic wars and Tory repression were uncongenial to liberal and radical ideas. But there was in the early 1790s this brief period of dawn that so dazzled Wordsworth and Shelley, when it appeared that all tyrants would be toppled from their throne, all ignorance banished, all men freed. No surprise then that in this heady atmosphere of freedom some should even dare write of women being free. Paine, perhaps the greatest English publicist for freedom in the 1790s, himself saw fit to note the subordinate and inferior status of women.

> Even in countries where they may be esteemed the most happy [women are] constrained in their desires in the disposal of their goods; robbed of freedom and will by the laws; slaves of opinion which rules them with absolute sway and construes the slightest appearances into guilt; surrounded on all sides by judges who are at once tyrants and their seducers ... for even with changes in attitudes and laws, deeply engrained and oppressing social prejudices remain which confront women minute by minute, day by day.[23]

But in Paine's whole corpus of writing, there are only these few lines which deal with the subjection of women. He is, after all, the author of *The Rights of Man*. It remained for a woman to apply the 1790s theme of freedom and liberty to women.

'A WOMAN'S PLACE' – THE FEMINIST BACKGROUND TO THE *VINDICATION*

A Vindication of the Rights of Woman is unique, but it does not emerge out of the eighteenth century without antecedents, other works concerned about the role and rights of woman. As it was essential to know its political setting, the *Vindication* is read far more profitably against this background of English feminism – the social and economic realities of women's place in society and the various writers concerned about that place. Still, Wollstonecraft is not so much the inheritor of a feminist tradition as she is the writer of its manifesto. Before Wollstonecraft, there were works suggesting the reform of female manners or proposals for improving female education, but there was no single-minded criticism of the social and economic system which created a double standard of excellence for male and female and relegated women to an inferior status.

The eighteenth century inherited an unfavourable amalgam of attitudes about women. The puritan reformers, good religious fundamentalists, encouraged submissiveness in women, passivity, dependence on men, limited education, a general containment and restriction of the 'weaker vessel'. The cavalier court of Charles II replaced puritanical disdain and restriction with ribald licentiousness, a thorough-going contempt and sexual exploitation of females, having no place for Renaissance idealism. But if the seventeenth-century woman was kept from books, or insulted at court, the workaday life of the rural or urban woman in the economy of the community had remained relatively unchanged since medieval times, and was a far more independent one than her sister's would be one hundred years later. The aristocratic woman, to be sure, led a non-productive life, divorced from the working routine of the community, but the wife of the farmer, small shopkeeper or tradesman, actively participated in the productive work which maintained the economy of the household. No man would consider, when marrying a woman, that he was obliged to undertake the burden of her support until she died. If she were the wife of a farmer she generally kept a dairy business, bringing eggs, butter and cheese regularly to market. She participated in seasonal harvests, and kept the accounts, if it were a large farm, superintending the servants and managing the care of the small children. While domestic industries thrived, the entire household, including children, participated in spinning and weaving cloth within the home. The wife of the shopkeeper in town worked alongside her husband behind the counter, with the entire household, servants and children living above the shop. One need not imply by this that women enjoyed an equal status with men in the working world. The trade guilds had restricted the training of women and had, for centuries, maintained them as a cheap pool of surplus labour. But women traditionally shared through their husbands the social and religious life of the guild, and if a woman, wife or daughter, survived the death of her male relation, she often carried on in his craft, a practice she continued well into the eighteenth century.

But apart from sharing her husband's work, there were a number of specific trades which were entirely dominated by women until the eighteenth century, in which a woman owned her own property, maintained her own apprentices and was responsible for her own debts as an independent trader. Most of these trades were based in the manufacture of food or functioning of the household, such as brewing, baking, dyeing cloth and preparing meat. Paradoxically, then, while the eighteenth century would be notable in calling for reform of female manners, the seventeenth-century woman, in spite of vilification by seventeenth-century puritanism and cavalier poets, was an active, productive member of the economic life of the community. The range of her activities was limited, but she had far more of the economic independence which Mary Wollstonecraft tried to reclaim for her sex a century later.

The reformers who wrote about women interest us not only in what they proposed but also in what they assumed. Many appear progressive, proposing the advancement of female learning, but often they clung like the puritans to biblical injunctions that necessarily limited any substantive change in the status of women. The rationale often cited for limiting the sphere of women was biblical, that they had been divinely ordained the mental and physical inferior of men. Adam says in Genesis, 'This is now bone of my bones, and flesh of my flesh: she shall be called Woman, because she was taken out of Man.' Corinthians elaborates a little. 'For the man is not of the woman; but the woman of the man. Neither was the man created for the woman; but the woman for the man.' And St Paul had said plainly, 'wives submit to your husbands'. Mary Wollstonecraft insisted that these basic attitudes and principles which subordinated women must be repudiated before a real change in a woman's condition could be gained permanently. But the overwhelming majority who wrote on women either assumed these traditional axioms were correct, or chose not to argue with them.

One of the first proposals for reform was Mary Astell's *A*

Serious Proposal to the Ladies for the Advancement of their True and Greatest Interest (1694), suggesting a college for women to which they might withdraw temporarily to return inured against worldly evils. When Astell wrote, and indeed for a long while after, genteel education for women was provided, if at all, by private tutors at home, instruction only within the ability of the very rich, even as Astell herself plainly intended her academy for daughters of noble families. Although she does not challenge traditional attitudes about female inferiority, she does imply, as Wollstonecraft will later argue explicitly, that the character of women is developed by their environment. 'Women are,' complains Astell, one hundred years before Wollstonecraft, 'from their very infancy debarr'd those advantages with the want of which they are afterwards reproached and nursed up in those vices which will hereafter be upbraided to them.'[24] Astell wanted to shore up the religious faith of women by educating them. In fact her proposal for monastic withdrawal from the world drew more fire from those who thought it 'popish' than from traditionalists. Wollstonecraft would have agreed with Astell that virtue is dependent on knowledge and that an educated mother is a better one, but Wollstonecraft will give these notions the twist of Enlightenment liberalism: the educated woman will go into society to facilitate its progress and development; the educated woman may even make contributions to human wisdom; if she is talented, and wants to enough, she may be a vital constructive participant in reorganizing society. Astell didn't envision a woman doing more than engaging in benevolent charity.

Even while Astell was writing, social and domestic changes were altering the nature of domestic life, a life which had for so long given women some direct participation in the economy of the community. The changes would create vast numbers of dependent women who, if their husbands had enough money, would turn to a kind of useless and frivolous routine, inspiring in its very insipidity a fusillade of attacks on women's manners. With commercial and mechanical innovations in the Industrial Revolution demanding centralization of manufacture, the business premises were removed permanently from the home and built on a larger scale, leaving domestic life substantially altered. Women not only ceased to have an active share in their husband's work, but, since they seldom had capital enough, they were prevented from setting up competing enterprises in what had traditionally been their own trades. Changes in the farmhouse followed the same pattern. Small farm owners were forced from their land by the reorganization of rural life which had been going on slowly for centuries and which accelerated in the eighteenth century. The scattered holdings and strip system was considered wasteful. Population became concentrated in newly industrialized cities, creating an increased demand for food production. Landlords dispossessed small farmers in favour of larger corn-growing farmers who could pay higher rents. Eventually the dispossessed found their way into the labour pools of the cities, or became agricultural workers. Neither employment was particularly enviable.

The lower-class woman, forced from small business or farm into long hours of employment far from home – as a seasonal harvester in the country or eventually as a factory worker in the city – was less able than ever to care for her family. While Wollstonecraft would continually emphasize the importance of economic independence, and longed to put all useless women behind a counter in a shop, she alone among writers on women seemed to be aware of the desperately poor woman, produced by the early stages of industrialization in England, who had neither the leisure nor the indirect income for vanity, and was quite beyond the protection of male chivalry which traditionalists liked to claim for women. While the central concern of *A Vindication of the Rights of Woman* will be seen to provide for the rehabilitation of the socially useless middle-class woman, Wollstonecraft, to her credit, understood the difference between drudgery, what she calls in the *Vindication* the 'mindless toil' of the poor, and the kind of rewarding labour she felt was necessary for building character and instilling virtue.

The kinds of skilled trades available to women whose husbands had not grown rich enough to support them were severely limited. The domestic industry continued to decline, although women could find employment in the clothing trade throughout

the eighteenth century and it was not finally until the middle of
the nineteenth that they had seriously to compete with machines.
They might be milliners, mantua-makers and seamstresses,
although one needed, again, some capital to set up a shop and
apprentices were paid little for long hours and poor food and
accommodation. For the most part, with food costs rising
and employment not readily available, the woman who must
support herself or, worse, dependent relatives as well, was hard
pressed indeed. Single women like Mary Wollstonecraft, who
were trying to achieve some kind of economic independence,
were lucky to find, as she did, jobs as companions or governesses, but these positions were invariably poorly paid and the
governess could expect to be treated little better than a household servant. So when Wollstonecraft plied her pen in the latter
part of the century, the traditional economic function of the
woman in the household had been displaced by a new ideal, of
a woman dependent for total support upon her husband and,
at least in theory, protected by him.

Nothing announces this changing concept of the woman's
role quite so dramatically as the 'civil death' of women written
into the *Commentaries on the English Constitution* (1758) by
William Blackstone, the distinguished and learned professor of
law at Oxford. 'By marriage', interprets Blackstone,

> the husband and wife are one person in law; that is, the very being
> or legal existence of the woman is suspended during the marriage
> or at least is incorporated and consolidated into that of the
> husband; under whose wing, protection and cover, she performs
> everything.[25]

A married woman, then, could legally hold no property in her
own right, nor enter into any legal contract, nor for that matter
claim any rights over her own children. To be sure, families had
got round these laws for many years and would continue to do
so; still, the woman's dependence on the economic productivity
of her husband, a dependence which was becoming more and
more manifest in the course of the eighteenth century, achieved
a legal sanctity in Blackstone which formed the spirit, as well as

the letter, of all traditional injunctions to women which writers on the subject would make.

For the most part, writers bent upon reforming female manners were speaking critically of the new middle class. The wives of the large farm owners, the wives of the new and prospering businessmen, no longer managing dairies, or working with their husbands behind a counter, turned towards the manners of the aristocracy for a model of proper behaviour. As early as 1697 Daniel Defoe, who had read Mary Astell, was proposing equal education for women in *Essay on Projects*, and criticizing the new style of female manners. 'They act,' he wrote, 'as if they were ashamed of being tradesmen's wives' and 'scorn to be seen in the counting house'.[26] In the course of the eighteenth century boarding schools grew up to educate daughters of the newly affluent, schools which taught how to while away elegantly the leisure hours until marriage, and then the leisure hours after. One farmer complained:

> Our Daughters, instead of being taught their Duty, and the Business of a Dairy at home, receive their Education at a Boarding School, are taught to dance, to speak French, and to play upon the Harpsichord.[27]

History, philosophy and classical languages were considered too rigorous for minds born uniformly unequal to the task. Indelicate subjects like botany were proscribed. Nor, unless one includes dancing and posture exercises, was the young girl encouraged in any manner of physical exercise. The new feminine ideal to which the young girl was taught to aspire would obviously have been rather remote to the busy life of a manageress of a dairy, or the active wife of a town shopkeeper.

Learned and moral men began to object. But these would-be reformers of female manners never called into question the economic dependence of woman, which had rendered her useless, or the axiom of female inferiority which rationalized her superficial education. Addison and Steele, writing in the *Tatler*, the *Spectator* and the *Guardian* in the early years of the eighteenth century, deplore the vanity of the 'accomplished' young girl.

To make her an agreeable person is the main purpose of her parents; to that is all their cost, to that all their care directed, and from this general folly of parents we owe all our present numerous race of coquettes.[28]

But did these reformers wish to improve the coquette for her own sake, or for theirs? Even such a friend of women as Defoe had rationalized: 'I would have men take women for companions, and educate them to be fit for it.'[29] Still, such well-intentioned reformers may be distinguished from their Augustan contemporaries like Pope and Swift, who criticized female manners and the vogue of mawkish sentimentality with which women were newly regarded without advocating any serious reform of their education. Jonathan Swift, in 'The Furniture of a Woman's Mind', complained in 1727:

> A set of Phrases learn't by Rote;
> A Passion for a Scarlet-Coat;
> When at a Play to laugh, or cry,
> Yet cannot tell the Reason why:
> Never to hold her Tongue a Minute;
> While all she prates has nothing in it.[30]

And were she to attempt her own reform, Hannah More recommended later, the young girl should remember Swift's advice that 'after all her boasted acquirements a woman will, generally speaking, be found to possess less of what is called learning than a common school boy'.[31] Pope and Swift recommended no reform because they guessed that little was possible. Those who did attempt to awaken some seriousness in the female mind did so without threatening the dependent and submissive role in the relationship of women with their husbands and fathers. The most widely read books for girls on the subject of moral instruction, Dr James Fordyce's *Sermons to Young Women* (1766) and Dr John Gregory's *Father's Legacy to His Daughters* (1774), echoed what the luminaries of London's literary world implied or directly advised – that the proper duty of the female was to make herself pleasing to men.

Such skill was woman's by nature. She didn't need to be dedicated to academic study to play the role of charming wife or loving mother satisfactorily. Understandably, in the face of these traditional injunctions to be good, to get married, and to be quiet, very few women triumphed intellectually. The 'Blue-stockings' were an interesting exception, but if they furthered the cause of women's education in the eighteenth century it was in spite of, rather than because of, any position they took favourably on the subject. These decorous, learned and loquacious women, unwilling to jeopardize their own precarious hold on convention, accepted without cavil the traditional notions about a woman's limited rational capacity and her proper domestic sphere. But while they made no attempt themselves to combat the system of limited education for women, they helped by their own intellectual achievements to cast some doubt on pessimistic attitudes about female intelligence; and such pioneering authors as Fanny Burney introduced women to the publishing world. Assembled in their various drawing-rooms, the 'Blues' included, in the latter part of the century, Elizabeth Carter, the classical scholar, Fanny Burney, author of the widely read and respected *Evelina*, Mrs Elizabeth Montagu, author and social leader, Mrs Thrale, woman of letters and Dr Johnson's companion, Mrs Barbauld, writer of children's stories, and Hannah More, who wrote religious and conservative political tracts for the poor. Not only did none of these women, contemporaries of Wollstonecraft, embrace her principles, but they were scrupulously careful to avoid any contamination by feminism. Mrs Barbauld refused to join Mrs Montagu's short-lived scheme for founding a woman's college, replying to her friend without embarrassment that 'The best way for a woman to acquire knowledge is from conversation with a father or brother and such a course of reading as they may recommend.'[32]

Bluestocking Hannah More was one of the more outspoken of Wollstonecraft's detractors, and invites an interesting contrast with her since they wrote on the subject of women's education within a few years of each other and from widely divergent positions on the political spectrum. In her criticism of the existing education for girls, More sounds a great deal like Wollstone-

craft. Indeed, since both were criticizing the failures of the
present society to achieve what each considered virtue in a
woman, they often sound similar. Like Wollstonecraft, Hannah
More condemns a girl's enervating indoor routine, her nonsensi-
cal curriculum with its emphasis on fashion and manners, and
she emphasizes, like Wollstonecraft, that women must be educated to be better mothers. But whereas *A Vindication of the
Rights of Woman* is built on an assumption that the sexes are
equal, that, environmental impediments aside, a woman will
rise as high as motivation and hard work will take her in
intellectual life, Hannah More's view of women ultimately
returns to the limited and traditional attitude of her conservative
politics. 'Far be it from me,' she writes, 'to make scholastic
ladies or female dialecticians.' It is only 'the vulgar and the ill
informed' who struggle most vehemently for power. Clearly
answering Wollstonecraft, in *Strictures on the Modern System
of Female Education* (1799), Hannah More is contemptuous of
the 'woman who is vain of her wit', who attempts to vindicate
the 'rights of women'. The more a woman's understanding is
improved, assures Hannah More, 'the more accurate views will
she take of the station she was born to fill.'[33]

This dreary round of learned women acquiescing in the notion
of their own natural inferiority was not uninterrupted. The
learned Mary Wortley Montagu, contemporary and one-time
friend of Alexander Pope, had much to say about her own sex.
In self-imposed exile in Italy for much of her life, Lady Mary
wrote long candid letters home to her daughter in which she
complained, often bitterly, about a woman's lot. Women are
everywhere in an appalling state of ignorance, she wrote, but
the pity of it all is that 'our knowledge must rest concealed and
be as useless to the world as gold in a mine',[34] a vast resource, a
creative potential which might have served the world if it had
been developed. But Lady Mary is cautious. Women might as
well accept that they pursue education to while away the leisure
hours life gives them in abundance. With a kind of sad anxious-
ness not to offend, she is careful to tailor her philosophy to suit
her correspondent, and when writing to the Bishop of Salisbury,
regretting that women are not encouraged to learn, she hastens

to assure him that she is not disputing women's essential inferiority. Only to her married daughter, and then with some apprehension that her daughter's husband (the influential Lord Bute) might read the letter and become angry, she confides that a woman's character is more likely formed by education 'which inclines me to think (if I dare say it) that nature has not placed us in an inferior rank to men, no more than the females of other animals, where we set no distinction of capacity though I am persuaded if there was a commonwealth of rational horses (as Doctor Swift has supposed) it would be an established maxim amongst them that a mare could not be taught to pace'.[35] It is not unlikely, considering Lady Mary's caution, that she is the anonymous author of a pamphlet published in 1737 by 'Sophia'. The pamphlet goes much further. The anonymous writer exalts motherhood, but also demands admission for women to all employment. Sophia asks 'why is learning useless to us?' and answers, 'Because we have no share in public offices, and why have we no share in public offices? Because we have no learning.'

The historian Catherine Macaulay agreed, and one of her readers was Mary Wollstonecraft. Writing *Letters on Education* in 1790, Macaulay does not criticize female manners so much as question the axioms themselves which control and limit a woman's environment. Wollstonecraft reviewed the *Letters* for Johnson's periodical, *Analytical Review*, and spoke warmly of Macaulay's achievements in the *Vindication* itself. Macaulay had argued that women were limited mentally and physically by their environment. She urged physical exercise and academic studies for women, equal to those of men, dismissing the concept of innate inferiority and claiming in a principle which Wollstonecraft would urge tirelessly, 'there is but one rule of right for the conduct of all rational beings.'[36] But the issue of female emancipation was not a central concern for Macaulay. Macaulay is concerned equally with the management of infants and the education of princes. It was for Mary Wollstonecraft to take the argument of natural rights and make their application to women the subject of a sustained argument. It was for Wollstonecraft to isolate and emphasize the issue of education for women, taking Lady Mary's 'unmined gold' and urging it to be used to enrich all of human society.

THE 'FEMINIST MANIFESTO' – THE ARGUMENT OF THE *VINDICATION*

A Vindication of the Rights of Woman is not polite or ladylike. As Wollstonecraft says in the Introduction to the first edition, she means to be useful, not entertaining, and she will write with 'energetic emotions'. One does not go far into the *Vindication* before being plunged into the very heart of her subject. She has lived the hardships of a woman who wanted to earn her own living and she means to be blunt. The energy and volatile personality of Mary Wollstonecraft are all here in its pages; her sense of humour and her anger are both easily apparent. How often she compares English middle-class women to inmates of a Turkish seraglio, or mutters indignantly of one man's portrayal of a patient wife – 'Such a woman ought to be an angel – or she is an ass' (p. 121). 'Idle empty words!' she exclaims of an author's description of romantic love, 'lover-like phrases of pumped up passion' (pp. 120, 119).

Godwin says the *Vindication* was written hastily in six weeks, and we accept that she probably dashed it off quickly to her publisher, Joseph Johnson, and as quickly set about another project. There are many digressions in the text, with the argument turning suddenly from one subject to another, as in the chapter on physical weaknesses in women when she trails off into a discussion of casuistry and religion. Wollstonecraft would probably have been somewhat defensive about her digression, however, for she says in Chapter II, when a train of thought invited her to digress on standing armies, that she would follow the associations that sprang naturally to mind, as if motivated by a natural order.

Mary Wollstonecraft set forth to vindicate the rights of women, but one of her earlier stipulations (p. 13), which may seem curious to the modern reader, is that her argument is intended to be directed towards middle-class women only; what is more, she is herself frankly dubious (p. 30) that she will effect any great change with the *Vindication*. Both of these assertions, actually qualifications, raise such interesting issues that before proceeding into the heart of her argument one ought to attempt to reconstruct Wollstonecraft's justification for excluding the upper- and lower-class woman from her call to reform, and suggesting limitations on even a middle-class woman's capacity to change. These qualifications form the perimeters of the argument of the *Vindication*, and Wollstonecraft's work is thrown into better perspective against them.

Wollstonecraft directs her argument to the middle-class woman because this woman lives in a 'natural state'. By contrast the aristocratic woman, Wollstonecraft explains in her Introduction (p. 13), is dissipated by great wealth and is incapable of any redemption by education. Eventually the aristocratic woman's class will be eradicated in a reformed society. Wollstonecraft does not explain, however, why she has excluded the poor woman from her audience, nor can her reader be certain what the status of the poor will be after reform, except that they will be less miserable. Wollstonecraft was far from indifferent to the sufferings of the poor, which makes her failure to provide for their relief in the *Vindication* all the more curious. Her pity for the poor had been sincere and profound throughout all her writing, and continued to be so after the *Vindication* was written. Three years later, while travelling in Scandinavia and preparing the *Letters* Johnson published, Wollstonecraft was moved to write with a mixture of sorrow and anger when watching peasant women scrub linen in cold water, their hands already cracked and bleeding. These were women 'to whom the most menial and even laborious offices' are left while 'men stand up for the dignity of men'.[37] And years earlier, Wollstonecraft's most memorable criticism of Burke in the *Rights of Men* was that his proud chivalry was callous and indifferent to the brutality inflicted on poor women.[38]

While Wollstonecraft obviously sincerely pitied poor women, and while she found, individually, their simplicity and 'frankness of heart' appealing, she is not concerned in the bulk of her

writing to suggest what kind of change they may look for in a
reformed society, except that in overthrowing the tyranny of
the aristocracy they will be restored to happiness. Except for an
occasional suggestion for dividing up large estates into smaller
farms in the *Letters* from Scandinavia,[39] and a suggestion to
Burke that he find employment for women rather than 'squandering alms' in the *Rights of Men*,[40] Wollstonecraft leaves the
issue of what the poor woman may expect after reform for the
reader of the *Vindication* to determine alone. But the reader
may easily assume from the *Vindication* that Wollstonecraft did
not believe the poor lived in a 'natural state'. The mind-numbing
routine of domestic drudgery put the poor woman beyond the
call of abstract argument. Wollstonecraft was not one to idealize
the state of poverty. She had been too close to it herself. The life
of the poor was more brutalizing than ennobling. The ideal
existence, as this one described in the *Vindication*, was one in
which women were

> Raised sufficiently above abject poverty not to be obliged to
> weigh the consequence of every farthing they spend, and having
> sufficient to prevent their attending to a frigid system of œconomy,
> which narrows both heart and mind ... (p. 178)

Addressing her reforms to the middle-class woman and to the
men who could legislate these improvements, Wollstonecraft
felt it was possible, but unlikely, that the middle-class woman
could rise above the inhibiting influence of her own environment. Although she was not dissipated by great wealth, nor
stupefied by hard work, the middle-class woman was enmeshed
in a tradition which discouraged reasoning and which certainly
discouraged defiance. Wollstonecraft was aware that, paradoxically, she was attempting to argue rationally with women, who,
according to Wollstonecraft's own understanding of the force
of environmental influence, might be uninclined to follow her
hard logic. The author of the *Vindication* was clearly hoping to
reach an ambitious and courageous few, like herself. 'To prevent
any misconstruction', she explains early in her argument,

> I must add, that I do not believe that a private education can work
> the wonders which some sanguine writers have attributed to it.
> Men and women must be educated, in a great degree, by the
> opinions and manners of the society they live in. (p. 30)

The weight of 'popular opinion' might be stronger than any
single virtuous argument like her own, she continues. 'It may
then fairly be inferred, that, till society be differently constituted,
much cannot be expected from education.'

A Vindication of the Rights of Woman proceeds in spite of
the author's misgivings because some individuals, some talented
few, might resurrect themselves. But the misgivings explain the
anger and frustration which occasionally erupt behind such
exclamations as this: 'I have throughout supposed myself talking
to ignorant women, for ignorant ye are in the most emphatical
sense of the word' (p. 225).

The main work of the *Vindication*, putting these qualifications aside, is establishing the basic principles on which the case
for women's rights is made (Chapters I–III) and examining
closely the character of women as it is shaped by early environmental influences (Chapters IV, VI). Chapter V is a close reading
of and commentary on notable eighteenth-century authors of
conventional attitudes towards women, including sizeable quotations from Jean-Jacques Rousseau. The concluding chapters
of the *Vindication* (VII–XII) are a consideration of ethical problems related to the status of women, which allows Wollstonecraft to discuss family life, the education of children, and the
specific role to be played by a rehabilitated, educated woman.
But Wollstonecraft was by no means scrupulously faithful to
this organization, and the reader confronts an argument built
concentrically rather than logically, progressively. To be faithful
to the richness of Wollstonecraft's apprehension of women in
society, this presentation of her argument cannot follow strictly
a sequential consideration chapter by chapter. One must expect
to meet, even in the closing chapters of the work, defences of
principles made in its early pages, as if Wollstonecraft felt that
by dint of repetition alone she might make headway against the
opposition she knew quite well her argument would face.

And there was no questioning that the *Vindication* would be received largely by a sceptical, in fact, a hostile readership. The middle-class women to whom Wollstonecraft says she will address her argument, women neither dissipated by inherited wealth nor brutalized by poverty, were comfortable and content. There was, to be sure, a small receptive circle of liberal reformers who would welcome the *Vindication* with enthusiasm; but for the most part, once concern grew over the association of English radicalism with the ideas of the French Revolution, Wollstonecraft's assault on established authority, and her denial of the divine rights of kings and men, was greeted with predictable alarm and outrage.

In the first two chapters Wollstonecraft undertakes to refute the dogma on women which had long preceded her work. For hundreds of years people had written that God created woman inferior to man. Wollstonecraft simply said 'nonsense'. This violated basic and self-evident principles of human nature, principles she had absorbed at Stoke Newington with the liberal reformer Dr Price. Both men and women were born with an innate capacity to reason, an apprehension of 'the true nature of things'. God gave human beings reason so that they might, by acquiring knowledge, perfect themselves. Human beings formed societies which would become perfect through successive constructive experiences. If individuals in society did not educate themselves, they would remain in a flawed state of ignorance, never capable of true virtue, or what Wollstonecraft called 'morals', instead imitating what they thought was morality with what Wollstonecraft called 'manners'. To conceive, she writes, of a just God who would create a woman and then deny her the rational capacity to seek the knowledge that would make her virtuous – is impossible. Her reason will not permit such a conception of divinity.

But the progress of civilization, and the progress of individuals, has been impeded by enemies Wollstonecraft calls 'the pestiferous purple'. 'It is the pestiferous purple,' she says at the close of her first chapter (p. 27), 'which renders the progress of civilization a curse.' Any group which coerces the individual by force, or collectively coerces society, eventually corrupts itself,

and inhibits the development of reason in its victims. Wollstonecraft emphasizes again and again that power corrupts the powerful at the same time as it enslaves the weak. Institutions and
individuals which exercise over others authority based on artificial criteria such as inherited wealth or noble names gradually
undermine themselves, become slaves to flattery and are
weakened by indolence. Her criticism of the aristocracy, the
army and the Church in Chapter II is part of a longstanding
Wollstonecraftian hostility to arbitrary authority. When these
tyrannies are overcome, the natural order of equality will
reassert itself and the sexes will find their proper spheres. It is
useless, then, to seek changes in society until these institutions
are put down and reason is allowed to assert itself. To suggest
superficial changes in the condition of women, to alleviate an
isolated grievance here or there, or to allow an élite number of
women to rise in the social order, is not a direct confrontation
with the problem. There can be no significant improvement in
society while the social and economic system prevails which
honours aristocratic titles and passes on great wealth from
father to son without either having needed to exercise reason to
attain status or comfort. Inherited property weakens character
and is the great foe of reason.

It is useless, then, to seek reform for women alone, without
speaking about a general reformation of all society. For the
same economic and social system which oppresses women and
limits their rational development, constrains and restricts with
the exercise of arbitrary power vast numbers of men as well.
These criticisms of established power are repeated often in the
Vindication and, indeed, were a vital part of Wollstonecraft's
previous political writing. For the most part her criticism of
established power is general and does not allude to the specific
issues of parliamentary reform which were as familiar to her
through her association with Dr Price and the circle around
Joseph Johnson as the exploitation of women itself. But
occasionally the radical dimension of her politics emerges, and,
of course, it had been apparent enough all along in her descriptions of the 'unnatural distinctions and pernicious effects' of
inherited property. It is a sharp reminder of how solidly Woll-

stonecraft adhered to radical proposals for political reforms when she says in Chapter IX, that 'The whole system of British politics, if system it may courteously be called', consists of 'multiplying dependents and contriving taxes which grind the poor to pamper the rich' (p. 179). Ministers, she complained, were only interested in patronage and keeping their places. 'Yet it is not necessary that a minister should feel like a man, when a bold push might shake his seat.'

The 'bold push' will reform women, as it reforms all of society by eliminating the degenerating influence of property and reconstructing an environment more favourable to the growth of enlightened, virtuous citizens. In arguing for reform, Wollstonecraft, like liberals before and after her, is led to manipulate the environment to improve the product. Wollstonecraft inherits a tradition of sensationalist psychology associated with John Locke and his notion that upon the *tabula rasa* or 'clean slate' of a person's mind at birth are written all the experiences which will shape his or her character. Chapter VI, 'The effect which an early association of ideas has upon the character', will be a formal presentation of this principle, but the whole of the *Vindication* is based on this set of Lockean associational and environmental assumptions. To answer traditional dogma on women, Wollstonecraft must confront directly the conservative attitude that found women inferior by divine ordination, but an inferiority they proved daily with foolishness and ignorance.

Wollstonecraft does not for a moment pretend that her feminine contemporaries were more serious and more virtuous than they were. Her own criticism of the rich, indolent, aristocratic and would-be aristocratic ladies resembles the more scathing of the misogynist satirists of the eighteenth century. She is angry because of what she perceived was a waste of potential and because she realized that it was women themselves who, by their ignorance and uselessness, provided the fuel for the traditional anti-feminists. '[I]t is your own conduct, O ye foolish women!' she says, 'which throws an odium on your sex' (p. 225). But as she said elsewhere of Marie Antoinette, the idle aristocrat of Wollstonecraft's time, 'In such a voluptuous atmosphere, how could she escape contagion'?[41] The fault lay not in their stars, nor even in themselves, but in their environment.

Young girls, Chapter VI of the *Vindication* argues, are encouraged by their parents, their teachers, by the very structure and sedentary nature of their daily routine, to become the kind of woman conceived of popularly as the feminine ideal. Few rebels can escape this moulding, not only because Wollstonecraft thought only a native genius was free from the influence of environment, but because young girls soon perceive that pleasure and power will be theirs only in proportion to their ability to please men. More than likely, then, a girl will be a willing participant in a process of socialization which leaves her finally dependent and feeble, intellectually and physically. Rather than robust, she would be delicate, instead of prudent, she'd be foolish; she'd not be learned, she'd be ignorant, not clever, but cunning, vain rather than self-respecting, sentimental rather than sensible, and good mannered rather than moral. But how does this happen?

The small girl, even before she was self-consciously instructed in femininity, had before her the example of her own mother. One of Wollstonecraft's more amusing vignettes is set forth in Chapter III, where she argues that women are enervated by an inactive domestic routine.

I once knew a weak woman of fashion, who was more than commonly proud of her delicacy and sensibility. She thought a distinguishing taste and puny appetite the height of all human perfection, and acted accordingly. – I have seen this weak sophisticated being neglect all the duties of life, yet recline with self-complacency on a sofa, and boast of her want of appetite as a proof of delicacy that extended to, or, perhaps, arose from, her exquisite sensibility. (p. 58)

Little girls imitate their mothers, and physical delicacy was one of the ideals imitated. All too soon the delicacy would be real frailty, reinforced by a sedentary life. Boys frolic in the open air, complained Wollstonecraft, while girls are kept indoors and advised not to soil their frocks. Wollstonecraft allows men a natural superiority in bodily strength, but she feels that female frailty is no incurable affliction. 'But should it be proved that woman is naturally weaker than man, whence does it follow that it is natural for her to labour to become still weaker than nature intended her to be?' (p. 55). Not only is this carefully cultivated physical frailty achieved at the expense of the natural pleasures a young girl would find in playing hard out of doors, but it also undermines intellectual achievement. 'Shakspeare never grasped the airy dagger with a nerveless hand, nor did Milton tremble when he led Satan far from the confines of his dreary prison' (p. 52). Wollstonecraft is quite evidently talking about the real physical infirmity, not at all unusual in young women who seldom saw the light of day except from the windows of their carriages. The *Vindication* argues that the rigours of intellectual life, its long hours of study, demand a more sturdy physical constitution than the fashionably delicate standard of femininity would allow.

The domestic routine is not only sedentary, explains Wollstonecraft, it is noisy, crowded and disjointed. A girl's academic curriculum, superficial at best, is offered her 'by snatches' (p. 33). Interrupted, distracted, seldom alone, she is denied the long concentration necessary for good study. It was, after all, not at all unusual for several women to be part of the same household – sisters, sisters-in-law, cousins, a wife, a mother – all continually thrown into each other's company, willing or not. The *Vindication* argues in Chapter IV, 'Observations on the state of degradation to which woman is reduced by various causes', that this familiarity among women denies them the solitude necessary for reflection. John Stuart Mill makes the same point almost one hundred years later in *The Subjection of Women*.[42] Nor will the young girl read anything which might be considered indelicate, like botany or biology, so widespread was the notion that subjects like these were improper for women. In fact, that a lady should be knowledgeable enough to converse easily and learnedly with men at all offended, in itself, traditional notions of female modesty. The *Vindication* will confront this problem directly in Chapter VII, 'Modesty', arguing that nothing in God's creation could be unlovely or unfit for human understanding, male or female. True modesty is not blushing ignorance. True modesty is a soberness of mind which knows its own worth. Not only is education compatible with modesty, education is its necessary precursor. It is impossible to be modest, obviously self-respecting in Wollstonecraft's understanding of the word, without education.

When she does turn to read, then, this 'delicate' girl does not read the substantial material which will build her character and contribute to her store of wisdom. She will read little or no history, no philosophy. She will read mainly novels. Mary Wollstonecraft did not wholly disparage novels; 'any kind of reading I think better than leaving a blank still a blank . . .' (p. 229). And noble sentiments could be found in novels, indeed she had written one herself. But a steady diet of novel-reading, interrupted only by music and poetry, the whole undertaken in the cloying company of women much like herself, was no education. 'All their thoughts', said Wollstonecraft of young girls, 'turn on things calculated to excite emotion; and feeling, when they should reason, their conduct is unstable, and their opinions are wavering' (pp. 78–9). Furthermore, novel-reading was an exercise in fantasy. Girls, hopelessly sheltered from life, ignorant and vulnerable, were fed romantic illusions about their future which made them the natural prey of fortune hunters and rakes. Ignorance, as Wollstonecraft was fond of saying, was a frail base for virtue, and was frailer still if sensibility was for ever supplanting sense. But of course Wollstonecraft and the traditional educators of women did not agree about what constituted virtue in a woman. Wollstonecraft distinguishes between 'decorum' which is manners, such as any puppet might learn, and 'morals' which is based on an educated understanding. And the kind of 'decorum' considered feminine, cunning, vanity, immaturity, is often an offence against morality itself.

Chapter V of the *Vindication* surveys the field of important writers on women in the eighteenth century; but the figure who looms largest in this company is Jean-Jacques Rousseau. Wollstonecraft's political ideas are not that far removed from those of Jean-Jacques. She had read *Émile* while a governess herself, approving its proposals for the education of a young boy, and she shared Rousseau's disdain for aristocratic claims to privilege and power. The message of his *Social Contract*, with its emphasis on popular sovereignty and its egalitarian vision of society, were part of Wollstonecraft's own radical sympathies, sympathies she would make quite clear in her defence of the French Revolution, in her answer to Burke, and in the *Vindication*. Like many English people, she had been impressed by Rousseau's *La Nouvelle Héloïse*, the most widely translated of Rousseau's books in England, with its lyrical description of romantic passion, and its moral resolution of willing submission to family and marriage. Rousseau was such a favourite of hers, she once teased Imlay, that she was half in love with Jean-Jacques all along. But favourite or not, Wollstonecraft would have no part of Rousseau's views on women.

When she came to treat Rousseau's opinion of women, Wollstonecraft was not remiss in explaining where Rousseau went astray. Much of the *Vindication* is a refutation of Rousseau's theories about women, and clearly, to Wollstonecraft, Rousseau's acceptance of traditional attitudes about female inferiority is a more painful betrayal of liberalism than the platitudinous fatherly preachings of a Gregory or a Fordyce. Wollstonecraft, like Catherine Macaulay before her, explains Rousseau's attitudes towards women as an error in reasoning arising out of his sensibility. 'When he should have reasoned,' explained Wollstonecraft in the *Vindication*, 'he became impassioned' (p. 115). Rousseau, according to Wollstonecraft, is a victim of his own philosophy, for after instructing all women to be adorable and alluring, he loses all ability to evaluate their essential humanity. 'Is this the man,' asks Wollstonecraft, introducing the subject of Rousseau into the *Vindication* (p. 35), 'who delights to paint the useful struggles of passion, the triumphs of good dispositions, and the heroic flights which carry the glowing soul out of itself? – How are these mighty sentiments lowered when he describes the pretty foot and enticing airs of his little favourite!'

'Sophie' is Rousseau's creation of a young girl bred to be the ideal wife for 'Émile' and the antithesis of Wollstonecraft's rational woman. Not only is she by nature inferior, but she exists only to provide entertainment for men. Wollstonecraft challenges Rousseau's major assumptions about women: that a state of dependence is natural to them, therefore they should be dependent on men; that they are naturally uninclined to learn, therefore they should be given little opportunity; that they should have little liberty, but become accustomed to 'habitual restraints' since dissipation, levity and inconstancy are also natural to them. Wollstonecraft argues with all these assumptions. That women were created for the entertainment of men is offensive to Wollstonecraft's notion of reason. She will argue that women's faults are not a proof of their natural inferiority but proof instead of the intrinsic inferiority of their environment.

What Wollstonecraft finds most pernicious in Rousseau are the ethics he teaches women. If a virtue is one which is applied differentially to men and women, Wollstonecraft calls it a 'sexual virtue'. Concern with one's reputation, cunning, dissimulation, patience and forgiveness are all sexual virtues, or praiseworthy in a woman while demeaning to a man. Wollstonecraft's evaluation of these feminine virtues is often pragmatic and seldom unconvincing. Concern for reputation alone, for example, is a shallow virtue, for

> If the honour of a woman, as it is absurdly called, be safe, she may neglect every social duty; nay, ruin her family by gaming and extravagance; yet still present a shameless front – for truly she is an honourable woman! (pp. 170–71)

Furthermore, to be concerned always with mere appearances inevitably inhibits a woman's adventurousness. But while, according to Rousseau, a young woman should cultivate a good reputation, she can be indifferent to the virtue of simple honesty, and rightly so. Rousseau enjoyed the notion of a feminine coquette, and he would actually encourage young girls to cultivate little schemes to have their own way with their teachers. But women, cautioned Wollstonecraft, having to exercise power only through men and at the same time to please them, were instructed enough in the fine art of deception. What Rousseau thought charming, Wollstonecraft thought immoral and dangerous. After all, if a woman thrives for many years wholly on flattery and admiration, and is schooled in deception, where will she turn when her husband no longer finds her amusing or attractive? Surely the appetite for flattery and the practice of deception can only lead her to infidelity and further neglect of her children.

The ideal woman Rousseau described was not only a mindless coquette but, according to Wollstonecraft in the *Vindication*, she was a cheerfully submissive one. It was not at all unlikely, Wollstonecraft reads from Rousseau on p. 105, that a husband might occasionally unfairly accuse his wife of a misdemeanour. Rather than defend herself, Rousseau teaches, a woman should bear the insults of her husband without complaining. Replies Wollstonecraft (p. 106), 'Of what materials can that heart be composed, which can melt when insulted, and instead of revolting at injustice, kiss the rod?' The character of a woman is continually corroded as she tries to mimic these unnatural manners. She cannot submit, dissimulate, flatter without finally doing permanent harm to the moral imperative to seek reason and justice with which she was born. Rousseau and teachers like him had encouraged the development of a non-reasonable human being, another kind of person, always seeming to be, never being. 'Why are girls to be told that they resemble angels,' she asks (p. 120), 'but to sink them below women?'

One apprehends in the *Vindication* Wollstonecraft's profound sense that the middle-class girl is not being raised in the world and for the world, but raised instead, protected from the world, for the man she will one day marry. Isolated, sequestered, she is taught that life is like an intricate dance she will one day be called upon to perform. She learns to move like a puppet on a string, imitating other puppets as artificial and as unreal as she is. She is applauded for accomplishments which are in themselves hollow, and encouraged to anticipate a future which is mostly fantasy. And why? To be called an angel, a truly feminine woman, to have handkerchiefs retrieved and doors shut behind her, which she could have done herself if she moved a pace or two – a false and empty sovereignty – raised upon a pedestal within a prison or as Wollstonecraft puts it, 'Confined, then, in cages like the feathered race,' pluming themselves, stalking 'with mock majesty from perch to perch' (p. 72).

But Wollstonecraft was more than merely contemptuous of this feathered majesty. She was genuinely concerned for the future of the often self-satisfied and self-confident middle-class girl who was so ill-prepared to leave the protection of a father's home. Nothing could be quite so illusory as a young girl's fantasies about romantic love. And nothing could so completely mislead her about the realities of married life. The reader may find a few of the pronouncements the *Vindication* makes on marriage and motherhood frankly surprising. '[T]he neglected wife is, in general, the best mother' is one sober suggestion, and 'an unhappy marriage is often very advantageous to a family' another (p. 42). One can scarcely accept such sentiments from the same woman who in a few short years will attempt suicide for the unrequited love of Gilbert Imlay. Recent Wollstonecraft scholarship, as I explain in my discussion of her reception in our own time, has described these beliefs in a richer context of what she believed it was possible for her to argue. In part, Wollstonecraft may have been trying to tip the scales against romantic love, so heavily weighted down were young girls in its illusions. In Chapter VI Wollstonecraft makes a careful distinction between romantic love and 'friendship'. The first, explains Wollstonecraft, is an 'arbitrary passion', a stalking mischief (p. 147), the very opposite of reason which cannot last long in marriage without exhausting itself. Friendship, on the other hand, is a more sublime affection, because it is founded on principle and cemented by time.

The young girl ought to look beyond superficial charms when she chooses a marriage partner, for a compatibility of interests and temperament which will endure. But unhappily for them, this kind of caution was unlikely in young girls, educated as they were to delight in flattery and chivalry, scarcely knowledgeable enough to recognize good sense in another if they should be so fortunate to find it. Perhaps later, Wollstonecraft would say, after a revolution in human affairs, love might be a nobler passion. If women were, says Wollstonecraft, 'in some future revolution of time, to become, what I sincerely wish them to be, even love would acquire more serious dignity, and be purified in its own fires' (p. 148).

Wollstonecraft is, then, no permanent detractor of romantic love; she is only wary of its excesses in an imperfect age. As she wrote, romantic love was the fantasy only of young girls, exhausting their imagination, starving their ambition while worldly experience and academic study modified this influence on the growing boy. Since marriage would inevitably dispel the rosy illusions, the young girl should be undeceived and expect to find satisfaction in life as a reward for achievements beyond that of finding an attractive husband. No woman ought 'to rely for all her happiness on a being subject to like infirmities with herself' (p. 39).

But, while girls were taught to exaggerate romantic love out of all proportion to reality, they were not taught to respect the duties of motherhood. That most women are destined to be mothers is Wollstonecraft's best argument for educating them – in terms of the ease with which these arguments would be accepted; so it is an argument she will bring out again and again. Moreover, assigning the work of motherhood to a woman's exercise of civic virtue rescues women from the corruption of uselessness. Not only does Enlightenment social meliorism require the agency of educated mothers, the cultivation of their own virtue depends upon it.

One must realize again, however, that the fundamental imperative for education in Wollstonecraft's *Vindication* is that a woman has an innate capacity to reason which is its own moral justification for development. Wollstonecraft asserts candidly that a woman's first responsibility is to herself as a rational creature, and should one conceive of a conflict between domestic duties, motherhood and reason, it is reason which should be served. But such a conflict was highly unlikely. Right conduct, motherhood and developing reason could never be at variance. '[R]eason is absolutely necessary to enable a woman to perform any duty properly,' explains Wollstonecraft (p. 83), and no duty was as important as her duty to her children.

The *Vindication* places a great deal of importance on the role of women in the home, although Wollstonecraft is by no means

convinced that this is the only place for her to be. 'When I treat
of the peculiar duties of women . . . it will be found that I do
not mean to insinuate that they should be taken out of their
families, speaking of the majority . . .' (p. 82). She is frankly
torn by this dilemma. On the one hand she believes that
mothering is crucially important to the ongoing process of per-
fecting civilizations, on the other hand she accepts that great
achievements and family life do not walk hand in hand. Her
attempt to resolve this dilemma is curious, and one she would
probably not have been long happy with. If the demands of
family life were such that it would be difficult for a woman to
achieve any worldly distinction, one was to be comforted with
the following: '[T]he welfare of society is not built on extraordinary exertions; and were it more reasonably organized, there
would be still less need of great abilities, or heroic virtues'
(p. 82). More progressive proposals for women were made later
in the *Vindication*; meanwhile in acknowledging motherhood
to be a responsibility, Wollstonecraft insists that education be
provided for the future mother. If government is to be based on
the consent of its citizens, then the citizens must be virtuous. If
a change in the affairs of society must be made, the need for a
change must be recognized by wise men and women. Not only
was it an inherent right of women to be educated, it was a social
imperative; if not, succeeding generations would inherit their
parents' ignorance, instead of their wisdom.

Wollstonecraft uses the same blend of environmentalist
eugenics and ideology when she describes sexual promiscuity.
When women are morally lax, the fault, argues the *Vindication*,
is the man's. Until her education is improved, it is unjust to
consider a poor, ignorant, foolish girl, brought up only to reverence sensibility, a free moral agent. The *Vindication* suggests (in
Chapter VIII, 'Morality'), that until such time as women are
educated, a man who fathers an illegitimate child should be
required to support the mother and child; '. . . all the causes of
female weakness . . . branch out of one grand cause – want of
chastity in men' (p. 172). But the real victim of moral laxity is
neither man nor woman, but society itself, since

The weak enervated women who particularly catch the attention
of libertines, are unfit to be mothers, though they may conceive; so
that the rich sensualist, who has rioted among women, spreading
depravity and misery, when he wishes to perpetuate his name,
receives from his wife only an half-formed being that inherits
both its father's and mother's weakness. (p. 173)

Ideology, ethics and simple humanity were not so well blended
again until William Blake's 'London':

> But most thro' midnight streets I hear
> How the youthful Harlot's curse
> Blasts the new-born Infant's tear,
> And blights with plagues the Marriage hearse.

Beyond the general argument for the emancipation of women
the *Vindication* advocates more specific social reforms in education and the family (Chapters X and XI, 'Parental affection'
and 'Duty to parents'). Wollstonecraft speaks now not of male
or female children, but of all children, given equal advantages.
The home, with an educated mother and father presiding over
it, looms large in shaping good character in the child. In an
affectionate and well-regulated home, children will develop a
love for family life which will inspire their own home-making
when they are adults. In return for parental affection and care,
children will respond with loyalty and protection when they
mature. Filial duty, in the *Vindication*, is treated in a manner
consistent with Wollstonecraft's progressive ideology. Children
should acknowledge the authority of their parents until they
have attained the age of reason. Then they must follow the
dictates of their own conscience. There must be no tyranny over
children when they are able to reason, just as the virtuous citizen
should be free of the tyranny of the state. When they are ready
for school, they will go, not to boarding school, where isolated
from adults they would compound each other's ignorance, but
to a day-school near their home. In Chapter XII, 'On national
education', Wollstonecraft, like Thomas Paine, considerably in
advance of her time, recommends the establishment of a national

system of instruction, which would operate co-educational day schools. Assuming a reformed state, which represents the collective wisdom of its citizenry, Wollstonecraft would, by nationalizing education, free schoolmasters from economic dependence on individual parents which might be injurious to good teaching. With a schoolteacher independent of individual prejudices, a child, in the more natural atmosphere of comradeship with both sexes, would receive basic instruction, after which the more able would continue academic work while the others learned a trade.

Girls, according to the *Vindication*, would not receive this excellent education merely for their eternal amusement. And it is with this distinction that Wollstonecraft must be so sharply distinguished from those who wanted to reform women's manners either to make them more attractive companions for men, or to enrich their moments of leisure. Independence, said Wollstonecraft, is derived from the ability to earn one's living. So long as women lean on another for support they will inevitably dissipate their native intelligence and imperil their virtue. 'Happy is it when people have the cares of life to struggle with; for these struggles prevent their becoming a prey to enervating vices, merely from idleness' (p. 71). Having to struggle with the cares of life is what Wollstonecraft calls the 'virtue of necessity', and she urges its embrace tirelessly.

Give a woman back, she says, the simple need to earn her own bread, take from her the false manners and artificial chivalry which isolate her and corrupt her, and put her to work. 'It is true,' she says of dependent women, 'they are provided with food and raiment, for which they neither toil nor spin; but health, liberty, and virtue, are given in exchange' (pp. 72–3). Wollstonecraft had her own remedy for the odd assortment of maladies and vapours which too often afflicted the delicate women of fashion. 'I have often wished, with Dr Johnson,' she said, 'to place some of them in a little shop with half a dozen children looking up to their languid countenances for support' (p. 182). Then some health and vigour might return to the pale cheeks, and a more thoughtful expression might accompany the dimples.

But what work was a woman to do? We have already seen that even as Wollstonecraft was writing, employment for women was becoming more limited. Not all women had capital enough to be a milliner or a mantua-maker with a shop, and the apprenticeship for these trades was gruelling. The women who had earned their living with a dairy farm, or a small brewery, or in domestic industry were finding employment eliminated by industrialization. Wollstonecraft is certain, however, that women should be allowed to rise as high as their industry and intelligence can take them. Chapter IX, with its ponderous title, would have left her reader breathless with its daring. If tradition and law stand as obstacles to a woman's rise in working society, argues the *Vindication*, referring to Blackstone's 'civil death' of women in marriage, such laws must be changed. '[I]n order to render their private virtue a public benefit, they must have a civil existence in the state,' says Wollstonecraft (p. 185); adding, 'How many women thus waste life away the prey of discontent, who might have practised as physicians, regulated a farm, managed a shop . . .' She goes so far as to say that they ought to be represented in government, although in 1792 they were well accompanied among the many disenfranchised.

The force of the *Vindication* is clearly to derive education for women so that they might be the virtuous mothers of a reform-minded new generation of citizens, extending the republican requirement of civic virtue to women by schooling them in rational motherhood. In Wollstonecraft's reformed society, the enlightened woman must inevitably depend on some assistance with domestic labour. She would have no flocks of servants to assist her, but she would be no household drudge. She would be 'an active citizen', says Wollstonecraft (p. 181), 'equally intent to manage her family, educate her children, and assist her neighbours'. If she is this, one understands, then she fulfils an obligation to the community which earns her the support she derives from her husband, and frees her at least from the spirit of economic dependence, if not its actuality. The *Vindication*, then, offers no romanticization of motherhood, nor of housework, just as Wollstonecraft herself, although she despised luxury, was no romanticizer of poverty. The ideal woman pictured in the *Vindication* is active and intelligent, blending civic and familial responsibilities, freed from drudgery and debasing frugality. But Wollstonecraft will not yield the principle that the reformation of the community and the socialization of children is the important work of educated parents; and that society could ill afford to delay, considering the immensity of the task, to offer an equal partnership to women. 'It is time', she says, thinking of the great waste of human resources, 'to effect a revolution in female manners – time to restore to them their lost dignity – and make them, as a part of the human species, labour by reforming themselves to reform the world' (p. 60).

'POSTERITY, HOWEVER, WILL BE MORE JUST' – FEMINISM AFTER THE *VINDICATION*

In *A Vindication of the Rights of Woman*, Mary Wollstonecraft pleaded for a more sympathetic reading from posterity for her radical mentor Catherine Macaulay (p. 131). Had Wollstonecraft also hoped that her immediate posterity would pay 'a sufficient respect' to her own memory, her expectations would have been disappointed. *A Vindication of the Rights of Woman* is so comprehensive an argument that one may say that all feminists, radical and conservative, who followed Wollstonecraft are her philosophic descendants. But for a long while after her death it was not the argument of the *Vindication* which formed the basis of the controversy surrounding it, but the personal life of its author. Wollstonecraft had openly challenged conventional morality by living with a man outside of marriage and bearing a child. Godwin, whose grief for Wollstonecraft was for a long while absorbed in writing her memoirs, had made this relationship with Imlay the subject of public knowledge. Wollstonecraft's name, in the years following her death, years of political repression and a fear of French radicalism, became virtually synonymous with free love and Jacobinism. Very few

who might have otherwise been sympathetic to feminist objec-
tives dared risk, in this atmosphere of political hysteria, being
tainted by association with her. The *Vindication* which espoused
the supremacy of reason was not, then, given a reasonable
rebuttal, but was answered instead with derision, ridicule and
abuse. Such a long reach were the pernicious effects of the
Vindication thought to have, that when the unhappy Fanny
Imlay committed suicide as a young woman, and Mary Godwin
eloped with the poet Shelley, many years after the death of their
mother, public opinion considered Wollstonecraft's feminism
responsible.

A few women, like Mary Hays and Mary Robinson, novelists
and essayists, did write about the emancipation of women in
the years immediately following Wollstonecraft's death, but
their reputations were not improved by being thought in the
'pernicious train of Mary Wollstonecraft's followers', one of
the 'impious amazons of Republican France'. Mary Hays, even
though she was a good friend of Godwin's and a disciple of
Wollstonecraft's, felt obliged to omit Wollstonecraft's name
from a volume on learned women which she prepared in 1803.
For the most part, as part of a national mood of political
conservatism, feminism was quiescent in England in the early
nineteenth century, and when the movement did begin to gather
force in the 1850s, with organizations to reform married
women's property rights, it was in a spirit uncongenial to the
ideological basis of the *Vindication*.

If one isolates a Wollstonecraft tradition in feminist reform,
it is an approach which considers all aspects of women's condition, economic, psychological, cultural, as inter-related, with
effective reform dependent on basic social changes in the distribution of political and economic power. Very few English or
American feminists in the nineteenth century worked for such
basic social change. The mainstream of feminism in both countries, after the *Vindication*, was concerned instead with achiev-
ing limited and specific reforms often for particular kinds of
women like unmarried and working-class women, who, it was
assumed, were without the conventional protection of the
male sex.

Nor were all reformers associated with the feminist movement interested in the problem of the unequal treatment of women. The suffrage movement, for example, was perceived by many women as the means by which certain benevolent reforms concerning moral welfare might be enacted, rather than representing a woman's right to participate fully in political and professional life. Some would say that the only tangible evidence of women's influence in American political life was the passing of the Temperance Act of 1919, outlawing the sale of alcoholic beverages.

Paradoxically, the kind of women's lives post-Wollstonecraft feminists were least interested in changing were lives like their own, middle-class, married and respectable, the very same Wollstonecraft wanted to galvanize into a new understanding of their potential as rational creatures. The fight for education, for suffrage, for job-training, for admission into the professions, seldom challenged the traditional verity that these were avenues for those who must of necessity make their own way. Among the limited piecemeal movements of the Victorians, there was little recognition of the unfulfilled potential of the married, economically secure, but dependent middle-class woman.

Seldom too in the nineteenth century was there anything like Wollstonecraft's challenge to conventional sexual morality. Sexual morality for Wollstonecraft was, after all, wholly dependent upon a rational and just social order. She had said that one couldn't call 'virtuous' a faithful wife whose freedom of choice was inhibited by the tyranny of the marriage contract. Similarly, how could one condemn a faithless woman if her education encouraged her to be coquettish, not reasonable. Most Victorian feminists, however, accepted prevailing notions of female modesty and were willing to attack individual bastions of male supremacy without actively challenging the notions of sexual morality, a morality which assumed that men needed to lead more active sexual lives than women and tolerated the infidelities of the husband, but not of the wife. When women did crusade for moral welfare, they often tried to pacify what they called male 'viciousness' rather than claim the right for sexual satisfaction themselves. Not only did the lack of awareness of had she written it, was to have treated the subject of laws concerning women.

Perhaps the most important written argument for feminism in the nineteenth century was John Stuart Mill's *The Subjection of Women*, published in 1869, which gave to a wider audience many of the concerns the *Vindication* had raised seventy-nine years earlier. Mill, who became an active feminist reformer, argued, as did Wollstonecraft, for improved education for women, disparaging the environmental forces which appeared to consign them to coquettish imbecility. He spoke also of the deleterious effects of Victorian prudishness on a woman's as well as a man's worldly ambitions, saying 'whoever has a wife and children has given hostages to Mrs Grundy'.[44] Like Wollstonecraft, he believed that 'the power of earning is essential to the dignity of women'.[45] The character of a married woman's life, however, must still be primarily domestic, her education a source of spiritual enrichment rather than the means by which she gains economic independence.

Although the mainstream of feminism in the nineteenth century challenged neither the basic social structure of society nor the quality of life of the married middle-class woman, it achieved important successes. By the end of the century women gained the right of entry to medical schools, the right to be educated at Cambridge University, entry to various professions and establishment of job-training programmes for working-class women. The great crusade of feminist reformers, however, was for the vote. From John Stuart Mill's presentation of the first petition to Parliament in 1866 until suffrage was achieved in England in 1927 (in the USA in 1919), the constitutional movement for women's suffrage, under the leadership of Millicent Fawcett, persevered against the hostile male legislators in whom they rested all their hopes. But in its single-minded pursuit, and its refusal to join forces with feminists whose work was tainted by the merest hint of scandal, the suffrage issue badly divided the feminist movement and exhausted the efforts of a generation of women who felt that when the vote was obtained, the struggle for equal rights was somehow won. The suffrage movement and the acquisition of a few places in higher education changed the lives of only a small group of women. The married woman's life was still circumscribed by her domesticity. The working-class woman worked hard at two jobs, the one she went to in the morning, and the other to which she returned at home.

By the time Emma Goldman was writing in 1917 she found reason to accuse feminists of having accepted so carefully the tenets of conventional sexual morality that they had sacrificed their own womanhood. Goldman, a Russian-born, American-Jewish anarchist, spoke passionately for a woman's right to be independent and yet still maintain a loving relationship with a man and rejoice in motherhood. 'The greatest shortcoming of the emancipation of the present day,' she wrote, 'lies in its artificial stiffness and its narrow respectabilities, which produce an emptiness in woman's soul that will not let her drink from the fountain of life.'[46] Emma Goldman acknowledged Mary Wollstonecraft as a 'pioneer of modern womanhood', a true rebel, like herself.[47] But victories at court or at the polls would be useless without a woman's claiming unrestricted freedom over her own body. Goldman told the 'majority of our emancipated professional women who fill the colleges, halls of learning, and various offices' to listen to the voice of nature, 'whether it call for life's greatest treasure, love for a man, or her most glorious privilege, the right to give birth to a child'. 'This does not mean a wish to return to the past,' she cautioned, 'nor does it condemn woman to her old sphere, the kitchen and the nursery.'[48]

As Mary Wollstonecraft had hoped for the works of her mentor Catherine Macaulay, by the late-twentieth-century readers had indeed taken the *Vindication* seriously. To be sure, readers had always been able to reshape Mary Wollstonecraft according to their own political literary and social agenda. She was either the philosophic and moral wanton of the conservatives who opposed the French Revolution, or she was the sentimental favourite of the early Romantics. She became the anarchist Emma Goldman's courageous sexual revolutionary and Virginia Woolf's reform-minded critic of women's education. Another generation to come to the drawing-board has been influenced in the 1960s and 1970s by a feminism born out of the progressive politics of the American civil rights movement and dissent against the Vietnam War. As have other generations of readers, this more sexually free and professionally emancipated readership reshaped the Wollstonecraft it found, reclaiming her as the founding mother of feminism's rebirth. Studying the corpus of her writings, newly issued in scholarly editions, these readers have brought Mary Wollstonecraft inside the academy and consecrated the *Vindication* as feminism's founding text. Submitting her texts to new scrutiny, they claimed to have rescued Wollstonecraft from the abuses of misunderstanding and underrating that had earlier dismissed her arguments as the ravings of an unfortunate woman who had simply met the wrong kind of man.

Far from denying the contradictory representations of 'wanton' or heroine, reformer or revolutionary, Wollstonecraft's more recent reception embraces and explains all of these paradoxes, without attempting their reconciliation. These readings stress an apparent paradox in the *Vindication*, her surprising denigration of sensibility and sexual passion in spite of her novel-writing, her own lived sexual liberation and her willingness to flout the conventions of bourgeois morality. In the *Vindication*, Wollstonecraft argued that 'In order to fulfil the duties of life . . . master and mistress of a family ought not to continue to love each other with passion' (p. 42). She claimed sexual feeling is itself only transient, 'creating intolerable disgust' (p. 240). 'Pleasure,' she argued, 'is the business of woman's life . . . and while it continues to be so, little can be expected from such weak beings' (pp. 71–2). Having extended the Enlightenment credo of the rights of man to woman, Wollstonecraft had insisted that there were no male or female virtues, but only human ones; she had appealed to men's reason to make women their companions not their slaves, and had claimed that there could be no improvement in women's morality until men were themselves moral. With hopes for human happiness and societal improvement lodging in men's capacity to reason, she found sexual passion not only useless but corrupting.

Although the logic of Wollstonecraft's argument is unassailable, many argue that she has apparently given away too much.

As Cora Kaplan has argued, 'it is Mary Wollstonecraft who first offered women this fateful choice between the opposed and moralized bastions of reason and feeling, which continues to determine much feminist thinking'.[49] In requiring that reason and passion could not cohabit the same conceptual space, Wollstonecraft bequeathed to her intellectual descendants a troubling dichotomy, not one the readers of her passionate letters to Gilbert Imlay would ever have imagined that she herself believed in.

Approaching such a paradox, the critics of the *Vindication* have divided themselves into several groups. The first of these, best exemplified by G. J. Barker-Benfield, imagines a Wollstonecraft who enters the political debate of the late Enlightenment to make a purposeful argument about women's oppression.[50] According to such a reading, Wollstonecraft offered her readers an argument for educating women to be virtuous. Influenced by the political thought of liberal Dissenters James Burgh and Richard Price, Wollstonecraft took her moral lexicon from the seventeenth-century British Commonwealth tradition and a masculine model of civic virtue that represented man's fulfilling of the duties of rational citizenship as he engaged in public life. As an analogue to the public-spirited republican man, the virtuous woman given in the *Vindication* fulfilled the duties of citizenship in motherhood, or at least would do so if she were properly educated.

This Wollstonecraft promulgated a republican motherhood to bring society to all the perfection that the Enlightenment imagined possible, arguing, 'When I treat of the peculiar duties of women, as I should treat of the peculiar duties of a citizen or father, it will be found that I do not mean to insinuate that they should be taken out of their families, speaking of the majority' (p. 82). Limited in sphere, the woman represented in this reading of the *Vindication* is equally limited in her capacity for erotic life, perhaps necessarily so. Such interpretations argue that Wollstonecraft omitted sexual passion from her construction of civic virtue because of its associations with aristocratic voluptuousness and decadence. She has taken as her lead the puritan reformers of the previous century who claimed that both men and women must practise marital fidelity because 'the tie is equal', and required of both sexes a suppression of desire that might trouble this practice.[51] A feminism derived from this reading of the *Vindication* places its hopes for improvement in men's reasonableness and their willingness to reform the conditions that protect their own privilege. A politics critical of such hopes argues that Wollstonecraft left intact the rigid separation of male and female duties that gave political and economic power to men. In so doing, according to feminist theorist Zillah Eisenstein, the *Vindication* fatally relegated women to a subordinate and dependent portion of human work.[52]

A second reading, based too on what is readily apparent in Wollstonecraft's argument, finds a more radical author, one quite willing to take women beyond the duties of motherhood so that they might support themselves 'by their own industry', practising as physicians, regulating a farm, or managing a shop (p. 185). Wollstonecraft had suggested as well, although she imagined laughter in response, that 'women ought to have representatives, instead of being arbitrarily governed without having any direct share allowed them in the deliberations of government' (p. 182). This more radical Wollstonecraft, as read by Elissa S. Guralnick, insisted that domestic spaces be governed by the same virtues that governed public ones, laying the basis, thereby, for a politics that militates against the rigid separation of middle-class social life into the private and domestic refuges provided by women, governed by sensibility, and the public, marketable work of men, governed by reason.[53] According to such readings, when Wollstonecraft refused women's identification with sensibility, she rejected as well the association of women with sentiment and feeling, an ideology that both trivialized their enterprises and legitimized their subordination.

A third reading, in which many contemporary critics participate, describes a Wollstonecraft less immediately apparent on the surface of the text, and her argument not as readily translatable into Enlightenment projects of reform or revolution.[54] These interpretations take as their theoretical beginnings that all texts are shaped profoundly at a conscious and unconscious level by gendered political, social and literary conventions. Because of such shaping, the *Vindication* takes its dimension not only from its historical moment in the late Enlightenment but also from its having been written by a woman. A woman writing political essays occupied a position from which, paradoxically, according to cultural convention, no public argument was considered either possible, or, in the unlikely event of its having emerged, of such substance that required serious consideration. To write as a woman to vindicate one's own rights is, by this culturally imposed contradiction, to bespeak oneself as some kind of mutant, a monstrosity which provoked the anti-Jacobins to laughter and ridicule. A woman who wrote and wanted to be taken seriously, therefore, must disguise this monstrosity as much as possible by blurring the seams of her sexual difference.

Writing as if she were a man, such a writer adopts the conventionalized rhetorical modes and values of the dominant masculine culture, even when they may seem to contradict her own felt experience as a woman. According to such interpretations, Wollstonecraft denied female passion as she responded to the constraints of a masculine public discourse. While suppressing her femaleness to write for masculinized public places, the female body which she attempted to submerge surfaced in her text in spite of herself to disrupt and qualify her argument. Interpretations of the *Vindication* taking these theories as their critical assumptions have not only tried to reconnect the body, which cultural convention required Wollstonecraft to sever from her head, these readings have gone a long way as well to rescuing and restoring significance to Wollstonecraft's style of writing.

By such lights Wollstonecraft has not quite rejected passion in order to claim reason, but has repressed it. Such repression has been compelled not by the conscious embrace of rational virtues but because cultural convention, either idealizing women as sexually passive or dismissing them as wantons, has predetermined the borders of articulation within which Wollstonecraft could make her argument. These readings claim that she has not quite given away a woman's body to acquire her mind, nor completely accepted the rigid dichotomy of passion and intellect to secure human virtues for women. This Wollstonecraft is ambivalent, contradictory and paradoxical, but in the double valences of these rhetorical positions, she has left space for an erotic female sentience. Writing about rationality, Wollstonecraft repressed her own sensibility and desire, but these have risen to the surface of the text elliptically, accounting for its apparent disorganization, digressiveness, sporadic examples, apostrophes and outbursts. All of these are the surface rumblings of the author's repression of feeling. It is as if a submerged, essential and undiscoursed woman is compelled to surface inside a conceptual terrain comprised of conventional political and literary shapes. The resulting earthquake is the prose tempest of the *Vindication*.

These several Wollstonecrafts, reformer and revolutionary, rationalist and woman of feeling, variously inhabit *A Vindication of the Rights of Woman* as it passed beyond its bicentenary. Mary Wollstonecraft has left a volatile and productive legacy for times momentous in political and social challenge. While we have, perhaps, less confidence than she in prospects for societal improvement based on the pure uncorrupted agency of human reason, we cannot do without her insistence on a single standard of human values. With her universal declaration of human rights, she has claimed the entitlement of all persons, however different from each other, in the long-standing project of creating social justice.

NOTES

1   *Anti-Jacobin Review and Magazine* 9 (1801), p. 518.
2   *Historical Magazine* 1 (1799), p. 34.
3   See unpublished manuscript, *Maria – The Wrongs of Woman*, in C. Kegan Paul, *William Godwin* (1876), p. 140. (*Mary, a Fiction* and *The Wrongs of Woman* have been republished and edited with an introduction by Gary Kelly (London: Oxford University Press, 1976).)
4   Paul, *William Godwin*, p. 187.

5   Mary Wollstonecraft, *Mary, A Fiction* (1788), p. 76.

6   Ibid., p. 187.

7   Paul, *William Godwin*, p. 191.

8   Mitzi Myers, 'Impeccable Governesses, Rational Dames, and Moral Mothers: Mary Wollstonecraft and the Female Tradition in Georgian Children's Books', *Children's Literature* 14 (1986), p. 54.

9   Moira Ferguson reprints the preface to *The Female Reader* and the four prayers in an archival note for *Signs: Journal of Women in Culture and Society* 3: 41 (1978), pp. 945–57.

10 Mary Wollstonecraft, *A Vindication of the Rights of Men* (1790), p. 92.

11 Ibid., pp. 25–6.

12 Thomas Cooper, *A Reply to Mr Burke's Invective* (1792), pp. 98–9.

13 *The Letters of Horace Walpole*, ed. Mrs Paget Toynbee (Oxford: Clarendon Press, 1905), Vol. XV, pp. 131–2, 337–8.

14 Mary Wollstonecraft, *An Historical and Moral View of the Origin and Progress of the French Revolution* (1794), p. 73.

15 Letter to Ruth Barlow, 20 May 1794, *The Collected Letters of Mary Wollstonecraft*, ed. Janet Todd (London: Penguin, 2003), no. 149.

16 Letters to Gilbert Imlay, December 1793, 12 January 1794, *Collected Letters*, ed. Todd, nos. 141, 132, 151.

17 See *British Critic* 7 (1796), pp. 602–10.

18 *Letters Written During a Short Residence in Sweden, Norway, and Denmark* (1796), pp. 214–15.

19 Ibid., p. 208.

20 William Godwin, *Memoirs of Mary Wollstonecraft* (London: Constable, 1927), p. 84.

21 Ralph Wardle, *Godwin and Mary* (Lawrence: Kansas University Press, 1966), p. 83.

22 See Marc Rubenstein, 'My Accursed Origin: the Search for the Mother in *Frankenstein*', *Studies in Romanticism* 15 (Spring 1976), pp. 165–94 and Ellen Moers, *New York Review of Books*, 21 March 1974, pp. 24–8.

23 Thomas Paine, 'An Occasional Letter to the Female Sex' (1775), in *The Writings of Thomas Paine*, ed. M. D. Conway and C. Putnam (New York, 1906), Vol. II, p. 60.

24 Mary Astell, *A Serious Proposal to the Ladies for the Advancement of their True and Greatest Interest* (1694), in *Mary Astell* (New York: Columbia University Press, 1916), Vol. II, p. 52.

25   William Blackstone, *Commentaries on the Laws of England* (New York, 1847), Vol. I, p. 441.

26   Daniel Defoe, *Compleat English Tradesman* (1738), Vol. I, pp. 279–80.

27   British Museum, ADD MSS. 27,827, f. 101.

28   Quoted from the *Spectator*, in Margaret Phillips and William S. Tomkinson, *English Women in Life and Letters* (Oxford: Oxford University Press, 1926), p. 114.

29   *Essay on Projects* (London, 1697), pp. 302–3.

30   *Swift, Poetical Works*, ed. Herbert Davis (London: Oxford University Press, 1967), p. 328.

31   Hannah More, *Works* (1857), Vol. I, p. 345.

32   *Life Works of Mrs Barbauld*, ed. Gran. A. Ellis (Boston, 1874), Vol. I, p. 57.

33   More, *Works*, Vol. I, pp. 345, 346.

34   *The Selected Letters of Lady Mary Wortley Montagu*, ed. Robert Halsband (New York, 1970), p. 246.

35   Ibid., p. 240.

36   Catherine Macaulay, *Letters on Education* (1790), p. 201.

37   Wollstonecraft, *Letters Written During a Short Residence*, p. 27.

38   Wollstonecraft, *A Vindication of the Rights of Men*, p. 26.

39   Wollstonecraft, *Letters Written During a Short Residence*, p. 75.

40   Wollstonecraft, *A Vindication of the Rights of Men*, pp. 138, 140.

41   Wollstonecraft, *An Historical and Moral View*, p. 33.

42   John Stuart Mill, *The Subjection of Women* (London, 1929), pp. 289–91.

43   Johanna Johnston, *Mrs Satan* (London: Macmillan, 1967), p. 92.

44   Mill, *The Subjection of Women*, p. 306.

45   Ibid., pp. 222–4.

46   Emma Goldman, 'The Tragedy of Woman's Emancipation', in *Anarchism and Other Essays* (Port Washington: Kennikat, 1969), p. 223.

47   Emma Goldman's lecture on Mary Wollstonecraft has been reprinted from the original manuscript in the New York Public Library by Alice Wexler in *Feminist Studies* no. 1 (Spring 1981), pp. 113–21.

48   Goldman, 'The Tragedy of Woman's Emancipation', pp. 222–4.

49   Cora Kaplan, 'Pandora's Box: Subjectivity, Class, and Sexuality in Socialist Feminist Criticism', in *Making a Difference*, ed. Gayle Greene and Coppelia Kahn (London: Methuen, 1985), pp. 146–76.

50   G. J. Barker-Benfield, 'Mary Wollstonecraft: Eighteenth-Century
     Commonwealthwoman', *Journal of the History of Ideas* 50:1
     (1989), pp. 95–115.

51   *Matrimonial Honour* (1642), pp. 181–2.

52   Zillah Eisenstein, 'Mary Wollstonecraft: The Feminist Embrace
     and Criticism of Liberalism', in *The Radical Future of Liberal
     Feminism* (New York: Longmans, 1981), pp. 89–112.

53   E. S. Guralnick, 'Radical Politics in Mary Wollstonecraft's *A
     Vindication of the Rights of Woman*', *Studies in Burke and His
     Time* 18:3 (1977), pp. 155–66.

54   See for example, Syndy McMillen Conger, 'The Sentimental Logic
     of Wollstonecraft's Prose', *Prose Studies: History, Theory, Criti-
     cism* 10:2 (Sept. 1987), pp. 143–8; Laurie A. Finke, 'A Philo-
     sophic Wanton: Language and Authority in Wollstonecraft's *A
     Vindication of the Rights of Woman*', in *The Philosopher as
     Writer*, ed. Robert Ginsberg (Selinsgrove: Susquehanna Univer-
     sity Press, 1987), pp. 155–76; Mary Poovey, *The Proper Lady
     and the Woman Writer: Ideology as Style in the Works of Mary
     Wollstonecraft, Mary Shelley, and Jane Austen* (Chicago: Univer-
     sity of Chicago Press, 1984).

Further Reading

Works by Mary Wollstonecraft*

The Collected Letters of Mary Wollstonecraft, ed. Janet Todd (London: Penguin, 2003).

Maria, or the Wrongs of Woman (1799), with an introduction by Anna K. Mellor (New York: Norton, 1994).

Mary, A Fiction (1788), ed. Gary Kelly (London: Oxford University Press, 1976).

Original Stories from Real Life, with conversations, calculated to regulate the affections, and form the mind to truth and goodness (1788; New York: Woodstock, 1990).

Political Writings of Mary Wollstonecraft: A Vindication of the Rights of Men, A Vindication of the Rights of Woman, An Historical and Moral View of the French Revolution (London: William Pickering, 1993).

Posthumous Works of the Author of 'A Vindication of the Rights of Woman', ed. William Godwin (1798), ed. Gina Luria (New York: Garland, 1974).

A Short Residence in Sweden, Norway, and Denmark (1796), ed. Richard Holmes (New York: Penguin, 1987).

Thoughts on the education of daughters; with reflections on female conduct, in the more important duties of life (1787), ed. Gina Luria (New York: Garland, 1974).

A Wollstonecraft Anthology, ed. Janet Todd (1977; New York: Columbia University Press, 1989).

* An annotated bibliography of Wollstonecraft's works and critical reception is available in a volume by Janet Todd (New York: Garland Publishing Co., 1976).

Biographies of Mary Wollstonecraft

Godwin, William, *Memoirs of Mary Wollstonecraft*, ed. with a Preface, Supplement, and Bibliographical Note by W. Clark Durant (London: Constable, 1927).

Wardle, Ralph M., *Mary Wollstonecraft: A Critical Biography* (Lawrence, Kansas: University of Kansas Press, 1951).

George, Margaret, *One Woman's 'Situation'* (Urbana: University of Illinois Press, 1970).

Nixon, Edna, *Mary Wollstonecraft: Her Life and Times* (London: Dent, 1971).

Flexner, Eleanor, *Mary Wollstonecraft: A Biography* (New York: Coward, McCann & Geoghegan, 1972).

Tomalin, Claire, *Mary Wollstonecraft* (London: Weidenfeld & Nicolson, 1974).

Sunstein, Emily, *A Different Face: The Life of Mary Wollstonecraft* (New York: Harper and Row, 1975).

Detre, Jean, *A Most Extraordinary Pair: Mary Wollstonecraft and William Godwin* (New York: Doubleday, 1975).

Lorch, Jennifer, *Mary Wollstonecraft: The Making of a Radical Feminist* (New York and Oxford: St Martin's Press, 1990).

Kelly, Gary, *Revolutionary Feminism: The Mind and Career of Mary Wollstonecraft* (New York: St Martin's Press, 1992).

Todd, Janet, *Mary Wollstonecraft: A Revolutionary Life* (London: Weidenfeld & Nicolson, 2000).

Jacobs, Diane, *Her Own Woman: The Life of Mary Wollstonecraft* (New York: Simon and Schuster, 2001).

A Selected Bibliography of Book-length and Periodical Critical Study of Mary Wollstonecraft

Barker-Benfield, G. J., 'Mary Wollstonecraft: Eighteenth-Century Commonwealthwoman', *Journal of the History of Ideas* 50:1 (1989), pp. 95–115.

Brody, Miriam, 'Mary Wollstonecraft: Sexuality and Women's Rights', in *Feminist Theorists*, ed. Dale Spender (London: Women's Press, 1982).

Conger, Syndy McMillen, 'The Sentimental Logic of Wollstonecraft's Prose', *Prose Studies: History, Theory, Criticism* 10:2 (Sept. 1987), pp. 143–8.

Eisenstein, Zillah, 'Mary Wollstonecraft: The Feminist Embrace and Criticism of Liberalism', in *The Radical Future of Liberal Feminism* (New York: Longmans, 1981).

Falco, Maria J. (ed.), *Feminist Interpretations of Mary Wollstonecraft* (University Park: Pennsylvania State University Press, 1996).

Ferguson, Moira and Janet Todd, *Mary Wollstonecraft* (Boston: Twayne, 1984).

Finke, Laurie A., 'A Philosophic Wanton: Language and Authority in Wollstonecraft's *A Vindication of the Rights of Woman*', in *The Philosopher As Writer*, ed. Robert Ginsberg (Selinsgrove: Susquehanna University Press, 1987).

Guralnick, E. S., 'Rhetorical Strategy on Mary Wollstonecraft's *A Vindication of the Rights of Woman*', *Humanitus Association Review* 30:3 (1989), pp. 174–85.

—, 'Radical Politics in Mary Wollstonecraft's *A Vindication of the Rights of Woman*', *Studies in Burke and His Time* 18:3 (1977), pp. 155–66.

Kaplan, Cora, 'Pandora's Box: Subjectivity, Class, and Sexuality in Socialist Feminist Criticism', in *Making a Difference: Feminist Literary Criticism*, ed. Gayle Greene and Coppelia Kahn (London: Methuen, 1985), pp. 146–76.

Kelly, Gary, 'Mary Wollstonecraft as Vir-Bonus', *English Studies in Canada* S:3 (1979), pp. 275–91.

Myers, Mitzi, 'Godwin's Memoirs of Wollstonecraft: The Shaping of Self and Subject', *Studies in Romanticism* 20:e (Fall 1981), pp. 299–316.

—, 'Impeccable Governesses, Rational Dames, and Moral Mothers: Mary Wollstonecraft and the Female Tradition in Georgian Children's Books', *Children's Literature: An International Journal. Annual of the Modern Language Association Division on Children's Literature* 14 (1986), pp. 31–59.

Poovey, Mary, *The Proper Lady and the Woman Writer: Ideology as Style in the Works of Mary Wollstonecraft, Mary Shelley, and Jane Austen* (Chicago: University of Chicago Press, 1984).

Rubenstein, M. A., 'My Accursed Origin: The Search for the Mother in Frankenstein', *Studies in Romanticism* 15 (Spring 1976), pp. 165–94.

A Note on the Text

The first edition of *A Vindication of the Rights of Woman* was published in London by Joseph Johnson early in 1792. Mary Wollstonecraft had written the *Vindication* in such haste that it went into print with many errors. Later the same year, she produced a corrected second edition, which is considered to be the last authoritative edition. In the course of numerous subsequent reprintings, changes in diction and spelling and in punctuation have entered the text. This reprinting of the *Vindication* has been set from a photocopy of the second edition in the possession of the British Library.

Minimal emendations have been made for the Penguin reader. House styling, without further notification, is limited to: (1) quotation marks: the occasional double quotation marks are made singles (and doubles inside singles); for a quotation, the quotation marks at the start of second and following lines (as was the printing style of the period) have been removed; omitted closing quotation marks have been added; (2) full stops have been omitted at the end of chapter numbers and titles, and in personal titles (e.g. Dr, Mr, Mrs); (3) the unspaced M-dashes have been printed as spaced N-dashes (and 2M-dashes as M-dashes); (4) the symbols for Wollstonecraft's footnotes have been printed after the punctuation; (5) the long s (*f*), a feature of eighteenth-century printing (e.g. di*f*cu*ff*ion) has been printed as 's'.

The spelling of the second edition has been retained, even when it looks strange to the modern eye, e.g. expence, every thing, tythe, superiour, subtilty, haram, uncontrouled, relicks, cumberous, œconomy, imbitter, bawble. All other emendations

of wording and punctuation are given here (this edition] 2nd
edition):

7:15 Yours] Your's
8:4 occurring] ocurring
49:9 sceptre] scepter
55:20 conformable] comformable
56:33 fuel] fewel
63:4 viceregents] vicegerents
70:38 to PLEASE] PLEASE
72:21 Your] You
83:19 example,] example;
85:18 worldly] wordly
95:16 other's] others
95:32 passions,] passions;
103:25 it is] it it
109:7 hers] her's
148:14 fuel] fewel
148:32 expressions] xpressions
149:28 foolishly] foolishy
149:29 wooers] woers
153:36 Modesty] Modesty,
155:14 November] november
158:6 remarks] remaks
160:23 mean] mean,
162:38 fuel] fewel
175:1 from] form
193:9 sense of] sense f
199:35 talk] task
203:2 boy's] boys
209:37 Bishop] bishop
217:23 hers] her's
233:21 other's] others
240:10 weight] wight

Facing page: Quasi-facsimile of the title-page of the first edition

A VINDICATION

OF THE

RIGHTS OF WOMAN:

WITH

STRICTURES

ON

POLITICAL AND MORAL SUBJECTS.

———

By MARY WOLLSTONECRAFT.

———

LONDON:
PRINTED FOR J. JOHNSON, Nº 72, ST. PAUL'S CHURCH YARD.

———

1792.

TO
M. TALLEYRAND-PÉRIGORD,[1]
LATE BISHOP OF AUTUN

SIR,

Having read with great pleasure a pamphlet which you have lately published, I dedicate this volume to you;[2] to induce you to reconsider the subject, and maturely weigh what I have advanced respecting the rights of woman and national education: and I call with the firm tone of humanity; for my arguments, Sir, are dictated by a disinterested spirit – I plead for my sex – not for myself. Independence I have long considered as the grand blessing of life, the basis of every virtue – and independence I will ever secure by contracting my wants, though I were to live on a barren heath.

It is then an affection for the whole human race that makes my pen dart rapidly along to support what I believe to be the cause of virtue: and the same motive leads me earnestly to wish to see woman placed in a station in which she would advance, instead of retarding, the progress of those glorious principles that give a substance to morality. My opinion, indeed, respecting the rights and duties of woman, seems to flow so naturally from these simple principles, that I think it scarcely possible, but that some of the enlarged minds who formed your admirable constitution, will coincide with me.

In France there is undoubtedly a more general diffusion of knowledge than in any part of the European world, and I attribute it, in a great measure, to the social intercourse which has long subsisted between the sexes. It is true, I utter my sentiments with freedom, that in France the very essence of sensuality has been extracted to regale the voluptuary, and a kind of sentimental lust has prevailed, which, together with the system of duplicity that the whole tenour of their political and civil government taught, have given a sinister sort of saga- city to the French character, properly termed finesse; from which naturally flow a polish of manners that injures the sub- stance, by hunting sincerity out of society. – And, modesty, the fairest garb of virtue! has been more grossly insulted in France than even in England, till their women have treated as *prudish* that attention to decency, which brutes instinctively observe.

Manners and morals are so nearly allied that they have often been confounded; but, though the former should only be the natural reflection of the latter, yet, when various causes have produced factitious and corrupt manners, which are very early caught, morality becomes an empty name. The personal reserve, and sacred respect for cleanliness and delicacy in domestic life, which French women almost despise, are the graceful pillars of modesty; but, far from despising them, if the pure flame of patriotism have reached their bosoms, they should labour to improve the morals of their fellow-citizens, by teaching men, not only to respect modesty in women, but to acquire it them- selves, as the only way to merit their esteem.

Contending for the rights of woman, my main argument is built on this simple principle, that if she be not prepared by education to become the companion of man, she will stop the progress of knowledge and virtue; for truth must be common to all, or it will be inefficacious with respect to its influence on general practice. And how can woman be expected to co-operate unless she know why she ought to be virtuous? unless freedom strengthen her reason till she comprehend her duty, and see in what manner it is connected with her real good? If children are to be educated to understand the true principle of patriotism, their mother must be a patriot; and the love of mankind, from which an orderly train of virtues spring, can only be produced by considering the moral and civil interest of mankind; but the education and situation of woman, at present, shuts her out from such investigations.

In this work I have produced many arguments, which to me were conclusive, to prove that the prevailing notion respecting a sexual character was subversive of morality, and I have contended, that to render the human body and mind more perfect, chastity must more universally prevail, and that chastity will never be respected in the male world till the person of a woman is not, as it were, idolized, when little virtue or sense embellish it with the grand traces of mental beauty, or the interesting simplicity of affection.

Consider, Sir, dispassionately, these observations – for a glimpse of this truth seemed to open before you when you observed, 'that to see one half of the human race excluded by the other from all participation of government, was a political phænomenon that, according to abstract principles, it was impossible to explain.' If so, on what does your constitution rest? If the abstract rights of man will bear discussion and explanation, those of woman, by a parity of reasoning, will not shrink from the same test: though a different opinion prevails in this country, built on the very arguments which you use to justify the oppression of woman – prescription.

Consider, I address you as a legislator, whether, when men contend for their freedom, and to be allowed to judge for themselves respecting their own happiness, it be not inconsistent and unjust to subjugate women, even though you firmly believe that you are acting in the manner best calculated to promote their happiness? Who made man the exclusive judge, if woman partake with him the gift of reason?

In this style, argue tyrants of every denomination, from the weak king to the weak father of a family; they are all eager to crush reason; yet always assert that they usurp its throne only to be useful. Do you not act a similar part, when you *force* all women, by denying them civil and political rights, to remain immured in their families groping in the dark? for surely, Sir, you will not assert, that a duty can be binding which is not founded on reason? If indeed this be their destination, arguments may be drawn from reason: and thus augustly supported, the more understanding women acquire, the more they will be attached to their duty – comprehending it – for unless they comprehend it, unless their morals be fixed on the same immutable principle as those of man, no authority can make them discharge it in a virtuous manner. They may be convenient slaves, but slavery will have its constant effect, degrading the master and the abject dependent.

But, if women are to be excluded, without having a voice, from a participation of the natural rights of mankind, prove first, to ward off the charge of injustice and inconsistency, that they want reason – else this flaw in your NEW CONSTI-TUTION will ever shew that man must, in some shape, act like a tyrant, and tyranny, in whatever part of society it rears its brazen front, will ever undermine morality.

I have repeatedly asserted, and produced what appeared to me irrefragable arguments drawn from matters of fact, to prove my assertion, that women cannot, by force, be confined to domestic concerns; for they will, however ignorant, intermeddle with more weighty affairs, neglecting private duties only to disturb, by cunning tricks, the orderly plans of reason which rise above their comprehension.

Besides, whilst they are only made to acquire personal accomplishments, men will feek for pleasure in variety, and faithless husbands will make faithless wives; such ignorant beings, indeed, will be very excusable when, not taught to respect public good, nor allowed any civil rights, they attempt to do themselves justice by retaliation.

The box of mischief[3] thus opened in society, what is to preserve private virtue, the only security of public freedom and universal happiness?

Let there be then no coercion *established* in society, and the common law of gravity prevailing, the sexes will fall into their proper places. And, now that more equitable laws are forming your citizens, marriage may become more sacred: your young men may choose wives from motives of affection, and your maidens allow love to root out vanity.

The father of a family will not then weaken his constitution and debase his sentiments, by visiting the harlot, nor forget, in obeying the call of appetite, the purpose for which it was implanted. And, the mother will not neglect her children to practise the arts of coquetry, when sense and modesty secure her the friendship of her husband.

But, till men become attentive to the duty of a father, it is vain to expect women to spend that time in their nursery which they, 'wise in their generation,'[4] choose to spend at their glass; for this exertion of cunning is only an instinct of nature to enable them to obtain indirectly a little of that power of which they are unjustly denied a share: for, if women are not permitted to enjoy legitimate rights, they will render both men and themselves vicious, to obtain illicit privileges.

I wish, Sir, to set some investigations of this kind afloat in France; and should they lead to a confirmation of my principles, when your constitution is revised the Rights of Woman may be respected, if it be fully proved that reason calls for this respect, and loudly demands JUSTICE for one half of the human race.

I am, Sir,

Yours respectfully,

M. W.

ADVERTISEMENT

When I began to write this work, I divided it into three parts, supposing that one volume would contain a full discussion of the arguments which seemed to me to rise naturally from a few simple principles; but fresh illustrations occurring as I advanced, I now present only the first part to the public.

Many subjects, however, which I have cursorily alluded to, call for particular investigation, especially the laws relative to women, and the consideration of their peculiar duties. These will furnish ample matter for a second volume,[1] which in due time will be published, to elucidate some of the sentiments, and complete many of the sketches begun in the first.

CONTENTS

INTRODUCTION

After considering the historic page, and viewing the living world with anxious solicitude, the most melancholy emotions of sorrowful indignation have depressed my spirits, and I have sighed when obliged to confess, that either nature has made a great difference between man and man, or that the civilization which has hitherto taken place in the world has been very partial. I have turned over various books written on the subject of education, and patiently observed the conduct of parents and the management of schools; but what has been the result? – a profound conviction that the neglected education of my fellow-creatures is the grand source of the misery I deplore; and that women, in particular, are rendered weak and wretched by a variety of concurring causes, originating from one hasty conclusion. The conduct and manners of women, in fact, evidently prove that their minds are not in a healthy state; for, like the flowers which are planted in too rich a soil, strength and usefulness are sacrificed to beauty; and the flaunting leaves, after having pleased a fastidious eye, fade, disregarded on the stalk, long before the season when they ought to have arrived at maturity. – One cause of this barren blooming I attribute to a false system of education, gathered from the books written on this subject by men who, considering females rather as women than human creatures, have been more anxious to make them alluring mistresses than affectionate wives and rational mothers; and the understanding of the sex has been so bubbled by this specious homage, that the civilized women of the present century, with a few exceptions, are only anxious to inspire love, when they ought to cherish a nobler ambition, and by their abilities and virtues exact respect.

In a treatise, therefore, on female rights and manners, the works which have been particularly written for their improvement must not be overlooked; especially when it is asserted, in direct terms, that the minds of women are enfeebled by false refinement; that the books of instruction, written by men of genius, have had the same tendency as more frivolous productions; and that, in the true style of Mahometanism, they are treated as a kind of subordinate beings, and not as a part of the human species, when improveable reason is allowed to be the dignified distinction which raises men above the brute creation, and puts a natural sceptre in a feeble hand.

Yet, because I am a woman, I would not lead my readers to suppose that I mean violently to agitate the contested question respecting the equality or inferiority of the sex; but as the subject lies in my way, and I cannot pass it over without subjecting the main tendency of my reasoning to misconstruction, I shall stop a moment to deliver, in a few words, my opinion. – In the government of the physical world it is observable that the female in point of strength is, in general, inferior to the male. This is the law of nature; and it does not appear to be suspended or abrogated in favour of woman. A degree of physical superiority cannot, therefore, be denied – and it is a noble prerogative! But not content with this natural pre-eminence, men endeavour to sink us still lower, merely to render us alluring objects for a moment; and women, intoxicated by the adoration which men, under the influence of their senses, pay them, do not seek to obtain a durable interest in their hearts, or to become the friends of the fellow creatures who find amusement in their society.

I am aware of an obvious inference:– from every quarter have I heard exclamations against masculine women; but where are they to be found? If by this appellation men mean to inveigh against their ardour in hunting, shooting, and gaming, I shall most cordially join in the cry; but if it be against the imitation of manly virtues, or, more properly speaking, the attainment of those talents and virtues, the exercise of which ennobles the human character, and which raise females in the scale of animal being, when they are comprehensively termed mankind; – all those who view them with a philosophic eye must, I should think, wish with me, that they may every day grow more and more masculine.

This discussion naturally divides the subject. I shall first consider women in the grand light of human creatures, who, in common with men, are placed on this earth to unfold their faculties; and afterwards I shall more particularly point out their peculiar designation.

I wish also to steer clear of an error which many respectable writers have fallen into; for the instruction which has hitherto been addressed to women, has rather been applicable to *ladies*, if the little indirect advice, that is scattered through Sandford and Merton,[1] be excepted; but, addressing my sex in a firmer tone, I pay particular attention to those in the middle class, because they appear to be in the most natural state. Perhaps the seeds of false-refinement, immorality, and vanity, have ever been shed by the great. Weak, artificial beings, raised above the common wants and affections of their race, in a premature unnatural manner, undermine the very foundation of virtue, and spread corruption through the whole mass of society! As a class of mankind they have the strongest claim to pity; the education of the rich tends to render them vain and helpless, and the unfolding mind is not strengthened by the practice of those duties which dignify the human character. – They only live to amuse themselves, and by the same law which in nature invariably produces certain effects, they soon only afford barren amusement.

But as I purpose taking a separate view of the different ranks of society, and of the moral character of women, in each, this hint is, for the present, sufficient; and I have only alluded to the subject, because it appears to me to be the very essence of an introduction to give a cursory account of the contents of the work it introduces.

My own sex, I hope, will excuse me, if I treat them like rational creatures, instead of flattering their *fascinating* graces, and viewing them as if they were in a state of perpetual childhood, unable to stand alone. I earnestly wish to point out in what true dignity and human happiness consists – I wish to persuade women to endeavour to acquire strength, both of mind and body, and to convince them that the soft phrases, susceptibility of heart, delicacy of sentiment, and refinement of taste, are almost synonymous with epithets of weakness, and that those beings who are only the objects of pity and that kind of love, which has been termed its sister, will soon become objects of contempt.

Dismissing then those pretty feminine phrases, which the men condescendingly use to soften our slavish dependence, and despising that weak elegancy of mind, exquisite sensibility, and sweet docility of manners, supposed to be the sexual character-istics of the weaker vessel, I wish to shew that elegance is inferior to virtue, that the first object of laudable ambition is to obtain a character as a human being, regardless of the distinction of sex; and that secondary views should be brought to this simple touchstone.

This is a rough sketch of my plan; and should I express my conviction with the energetic emotions that I feel whenever I think of the subject, the dictates of experience and reflection will be felt by some of my readers. Animated by this important object, I shall disdain to cull my phrases or polish my style; – I aim at being useful, and sincerity will render me unaffected; for, wishing rather to persuade by the force of my arguments, than dazzle by the elegance of my language, I shall not waste my time in rounding periods, or in fabricating the turgid bombast of artificial feelings, which, coming from the head, never reach the heart. – I shall be employed about things, not words! – and, anxious to render my sex more respectable members of society, I shall try to avoid that flowery diction which has slided from essays into novels, and from novels into familiar letters and conversation.

These pretty superlatives, dropping glibly from the tongue, vitiate the taste, and create a kind of sickly delicacy that turns away from simple unadorned truth; and a deluge of false senti-ments and overstretched feelings, stifling the natural emotions of the heart, render the domestic pleasures insipid, that ought to sweeten the exercise of those severe duties, which educate a rational and immortal being for a nobler field of action.

The education of women has, of late, been more attended to

than formerly; yet they are still reckoned a frivolous sex, and ridiculed or pitied by the writers who endeavour by satire or instruction to improve them. It is acknowledged that they spend many of the first years of their lives in acquiring a smattering of accomplishments; meanwhile strength of body and mind are sacrificed to libertine notions of beauty, to the desire of establishing themselves, – the only way women can rise in the world, – by marriage. And this desire making mere animals of them, when they marry they act as such children may be expected to act: – they dress; they paint, and nickname God's creatures. – Surely these weak beings are only fit for a seraglio![2] – Can they be expected to govern a family with judgment, or take care of the poor babes whom they bring into the world?

If then it can be fairly deduced from the present conduct of the sex, from the prevalent fondness for pleasure which takes place of ambition and those nobler passions that open and enlarge the soul; that the instruction which women have hitherto received has only tended, with the constitution of civil society, to render them insignificant objects of desire – mere propagators of fools! – if it can be proved that in aiming to accomplish them, without cultivating their understandings, they are taken out of their sphere of duties, and made ridiculous and useless when the short-lived bloom of beauty is over,* I presume that *rational* men will excuse me for endeavouring to persuade them to become more masculine and respectable.

Indeed the word masculine is only a bugbear: there is little reason to fear that women will acquire too much courage or fortitude; for their apparent inferiority with respect to bodily strength, must render them, in some degree, dependent on men in the various relations of life; but why should it be increased by prejudices that give a sex to virtue, and confound simple truths with sensual reveries?

Women are, in fact, so much degraded by mistaken notions of female excellence, that I do not mean to add a paradox when I assert, that this artificial weakness produces a propensity to

---

* A lively writer, I cannot recollect his name, asks what business women turned of forty have to do in the world?

tyrannize, and gives birth to cunning, the natural opponent of strength, which leads them to play off those contemptible infantine airs that undermine esteem even whilst they excite desire. Let men become more chaste and modest, and if women do not grow wiser in the same ratio, it will be clear that they have weaker understandings. It seems scarcely necessary to say, that I now speak of the sex in general. Many individuals have more sense than their male relatives; and, as nothing preponderates where there is a constant struggle for an equilibrium, without it has naturally more gravity, some women govern their husbands without degrading themselves, because intellect will always govern.

VINDICATION
OF THE
RIGHTS OF WOMAN
PART I

CHAP. I

THE RIGHTS AND INVOLVED DUTIES OF MANKIND CONSIDERED

In the present state of society it appears necessary to go back to first principles in search of the most simple truths, and to dispute with some prevailing prejudice every inch of ground. To clear my way, I must be allowed to ask some plain questions, and the answers will probably appear as unequivocal as the axioms on which reasoning is built; though, when entangled with various motives of action, they are formally contradicted, either by the words or conduct of men.

In what does man's pre-eminence over the brute creation consist? The answer is as clear as that a half is less than the whole; in Reason.

What acquirement exalts one being above another? Virtue; we spontaneously reply.

For what purpose were the passions implanted? That man by struggling with them might attain a degree of knowledge denied to the brutes; whispers Experience.

Consequently the perfection of our nature and capability of happiness, must be estimated by the degree of reason, virtue, and knowledge, that distinguish the individual, and direct the laws which bind society: and that from the exercise of reason, knowledge and virtue naturally flow, is equally undeniable, if mankind be viewed collectively.

The rights and duties of man thus simplified, it seems almost impertinent to attempt to illustrate truths that appear so incontrovertible; yet such deeply rooted prejudices have clouded reason, and such spurious qualities have assumed the name of virtues, that it is necessary to pursue the course of reason as it has been perplexed and involved in error, by various adventitious circumstances, comparing the simple axiom with casual deviations.

Men, in general, seem to employ their reason to justify prejudices, which they have imbibed, they can scarcely trace how, rather than to root them out. The mind must be strong that resolutely forms its own principles; for a kind of intellectual cowardice prevails which makes many men shrink from the task, or only do it by halves. Yet the imperfect conclusions thus drawn, are frequently very plausible, because they are built on partial experience, on just, though narrow, views.

Going back to first principles, vice skulks, with all its native deformity, from close investigation; but a set of shallow reasoners are always exclaiming that these arguments prove too much, and that a measure rotten at the core may be expedient. Thus expediency is continually contrasted with simple principles, till truth is lost in a mist of words; virtue, in forms, and knowledge rendered a sounding nothing, by the specious prejudices that assume its name.

That the society is formed in the wisest manner, whose constitution is founded on the nature of man, strikes, in the abstract, every thinking being so forcibly, that it looks like presumption to endeavour to bring forward proofs; though proof must be brought, or the strong hold of prescription will never be forced by reason; yet to urge prescription as an argument to justify the depriving men (or women) of their natural rights, is one of the absurd sophisms which daily insult common sense.

The civilization of the bulk of the people of Europe is very partial; nay, it may be made a question, whether they have acquired any virtues in exchange for innocence, equivalent to the misery produced by the vices that have been plastered over unsightly ignorance, and the freedom which has been bartered for splendid slavery. The desire of dazzling by riches, the most certain pre-eminence that man can obtain, the pleasure of commanding flattering sycophants, and many other complicated low calculations of doting self-love, have all contributed to overwhelm the mass of mankind, and make liberty a convenient handle for mock patriotism. For whilst rank and titles are held of the utmost importance, before which Genius 'must hide its diminished head,'[1] it is, with a few exceptions, very unfortunate for a nation when a man of abilities, without rank or property, pushes himself forward to notice. – Alas! what unheard of misery have thousands suffered to purchase a cardinal's hat for an intriguing obscure adventurer, who longed to be ranked with princes, or lord it over them by seizing the triple crown!

Such, indeed, has been the wretchedness that has flowed from hereditary honours, riches, and monarchy, that men of lively sensibility have almost uttered blasphemy in order to justify the dispensations of providence. Man has been held out as independent of his power who made him, or as a lawless planet darting from its orbit to steal the celestial fire of reason; and the vengeance of heaven, lurking in the subtile flame, like Pandora's pent up mischiefs, sufficiently punished his temerity, by introducing evil into the world.

Impressed by this view of the misery and disorder which pervaded society, and fatigued with jostling against artificial fools, Rousseau became enamoured of solitude, and, being at the same time an optimist, he labours with uncommon eloquence to prove that man was naturally a solitary animal.[2] Misled by his respect for the goodness of God, who certainly – for what man of sense and feeling can doubt it! – gave life only to communicate happiness, he considers evil as positive, and the work of man; not aware that he was exalting one attribute at the expence of another, equally necessary to divine perfection.

Reared on a false hypothesis his arguments in favour of a state of nature are plausible, but unsound. I say unsound; for to assert that a state of nature is preferable to civilization, in all its possible perfection, is, in other words, to arraign supreme wisdom; and the paradoxical exclamation, that God has made all things right, and that error has been introduced by the creature, whom he formed, knowing what he formed, is as unphilosophical as impious.

When that wise Being who created us and placed us here, saw the fair idea, he willed, by allowing it to be so, that the passions should unfold our reason, because he could see that present evil would produce future good. Could the helpless creature whom he called from nothing break loose from his providence, and

boldly learn to know good by practising evil, without his permission? No. – How could that energetic advocate for immortality argue so inconsistently? Had mankind remained for ever in
the brutal state of nature, which even his magic pen cannot
paint as a state in which a single virtue took root, it would have
been clear, though not to the sensitive unreflecting wanderer,
that man was born to run the circle of life and death, and
adorn God's garden for some purpose which could not easily
be reconciled with his attributes.

But if, to crown the whole, there were to be rational creatures
produced, allowed to rise in excellence by the exercise of powers
implanted for that purpose; if benignity itself thought fit to call
into existence a creature above the brutes,* who could think
and improve himself, why should that inestimable gift, for a gift
it was, if man was so created as to have a capacity to rise above
the state in which sensation produced brutal ease, be called, in
direct terms, a curse? A curse it might be reckoned, if the whole
of our existence were bounded by our continuance in this world;
for why should the gracious fountain of life give us passions,
and the power of reflecting, only to imbitter our days and inspire
us with mistaken notions of dignity? Why should he lead us from
love of ourselves to the sublime emotions which the discovery of
his wisdom and goodness excites, if these feelings were not set
in motion to improve our nature, of which they make a part,†
and render us capable of enjoying a more godlike portion of
happiness? Firmly persuaded that no evil exists in the world

* Contrary to the opinion of anatomists, who argue by analogy from the
formation of the teeth, stomach, and intestines, Rousseau will not allow a man
to be a carnivorous animal. And, carried away from nature by a love of system,
he disputes whether man be a gregarious animal, though the long and helpless
state of infancy seems to point him out as particularly impelled to pair, the first
step towards herding.[3]
† What would you say to a mechanic whom you had desired to make a watch
to point out the hour of the day, if, to shew his ingenuity, he added wheels to
make it a repeater, &c. that perplexed the simple mechanism; should he urge,
to excuse himself – had you not touched a certain spring, you would have
known nothing of the matter, and that he should have amused himself by
making *an experiment* without doing you any harm: would you not retort fairly
upon him, by insisting that if he had not added those needless wheels and
springs, the accident could not have happened?

that God did not design to take place, I build my belief on the perfection of God.

Rousseau exerts himself to prove that all *was* right originally: a crowd of authors that all *is* now right: and I, that all will *be* right.[4]

But, true to his first position, next to a state of nature, Rousseau celebrates barbarism, and apostrophizing the shade of Fabricius,[5] he forgets that, in conquering the world, the Romans never dreamed of establishing their own liberty on a firm basis, or of extending the reign of virtue. Eager to support his system, he stigmatizes, as vicious, every effort of genius; and, uttering the apotheosis of savage virtues, he exalts those to demi-gods, who were scarcely human – the brutal Spartans,[6] who, in defiance of justice and gratitude, sacrificed, in cold blood, the slaves who had shewn themselves heroes to rescue their oppressors.

Disgusted with artificial manners and virtues, the citizen of Geneva,[7] instead of properly sifting the subject, threw away the wheat with the chaff, without waiting to inquire whether the evils which his ardent soul turned from indignantly, were the consequence of civilization or the vestiges of barbarism. He saw vice trampling on virtue, and the semblance of goodness taking place of the reality; he saw talents bent by power to sinister purposes, and never thought of tracing the gigantic mischief up to arbitrary power, up to the hereditary distinctions that clash with the mental superiority that naturally raises a man above his fellows. He did not perceive that regal power, in a few generations, introduces idiotism into the noble stem,[8] and holds out baits to render thousands idle and vicious.

Nothing can set the regal character in a more contemptible point of view, than the various crimes that have elevated men to the supreme dignity. – Vile intrigues, unnatural crimes, and every vice that degrades our nature, have been the steps to this distinguished eminence; yet millions of men have supinely allowed the nerveless limbs of the posterity of such rapacious prowlers to rest quietly on their ensanguined thrones.*

---

* Could there be a greater insult offered to the rights of man than the beds of justice in France, when an infant was made the organ of the detestable Dubois![9]

What but a pestilential vapour can hover over society when its chief director is only instructed in the invention of crimes, or the stupid routine of childish ceremonies? Will men never be wise? – will they never cease to expect corn from tares, and figs from thistles?[10]

It is impossible for any man, when the most favourable circumstances concur, to acquire sufficient knowledge and strength of mind to discharge the duties of a king, entrusted with uncontrouled power; how then must they be violated when his very elevation is an insuperable bar to the attainment of either wisdom or virtue; when all the feelings of a man are stifled by flattery, and reflection shut out by pleasure! Surely it is madness to make the fate of thousands depend on the caprice of a weak fellow creature, whose very station sinks him *necessarily* below the meanest of his subjects! But one power should not be thrown down to exalt another – for all power inebriates weak man; and its abuse proves that the more equality there is established among men, the more virtue and happiness will reign in society. But this and any similar maxim deduced from simple reason, raises an outcry – the church or the state is in danger, if faith in the wisdom of antiquity is not implicit; and they who, roused by the sight of human calamity, dare to attack human authority, are reviled as despisers of God, and enemies of man. These are bitter calumnies, yet they reached one of the best of men,* whose ashes still preach peace, and whose memory demands a respectful pause, when subjects are discussed that lay so near his heart. —

After attacking the sacred majesty of Kings, I shall scarcely excite surprise by adding my firm persuasion that every profession, in which great subordination of rank constitutes its power, is highly injurious to morality.

A standing army,[11] for instance, is incompatible with freedom; because subordination and rigour are the very sinews of military discipline; and despotism is necessary to give vigour to enterprizes that one will directs. A spirit inspired by romantic notions of honour, a kind of morality founded on the fashion of the age,

* Dr Price.[12]

can only be felt by a few officers, whilst the main body must be moved by command, like the waves of the sea; for the strong wind of authority pushes the crowd of subalterns forward, they scarcely know or care why, with headlong fury.

Besides, nothing can be so prejudicial to the morals of the inhabitants of country towns as the occasional residence of a set of idle superficial young men, whose only occupation is gallantry, and whose polished manners render vice more dangerous, by concealing its deformity under gay ornamental drapery. An air of fashion, which is but a badge of slavery, and proves that the soul has not a strong individual character, awes simple country people into an imitation of the vices, when they cannot catch the slippery graces, of politeness. Every corps is a chain of despots, who, submitting and tyrannizing without exercising their reason, become dead weights of vice and folly on the community. A man of rank or fortune, sure of rising by interest, has nothing to do but to pursue some extravagant freak; whilst the needy *gentleman*, who is to rise, as the phrase turns, by his merit, becomes a servile parasite or vile pander.

Sailors, the naval gentlemen, come under the same description, only their vices assume a different and a grosser cast. They are more positively indolent, when not discharging the ceremonials of their station; whilst the insignificant fluttering of soldiers may be termed active idleness. More confined to the society of men, the former acquire a fondness for humour and mischievous tricks; whilst the latter, mixing frequently with well-bred women, catch a sentimental cant. – But mind is equally out of the question, whether they indulge the horse-laugh, or polite simper.

May I be allowed to extend the comparison to a profession where more mind is certainly to be found; for the clergy have superior opportunities of improvement, though subordination almost equally cramps their faculties? The blind submission imposed at college to forms of belief serves as a novitiate to the curate, who must obsequiously respect the opinion of his rector or patron, if he mean to rise in his profession. Perhaps there cannot be a more forcible contrast than between the servile dependent gait of a poor curate and the courtly mien of a bishop.

And the respect and contempt they inspire render the discharge of their separate functions equally useless.

It is of great importance to observe that the character of every man is, in some degree, formed by his profession. A man of sense may only have a cast of countenance that wears off as you trace his individuality, whilst the weak, common man has scarcely ever any character, but what belongs to the body; at least, all his opinions have been so steeped in the vat consecrated by authority, that the faint spirit which the grape of his own vine yields cannot be distinguished.

Society, therefore, as it becomes more enlightened, should be very careful not to establish bodies of men who must necessarily be made foolish or vicious by the very constitution of their profession.

In the infancy of society, when men were just emerging out of barbarism, chiefs and priests, touching the most powerful springs of savage conduct, hope and fear, must have had unbounded sway. An aristocracy, of course, is naturally the first form of government. But, clashing interests soon losing their equipoise, a monarchy and hierarchy break out of the confusion of ambitious struggles, and the foundation of both is secured by feudal tenures. This appears to be the origin of monarchical and priestly power, and the dawn of civilization. But such combustible materials cannot long be pent up; and, getting vent in foreign wars and intestine insurrections, the people acquire some power in the tumult, which obliges their rulers to gloss over their oppression with a shew of right. Thus, as wars, agriculture, commerce, and litera-ture, expand the mind, despots are compelled, to make covert corruption hold fast the power which was formerly snatched by open force.* And this baneful lurking gangrene is most quickly spread by luxury and superstition, the sure dregs of ambition. The indolent puppet of a court first becomes a luxurious mon-ster, or fastidious sensualist, and then makes the contagion which his unnatural state spread, the instrument of tyranny.

* Men of abilities scatter seeds that grow up and have a great influence on the forming opinion; and when once the public opinion preponderates, through the exertion of reason, the overthrow of arbitrary power is not very distant.

It is the pestiferous purple[13] which renders the progress of civilization a curse, and warps the understanding, till men of sensibility doubt whether the expansion of intellect produces a greater portion of happiness or misery. But the nature of the poison points out the antidote; and had Rousseau mounted one step higher in his investigation, or could his eye have pierced through the foggy atmosphere, which he almost disdained to breathe, his active mind would have darted forward to contemplate the perfection of man in the establishment of true civilization,[14] instead of taking his ferocious flight back to the night of sensual ignorance.

CHAP. II

THE PREVAILING OPINION OF A SEXUAL
CHARACTER DISCUSSED

To account for, and excuse the tyranny of man, many ingenious arguments have been brought forward to prove, that the two sexes, in the acquirement of virtue, ought to aim at attaining a very different character: or, to speak explicitly, women are not allowed to have sufficient strength of mind to acquire what really deserves the name of virtue. Yet it should seem, allowing them to have souls, that there is but one way appointed by Providence to lead *mankind* to either virtue or happiness.

If then women are not a swarm of ephemeron triflers, why should they be kept in ignorance under the specious name of innocence? Men complain, and with reason, of the follies and caprices of our sex, when they do not keenly satirize our head-strong passions and groveling vices. – Behold, I should answer, the natural effect of ignorance! The mind will ever be unstable that has only prejudices to rest on, and the current will run with destructive fury when there are no barriers to break its force. Women are told from their infancy, and taught by the example of their mothers, that a little knowledge of human weakness, justly termed cunning, softness of temper, *outward* obedience, and a scrupulous attention to a puerile kind of propriety, will obtain for them the protection of man; and should they be beautiful, every thing else is needless, for, at least, twenty years of their lives.

Thus Milton describes our first frail mother; though when he tells us that women are formed for softness and sweet attractive grace,[1] I cannot comprehend his meaning, unless, in the true Mahometan strain, he meant to deprive us of souls,[2] and insinuate that we were beings only designed by sweet attractive grace, and docile blind obedience, to gratify the senses of man when he can no longer soar on the wing of contemplation.

How grossly do they insult us who thus advise us only to render ourselves gentle, domestic brutes! For instance, the winning softness so warmly, and frequently, recommended, that governs by obeying. What childish expressions, and how insignificant is the being – can it be an immortal one? who will condescend to govern by such sinister methods! 'Certainly,' says Lord Bacon, 'man is of kin to the beasts by his body; and if he be not of kin to God by his spirit, he is a base and ignoble creature!'[3] Men, indeed, appear to me to act in a very unphilosophical manner when they try to secure the good conduct of women by attempting to keep them always in a state of childhood. Rousseau was more consistent when he wished to stop the progress of reason in both sexes, for if men eat of the tree of knowledge, women will come in for a taste; but, from the imperfect cultivation which their understandings now receive, they only attain a knowledge of evil.

Children, I grant, should be innocent; but when the epithet is applied to men, or women, it is but a civil term for weakness. For if it be allowed that women were destined by Providence to acquire human virtues, and by the exercise of their understandings, that stability of character which is the firmest ground to rest our future hopes upon, they must be permitted to turn to the fountain of light, and not forced to shape their course by the twinkling of a mere satellite. Milton, I grant, was of a very different opinion; for he only bends to the indefeasible right of beauty, though it would be difficult to render two passages which I now mean to contrast, consistent. But into similar inconsistencies are great men often led by their senses.

> 'To whom thus Eve with *perfect beauty* adorn'd.
> My Author and Disposer, what thou bidst
> *Unargued* I obey; so God ordains;
> God is *thy law, thou mine*: to know no more
> Is Woman's *happiest* knowledge and her *praise*.'[4]

These are exactly the arguments that I have used to children; but I have added, your reason is now gaining strength, and, till it arrives at some degree of maturity, you must look up to me for advice – then you ought to *think*, and only rely on God.

Yet in the following lines Milton seems to coincide with me; when he makes Adam thus expostulate with his Maker.

> 'Hast thou not made me here thy substitute,
> And these inferior far beneath me set?
> Among *unequals* what society
> Can sort, what harmony or true delight?
> Which must be mutual, in proportion due
> Giv'n and receiv'd; but in *disparity*
> The one intense, the other still remiss
> Cannot well suit with either, but soon prove
> Tedious alike: of *fellowship* I speak
> Such as I seek, fit to participate
> All rational delight – '[5]

In treating, therefore, of the manners of women, let us, disregarding sensual arguments, trace what we should endeavour to make them in order to co-operate, if the expression be not too bold, with the supreme Being.

By individual education, I mean, for the sense of the word is not precisely defined, such an attention to a child as will slowly sharpen the senses, form the temper, regulate the passions as they begin to ferment, and set the understanding to work before the body arrives at maturity; so that the man may only have to proceed, not to begin, the important task of learning to think and reason.

To prevent any misconstruction, I must add, that I do not believe that a private education can work the wonders which some sanguine writers have attributed to it. Men and women must be educated, in a great degree, by the opinions and manners of the society they live in. In every age there has been a stream of popular opinion that has carried all before it, and given a family character, as it were, to the century. It may then fairly be inferred, that, till society be differently constituted, much cannot be expected from education. It is, however, sufficient for my present purpose to assert, that, whatever effect circumstances have on the abilities, every being may become virtuous by the exercise of its own reason; for if but one being was created with vicious inclinations, that is positively bad, what can save us from atheism? or if we worship a God, is not that God a devil?

Consequently, the most perfect education, in my opinion, is such an exercise of the understanding as is best calculated to strengthen the body and form the heart. Or, in other words, to enable the individual to attain such habits of virtue as will render it independent. In fact, it is a farce to call any being virtuous whose virtues do not result from the exercise of its own reason. This was Rousseau's opinion respecting men: I extend it to women,[6] and confidently assert that they have been drawn out of their sphere by false refinement, and not by an endeavour to acquire masculine qualities. Still the regal homage which they receive is so intoxicating, that till the manners of the times are changed, and formed on more reasonable principles, it may be impossible to convince them that the illegitimate power, which they obtain, by degrading themselves, is a curse, and that they must return to nature and equality, if they wish to secure the placid satisfaction that unsophisticated affections impart. But for this epoch we must wait – wait, perhaps, till kings and nobles, enlightened by reason, and, preferring the real dignity of man to childish state, throw off their gaudy hereditary trappings: and if then women do not resign the arbitrary power of beauty – they will prove that they have *less* mind than man.

I may be accused of arrogance; still I must declare what I firmly believe, that all the writers who have written on the subject of female education and manners from Rousseau to Dr Gregory,[7] have contributed to render women more artificial, weak characters, than they would otherwise have been; and, consequently, more useless members of society. I might have expressed this conviction in a lower key; but I am afraid it would have been the whine of affectation, and not the faithful expression of my feelings, of the clear result, which experience and reflection have led me to draw. When I come to that division of the subject, I shall advert to the passages that I more particularly disapprove of, in the works of the authors I have just alluded to; but it is first necessary to observe, that my objection extends to the whole purport of those books, which tend, in my opinion, to degrade one half of the human species, and render women pleasing at the expence of every solid virtue.

Though, to reason on Rousseau's ground, if man did attain a degree of perfection of mind when his body arrived at maturity, it might be proper, in order to make a man and his wife *one*, that she should rely entirely on his understanding; and the graceful ivy, clasping the oak that supported it, would form a whole in which strength and beauty would be equally conspicuous. But, alas! husbands, as well as their helpmates, are often only overgrown children; nay, thanks to early debauchery, scarcely men in their outward form – and if the blind lead the blind, one need not come from heaven to tell us the consequence.

Many are the causes that, in the present corrupt state of society, contribute to enslave women by cramping their understandings and sharpening their senses. One, perhaps, that silently does more mischief than all the rest, is their disregard of order.

To do every thing in an orderly manner, is a most important precept, which women, who, generally speaking, receive only a disorderly kind of education, seldom attend to with that degree of exactness that men, who from their infancy are broken into method, observe. This negligent kind of guess-work, for what other epithet can be used to point out the random exertions of a sort of instinctive common sense, never brought to the test of reason? prevents their generalizing matters of fact – so they do to-day, what they did yesterday, merely because they did it yesterday.

This contempt of the understanding in early life has more baneful consequences than is commonly supposed; for the little knowledge which women of strong minds attain, is, from various circumstances, of a more desultory kind than the knowledge of men, and it is acquired more by sheer observations on real life, than from comparing what has been individually observed with the results of experience generalized by speculation. Led by their dependent situation and domestic employments more into society, what they learn is rather by snatches; and as learning is with them, in general, only a secondary thing, they do not pursue any one branch with that persevering ardour necessary to give vigour to the faculties, and clearness to the judgment. In the present state of society, a little learning is required to support the character of a gentleman; and boys are obliged to submit to a few years of discipline. But in the education of women, the cultivation of the understanding is always subordinate to the acquirement of some corporeal accomplishment; even while enervated by confinement and false notions of modesty, the body is prevented from attaining that grace and beauty which relaxed half-formed limbs never exhibit. Besides, in youth their faculties are not brought forward by emulation; and having no serious scientific study, if they have natural sagacity it is turned too soon on life and manners. They dwell on effects, and modifications, without tracing them back to causes; and complicated rules to adjust behaviour are a weak substitute for simple principles.

As a proof that education gives this appearance of weakness to females, we may instance the example of military men, who are, like them, sent into the world before their minds have been stored with knowledge or fortified by principles. The consequences are similar; soldiers acquire a little superficial knowledge, snatched from the muddy current of conversation, and, from continually mixing with society, they gain, what is termed a knowledge of the world; and this acquaintance with manners and customs has frequently been confounded with a knowledge of the human heart. But can the crude fruit of casual observation, never brought to the test of judgment, formed by comparing speculation and experience, deserve such a distinction? Soldiers, as well as women, practise the minor virtues with punctilious politeness. Where is then the sexual difference, when the education has been the same? All the difference that I can discern, arises from the superior advantage of liberty, which enables the former to see more of life.

It is wandering from my present subject, perhaps, to make a political remark; but, as it was produced naturally by the train of my reflections, I shall not pass it silently over.

Standing armies can never consist of resolute, robust men;

they may be well disciplined machines, but they will seldom contain men under the influence of strong passions, or with very vigorous faculties. And as for any depth of understanding, I will venture to affirm, that it is as rarely to be found in the army as amongst women; and the cause, I maintain, is the same. It may be further observed, that officers are also particularly attentive to their persons, fond of dancing, crowded rooms, adventures, and ridicule.* Like the *fair* sex, the business of their lives is gallantry. – They were taught to please, and they only live to please. Yet they do not lose their rank in the distinction of sexes, for they are still reckoned superior to women, though in what their superiority consists, beyond what I have just mentioned, it is difficult to discover.

The great misfortune is this, that they both acquire manners before morals, and a knowledge of life before they have, from reflection, any acquaintance with the grand ideal outline of human nature. The consequence is natural; satisfied with common nature, they become a prey to prejudices, and taking all their opinions on credit, they blindly submit to authority. So that, if they have any sense, it is a kind of instinctive glance, that catches proportions, and decides with respect to manners; but fails when arguments are to be pursued below the surface, or opinions analyzed.

May not the same remark be applied to women? Nay, the argument may be carried still further, for they are both thrown out of a useful station by the unnatural distinctions established in civilized life. Riches and hereditary honours have made cyphers of women to give consequence to the numerical figure; and idleness has produced a mixture of gallantry and despotism into society, which leads the very men who are the slaves of their mistresses to tyrannize over their sisters, wives, and daughters. This is only keeping them in rank and file, it is true. Strengthen the female mind by enlarging it, and there will be an end to blind obedience; but, as blind obedience is ever sought

---

* Why should women be censured with petulant acrimony, because they seem to have a passion for a scarlet coat?[8] Has not education placed them more on a level with soldiers than any other class of men?

for by power, tyrants and sensualists are in the right when they endeavour to keep women in the dark, because the former only want slaves, and the latter a play-thing. The sensualist, indeed, has been the most dangerous of tyrants, and women have been duped by their lovers, as princes by their ministers, whilst dreaming that they reigned over them.

I now principally allude to Rousseau, for his character of Sophia is, undoubtedly, a captivating one, though it appears to me grossly unnatural;[9] however it is not the superstructure, but the foundation of her character, the principles on which her education was built, that I mean to attack; nay, warmly as I admire the genius of that able writer, whose opinions I shall often have occasion to cite, indignation always takes place of admiration, and the rigid frown of insulted virtue effaces the smile of complacency, which his eloquent periods are wont to raise, when I read his voluptuous reveries. Is this the man, who, in his ardour for virtue, would banish all the soft arts of peace, and almost carry us back to Spartan discipline? Is this the man who delights to paint the useful struggles of passion, the triumphs of good dispositions, and the heroic flights which carry the glowing soul out of itself? – How are these mighty sentiments lowered when he describes the pretty foot and enticing airs of his little favourite! But, for the present, I wave the subject, and, instead of severely reprehending the transient effusions of overweening sensibility, I shall only observe, that whoever has cast a benevolent eye on society, must often have been gratified by the sight of humble mutual love, not dignified by sentiment, or strengthened by a union in intellectual pursuits. The domestic trifles of the day have afforded matters for cheerful converse, and innocent caresses have softened toils which did not require great exercise of mind or stretch of thought: yet, has not the sight of this moderate felicity excited more tenderness than respect? An emotion similar to what we feel when children are playing, or animals sporting,* whilst the contemplation of the

* Similar feelings has Milton's pleasing picture of paradisiacal happiness ever raised in my mind; yet, instead of envying the lovely pair, I have, with conscious dignity, or Satanic pride, turned to hell for sublimer objects.[10] In the same style, when viewing some noble monument of human art, I have traced the emanation

noble struggles of suffering merit has raised admiration, and carried our thoughts to that world where sensation will give place to reason.

Women are, therefore, to be considered either as moral beings, or so weak that they must be entirely subjected to the superior faculties of men.

Let us examine this question. Rousseau declares that a woman should never, for a moment, feel herself independent, that she should be governed by fear to exercise her *natural* cunning, and made a coquetish slave in order to render her a more alluring object of desire, a *sweeter* companion to man, whenever he chooses to relax himself.[11] He carries the arguments, which he pretends to draw from the indications of nature, still further, and insinuates that truth and fortitude, the corner stones of all human virtue, should be cultivated with certain restrictions, because, with respect to the female character, obedience is the grand lesson which ought to be impressed with unrelenting rigour.

What nonsense! when will a great man arise with sufficient strength of mind to puff away the fumes which pride and sensuality have thus spread over the subject! If women are by nature inferior to men, their virtues must be the same in quality, if not in degree, or virtue is a relative idea; consequently, their conduct should be founded on the same principles, and have the same aim.

Connected with man as daughters, wives, and mothers, their moral character may be estimated by their manner of fulfilling those simple duties; but the end, the grand end of their exertions should be to unfold their own faculties and acquire the dignity of conscious virtue. They may try to render their road pleasant; but ought never to forget, in common with man, that life yields not the felicity which can satisfy an immortal soul, I do not mean to insinuate, that either sex should be so lost in abstract reflections or distant views, as to forget the affections and duties

---

of the Deity in the order I admired, till, descending from that giddy height, I have caught myself contemplating the grandest of all human fights; – for fancy quickly placed, in some solitary recess, an outcast of fortune, rising superior to passion and discontent.

that lie before them, and are, in truth, the means appointed to produce the fruit of life; on the contrary, I would warmly recommend them, even while I assert, that they afford most satisfaction when they are considered in their true, sober light.

Probably the prevailing opinion, that woman was created for man, may have taken its rise from Moses's poetical story; yet, as very few, it is presumed, who have bestowed any serious thought on the subject, ever supposed that Eve was, literally speaking, one of Adam's ribs,[12] the deduction must be allowed to fall to the ground; or, only be so far admitted as it proves that man, from the remotest antiquity, found it convenient to exert his strength to subjugate his companion, and his invention to shew that she ought to have her neck bent under the yoke, because the whole creation was only created for his convenience or pleasure.

Let it not be concluded that I wish to invert the order of things; I have already granted, that, from the constitution of their bodies, men seem to be designed by Providence to attain a greater degree of virtue. I speak collectively of the whole sex; but I see not the shadow of a reason to conclude that their virtues should differ in respect to their nature. In fact, how can they, if virtue has only one eternal standard? I must therefore, if I reason consequentially, as strenuously maintain that they have the same simple direction, as that there is a God.

It follows then that cunning should not be opposed to wisdom, little cares to great exertions, or insipid softness, varnished over with the name of gentleness, to that fortitude which grand views alone can inspire.

I shall be told that woman would then lose many of her peculiar graces, and the opinion of a well known poet might be quoted to refute my unqualified assertion. For Pope has said, in the name of the whole male sex,

> 'Yet ne'er so sure our passion to create,
> As when she touch'd the brink of all we hate.'[13]

In what light this sally places men and women, I shall leave to the judicious to determine; meanwhile I shall content myself with observing, that I cannot discover why, unless they are mortal, females should always be degraded by being made subservient to love or lust.

To speak disrespectfully of love is, I know, high treason against sentiment and fine feelings; but I wish to speak the simple language of truth, and rather to address the head than the heart. To endeavour to reason love out of the world, would be to out Quixote Cervantes,[14] and equally offend against common sense; but an endeavour to restrain this tumultuous passion, and to prove that it should not be allowed to dethrone superior powers, or to usurp the sceptre which the understanding should ever coolly wield, appears less wild.

Youth is the season for love in both sexes; but in those days of thoughtless enjoyment provision should be made for the more important years of life, when reflection takes place of sensation. But Rousseau, and most of the male writers who have followed his steps, have warmly inculcated that the whole tendency of female education ought to be directed to one point: – to render them pleasing.[15]

Let me reason with the supporters of this opinion who have any knowledge of human nature, do they imagine that marriage can eradicate the habitude of life? The woman who has only been taught to please will soon find that her charms are oblique sunbeams, and that they cannot have much effect on her husband's heart when they are seen every day, when the summer is passed and gone. Will she then have sufficient native energy to look into herself for comfort, and cultivate her dormant faculties? or, is it not more rational to expect that she will try to please other men; and, in the emotions raised by the expectation of new conquests, endeavour to forget the mortification her love or pride has received? When the husband ceases to be a lover – and the time will inevitably come, her desire of pleasing will then grow languid, or become a spring of bitterness; and love, perhaps, the most evanescent of all passions, gives place to jealousy or vanity.

I now speak of women who are restrained by principle or prejudice; such women, though they would shrink from an intrigue with real abhorrence, yet, nevertheless, wish to be convinced by the homage of gallantry that they are cruelly neglected by their husbands; or, days and weeks are spent in dreaming of the happiness enjoyed by congenial souls till their health is undermined and their spirits broken by discontent. How then can the great art of pleasing be such a necessary study? it is only useful to a mistress; the chaste wife, and serious mother, should only consider her power to please as the polish of her virtues, and the affection of her husband as one of the comforts that render her task less difficult and her life happier. – But, whether she be loved or neglected, her first wish should be to make herself respectable, and not to rely for all her happiness on a being subject to like infirmities with herself.

The worthy Dr Gregory fell into a similar error. I respect his heart; but entirely disapprove of his celebrated Legacy to his Daughters.

He advises them to cultivate a fondness for dress, because a fondness for dress, he asserts, is natural to them. I am unable to comprehend what either he or Rousseau mean, when they frequently use this indefinite term. If they told us that in a pre-existent state the soul was fond of dress, and brought this inclination with it into a new body, I should listen to them with a half smile, as I often do when I hear a rant about innate elegance. – But if he only meant to say that the exercise of the faculties will produce this fondness – I deny it. – It is not natural; but arises, like false ambition in men, from a love of power.

Dr Gregory goes much further; he actually recommends dissimulation, and advises an innocent girl to give the lie to her feelings, and not dance with spirit, when gaiety of heart would make her feet eloquent without making her gestures immodest. In the name of truth and common sense, why should not one woman acknowledge that she can take more exercise than another? or, in other words, that she has a sound constitution; and why, to damp innocent vivacity, is she darkly to be told that men will draw conclusions which she little thinks of?[16] – Let the libertine draw what inference he pleases; but, I hope, that no sensible mother will restrain the natural frankness of youth by instilling such indecent cautions. Out of the abundance of the heart the mouth speaketh; and a wiser than Solomon hath said, that the heart should be made clean,[17] – and not trivial ceremonies observed, which it is not very difficult to fulfil with scrupulous exactness when vice reigns in the heart.

Women ought to endeavour to purify their heart; but can they do so when their uncultivated understandings make them entirely dependent on their senses for employment and amusement, when no noble pursuit sets them above the little vanities of the day, or enables them to curb the wild emotions that agitate a reed over which every passing breeze has power? To gain the affections of a virtuous man is affectation necessary? Nature has given woman a weaker frame than man; but, to ensure her husband's affections, must a wife, who by the exercise of her mind and body whilst she was discharging the duties of a daughter, wife, and mother, has allowed her constitution to retain its natural strength, and her nerves a healthy tone, is she, I say, to condescend to use art and feign a sickly delicacy in order to secure her husband's affection? Weakness may excite tenderness, and gratify the arrogant pride of man; but the lordly caresses of a protector will not gratify a noble mind that pants for, and deserves to be respected. Fondness is a poor substitute for friendship!

In a seraglio, I grant, that all these arts are necessary; the epicure must have his palate tickled, or he will sink into apathy; but have women so little ambition as to be satisfied with such a condition? Can they supinely dream life away in the lap of pleasure, or the languor of weariness, rather than assert their claim to pursue reasonable pleasures and render themselves conspicuous by practising the virtues which dignify mankind? Surely she has not an immortal soul who can loiter life away merely employed to adorn her person, that she may amuse the languid hours, and soften the cares of a fellow-creature who is willing to be enlivened by her smiles and tricks, when the serious business of life is over.

Besides, the woman who strengthens her body and exercises her mind will, by managing her family and practising various virtues, become the friend, and not the humble dependent of her husband; and if she, by possessing such substantial qualities, merit his regard, she will not find it necessary to conceal

her affection, nor to pretend to an unnatural coldness of constitution to excite her husband's passions. In fact, if we revert to
history, we shall find that the women who have distinguished
themselves have neither been the most beautiful nor the most
gentle of their sex.

Nature, or, to speak with strict propriety, God, has made all
things right; but man has sought him out many inventions to
mar the work. I now allude to that part of Dr Gregory's treatise,
where he advises a wife never to let her husband know the extent
of her sensibility or affection.[18] Voluptuous precaution, and as
ineffectual as absurd. – Love, from its very nature, must be
transitory. To seek for a secret that would render it constant,
would be as wild a search as for the philosopher's stone,[19] or
the grand panacea: and the discovery would be equally useless,
or rather pernicious, to mankind. The most holy band of society
is friendship. It has been well said, by a shrewd satirist, 'that
rare as true love is, true friendship is still rarer.'[20]

This is an obvious truth, and the cause not lying deep, will
not elude a slight glance of inquiry.

Love, the common passion, in which chance and sensation
take place of choice and reason, is, in some degree, felt by the
mass of mankind; for it is not necessary to speak, at present, of
the emotions that rise above or sink below love. This passion,
naturally increased by suspense and difficulties, draws the mind
out of its accustomed state, and exalts the affections; but the
security of marriage, allowing the fever of love to subside, a
healthy temperature is thought insipid, only by those who have
not sufficient intellect to substitute the calm tenderness of friendship, the confidence of respect, instead of blind admiration, and
the sensual emotions of fondness.

This is, must be, the course of nature – friendship or indifference inevitably succeeds love. – And this constitution seems
perfectly to harmonize with the system of government which
prevails in the moral world. Passions are spurs to action, and
open the mind; but they sink into mere appetites, become a
personal and momentary gratification, when the object is
gained, and the satisfied mind rests in enjoyment. The man who
had some virtue whilst he was struggling for a crown, often

becomes a voluptuous tyrant when it graces his brow; and, when the lover is not lost in the husband, the dotard, a prey to childish caprices, and fond jealousies, neglects the serious duties of life, and the caresses which should excite confidence in his children are lavished on the overgrown child, his wife.

In order to fulfil the duties of life, and to be able to pursue with vigour the various employments which form the moral character, a master and mistress of a family ought not to continue to love each other with passion. I mean to say, that they ought not to indulge those emotions which disturb the order of society, and engross the thoughts that should be otherwise employed. The mind that has never been engrossed by one object wants vigour – if it can long be so, it is weak.

A mistaken education, a narrow, uncultivated mind, and many sexual prejudices, tend to make women more constant than men; but, for the present, I shall not touch on this branch of the subject. I will go still further, and advance, without dreaming of a paradox, that an unhappy marriage is often very advantageous to a family, and that the neglected wife is, in general, the best mother. And this would almost always be the consequence if the female mind were more enlarged: for, it seems to be the common dispensation of Providence, that what we gain in present enjoyment should be deducted from the treasure of life, experience; and that when we are gathering the flowers of the day and revelling in pleasure, the solid fruit of toil and wisdom should not be caught at the same time. The way lies before us, we must turn to the right or left; and he who will pass life away in bounding from one pleasure to another, must not complain if he acquire neither wisdom nor respectability of character.

Supposing, for a moment, that the soul is not immortal, and that man was only created for the present scene, – I think we should have reason to complain that love, infantine fondness, ever grew insipid and palled upon the sense. Let us eat, drink, and love, for to-morrow we die, would be, in fact, the language of reason, the morality of life; and who but a fool would part with a reality for a fleeting shadow? But, if awed by observing the improbable powers of the mind, we disdain to confine our wishes or thoughts to such a comparatively mean field of action;

that only appears grand and important, as it is connected with a boundless prospect and sublime hopes, what necessity is there for falsehood in conduct, and why must the sacred majesty of truth be violated to detain a deceitful good that saps the very foundation of virtue? Why must the female mind be tainted by coquetish arts to gratify the sensualist, and prevent love from subsiding into friendship, or compassionate tenderness, when there are not qualities on which friendship can be built? Let the honest heart shew itself, and *reason* teach passion to submit to necessity; or, let the dignified pursuit of virtue and knowledge raise the mind above those emotions which rather imbitter than sweeten the cup of life, when they are not restrained within due bounds.

I do not mean to allude to the romantic passion, which is the concomitant of genius. – Who can clip its wing? But that grand passion not proportioned to the puny enjoyments of life, is only true to the sentiment, and feeds on itself. The passions which have been celebrated for their durability have always been unfortunate. They have acquired strength by absence and constitutional melancholy. – The fancy has hovered round a form of beauty dimly seen – but familiarity might have turned admiration into disgust; or, at least, into indifference, and allowed the imagination leisure to start fresh game. With perfect propriety, according to this view of things, does Rousseau make the mistress of his soul, Eloisa, love St Preux,[21] when life was fading before her; but this is no proof of the immortality of the passion.

Of the same complexion is Dr Gregory's advice respecting delicacy of sentiment, which he advises a woman not to acquire, if she have determined to marry.[22] This determination, however, perfectly consistent with his former advice, he calls *indelicate*, and earnestly persuades his daughters to conceal it, though it may govern their conduct: – as if it were indelicate to have the common appetites of human nature.

Noble morality! and consistent with the cautious prudence of a little soul that cannot extend its views beyond the present minute division of existence. If all the faculties of woman's mind are only to be cultivated as they respect her dependence on man; if, when a husband be obtained, she have arrived at her goal, and meanly proud rests satisfied with such a paltry crown, let her grovel contentedly, scarcely raised by her employments above the animal kingdom; but, if, struggling for the prize of her high calling, she look beyond the present scene, let her cultivate her understanding without stopping to consider what character the husband may have whom she is destined to marry. Let her only determine, without being too anxious about present happiness, to acquire the qualities that ennoble a rational being, and a rough inelegant husband may shock her taste without destroying her peace of mind. She will not model her soul to suit the frailties of her companion, but to bear with them: his character may be a trial, but not an impediment to virtue.

If Dr Gregory confined his remark to romantic expectations of constant love and congenial feelings, he should have recollected that experience will banish what advice can never make us cease to wish for, when the imagination is kept alive at the expence of reason.

I own it frequently happens that women who have fostered a romantic unnatural delicacy of feeling, waste their* lives in *imagining* how happy they should have been with a husband who could love them with a fervid increasing affection every day, and all day. But they might as well pine married as single – and would not be a jot more unhappy with a bad husband than longing for a good one. That a proper education; or, to speak with more precision, a well stored mind, would enable a woman to support a single life with dignity, I grant; but that she should avoid cultivating her taste, lest her husband should occasionally shock it, is quitting a substance for a shadow. To say the truth, I do not know of what use is an improved taste, if the individual be not rendered more independent of the casualties of life; if new sources of enjoyment, only dependent on the solitary operations of the mind, are not opened. People of taste, married or single, without distinction, will ever be disgusted by various things that touch not less observing minds. On this conclusion the argument must not be allowed to hinge; but in the whole sum of enjoyment is taste to be denominated a blessing?

* For example, the herd of Novelists.

The question is, whether it procures most pain or pleasure? The answer will decide the propriety of Dr Gregory's advice, and shew how absurd and tyrannic it is thus to lay down a system of slavery; or to attempt to educate moral beings by any other rules than those deduced from pure reason, which apply to the whole species.

Gentleness of manners, forbearance and long-suffering, are such amiable Godlike qualities, that in sublime poetic strains the Deity has been invested with them; and, perhaps, no representation of his goodness so strongly fastens on the human affections as those that represent him abundant in mercy and willing to pardon. Gentleness, considered in this point of view, bears on its front all the characteristics of grandeur, combined with the winning graces of condescension; but what a different aspect it assumes when it is the submissive demeanour of dependence, the support of weakness that loves, because it wants protection; and is forbearing, because it must silently endure injuries; smiling under the lash at which it dare not snarl. Abject as this picture appears, it is the portrait of an accomplished woman, according to the received opinion of female excellence, separated by specious reasoners from human excellence. Or, they* kindly restore the rib, and make one moral being of a man and woman; not forgetting to give her all the 'submissive charms.'[23]

How women are to exist in that state where there is to be neither marrying nor giving in marriage,[24] we are not told. For though moralists have agreed that the tenor of life seems to prove that *man* is prepared by various circumstances for a future state, they constantly concur in advising *woman* only to provide for the present. Gentleness, docility, and a spaniel-like affection are, on this ground, consistently recommended as the cardinal virtues of the sex; and, disregarding the arbitrary economy of nature, one writer has declared that it is masculine for a woman to be melancholy. She was created to be the toy of man, his rattle, and it must jingle in his ears whenever, dismissing reason, he chooses to be amused.

* Vide Rousseau, and Swedenborg.[25]

To recommend gentleness, indeed, on a broad basis is strictly philosophical. A frail being should labour to be gentle. But when forbearance confounds right and wrong, it ceases to be a virtue; and, however convenient it may be found in a companion – that companion will ever be considered as an inferior, and only inspire a vapid tenderness, which easily degenerates into contempt. Still, if advice could really make a being gentle, whose natural disposition admitted not of such a fine polish, something towards the advancement of order would be attained; but if, as might quickly be demonstrated, only affectation be produced by this indiscriminate counsel, which throws a stumbling-block in the way of gradual improvement, and true melioration of temper, the sex is not much benefited by sacrificing solid virtues to the attainment of superficial graces, though for a few years they may procure the individuals regal sway.

As a philosopher, I read with indignation the plausible epithets which men use to soften their insults; and, as a moralist, I ask what is meant by such heterogeneous associations, as fair defects, amiable weaknesses, &c.? If there be but one criterion of morals, but one archetype for man, women appear to be suspended by destiny, according to the vulgar tale of Mahomet's coffin; they have neither the unerring instinct of brutes, nor are allowed to fix the eye of reason on a perfect model. They were made to be loved, and must not aim at respect, lest they should be hunted out of society as masculine.

But to view the subject in another point of view. Do passive indolent women make the best wives? Confining our discussion to the present moment of existence, let us see how such weak creatures perform their part? Do the women who, by the attainment of a few superficial accomplishments, have strengthened the prevailing prejudice, merely contribute to the happiness of their husbands? Do they display their charms merely to amuse them? And have women, who have early imbibed notions of passive obedience, sufficient character to manage a family or educate children? So far from it, that, after surveying the history of woman, I cannot help, agreeing with the severest satirist, considering the sex as the weakest as well as the most oppressed half of the species. What does history disclose but marks of inferiority, and how few women have emancipated themselves from the galling yoke of sovereign man? – So few, that the exceptions remind me of an ingenious conjecture respecting Newton:[26] that he was probably a being of a superior order, accidently caged in a human body. Following the same train of thinking, I have been led to imagine that the few extraordinary women who have rushed in eccentrical directions out of the orbit prescribed to their sex, were *male* spirits, confined by mistake in female frames. But if it be not philosophical to think of sex when the soul is mentioned, the inferiority must depend on the organs; or the heavenly fire, which is to ferment the clay, is not given in equal portions.

But avoiding, as I have hitherto done, any direct comparison of the two sexes collectively, or frankly acknowledging the inferiority of woman, according to the present appearance of things, I shall only insist that men have increased that inferiority till women are almost sunk below the standard of rational creatures. Let their faculties have room to unfold, and their virtues to gain strength, and then determine where the whole sex must stand in the intellectual scale. Yet let it be remembered, that for a small number of distinguished women I do not ask a place.

It is difficult for us purblind mortals to say to what height human discoveries and improvements may arrive when the gloom of despotism subsides, which makes us stumble at every step; but, when morality shall be settled on a more solid basis, then, without being gifted with a prophetic spirit, I will venture to predict that woman will be either the friend or slave of man. We shall not, as at present, doubt whether she is a moral agent, or the link which unites man with brutes. But, should it then appear, that like the brutes they were principally created for the use of man, he will let them patiently bite the bridle, and not mock them with empty praise; or, should their rationality be proved, he will not impede their improvement merely to gratify his sensual appetites. He will not, with all the graces of rhetoric, advise them to submit implicitly their understanding to the guidance of man. He will not, when he treats of the education of women, assert that they ought never to have the free use of reason, nor would he recommend cunning and dissimulation to beings who are acquiring, in like manner as himself, the virtues of humanity.

Surely there can be but one rule of right, if morality has an eternal foundation, and whoever sacrifices virtue, strictly so called, to present convenience, or whose *duty* it is to act in such a manner, lives only for the passing day, and cannot be an accountable creature.

The poet then should have dropped his sneer when he says,

> 'If weak women go astray,
> The stars are more in fault than they.'[27]

For that they are bound by the adamantine chain of destiny is most certain, if it be proved that they are never to exercise their own reason, never to be independent, never to rise above opinion, or to feel the dignity of a rational will that only bows to God, and often forgets that the universe contains any being but itself and the model of perfection to which its ardent gaze is turned, to adore attributes that, softened into virtues, may be imitated in kind, though the degree overwhelms the enraptured mind.

If, I say, for I would not impress by declamation when Reason offers her sober light, if they be really capable of acting like rational creatures, let them not be treated like slaves; or, like the brutes who are dependent on the reason of man, when they associate with him; but cultivate their minds, give them the salutary, sublime curb of principle, and let them attain conscious dignity by feeling themselves only dependent on God. Teach them, in common with man, to submit to necessity, instead of giving, to render them more pleasing, a sex to morals.

Further, should experience prove that they cannot attain the same degree of strength of mind, perseverance, and fortitude, let their virtues be the same in kind, though they may vainly struggle for the same degree; and the superiority of man will be equally clear, if not clearer; and truth, as it is a simple principle, which admits of no modification, would be common to both. Nay, the order of society as it is at present regulated would not be inverted, for woman would then only have the rank that reason assigned her, and arts could not be practised to bring the balance even, much less to turn it.

These may be termed Utopian dreams. – Thanks to that Being who impressed them on my soul, and gave me sufficient strength of mind to dare to exert my own reason, till, becoming dependent only on him for the support of my virtue, I view, with indignation, the mistaken notions that enslave my sex.

I love man as my fellow; but his sceptre, real, or usurped, extends not to me, unless the reason of an individual demands my homage; and even then the submission is to reason, and not to man. In fact, the conduct of an accountable being must be regulated by the operations of its own reason; or on what foundation rests the throne of God?

It appears to me necessary to dwell on these obvious truths, because females have been insulated, as it were; and, while they have been stripped of the virtues that should clothe humanity, they have been decked with artificial graces that enable them to exercise a short-lived tyranny. Love, in their bosoms, taking place of every nobler passion, their sole ambition is to be fair, to raise emotion instead of inspiring respect; and this ignoble desire, like the servility in absolute monarchies, destroys all strength of character. Liberty is the mother of virtue, and if women be, by their very constitution, slaves, and not allowed to breathe the sharp invigorating air of freedom, they must ever languish like exotics, and be reckoned beautiful flaws in nature.

As to the argument respecting the subjection in which the sex has ever been held, it retorts on man. The many have always been enthralled by the few; and monsters, who scarcely have shewn any discernment of human excellence, have tyrannized over thousands of their fellow-creatures. Why have men of superiour endowments submitted to such degradation? For, is it not universally acknowledged that kings, viewed collectively, have ever been inferior, in abilities and virtue, to the same number of men taken from the common mass of mankind – yet, have they not, and are they not still treated with a degree of reverence that is an insult to reason? China is not the only country where a living man has been made a God.[28] *Men* have

submitted to superior strength to enjoy with impunity the pleasure of the moment – *women* have only done the same, and
therefore till it is proved that the courtier, who servilely resigns
the birthright of a man, is not a moral agent, it cannot be
demonstrated that woman is essentially inferior to man because
she has always been subjugated.

Brutal force has hitherto governed the world, and that the
science of politics is in its infancy, is evident from philosophers
scrupling to give the knowledge most useful to man that determinate distinction.

I shall not pursue this argument any further than to establish
an obvious inference, that as sound politics diffuse liberty, mankind, including woman, will become more wise and virtuous.

CHAP. III

Bodily strength from being the distinction of heroes is now sunk into such unmerited contempt that men, as well as women, seem to think it unnecessary: the latter, as it takes from their feminine graces, and from that lovely weakness the source of their undue power; and the former, because it appears inimical to the character of a gentleman.

That they have both by departing from one extreme run into another, may easily be proved; but first it may be proper to observe, that a vulgar error has obtained a degree of credit, which has given force to a false conclusion, in which an effect has been mistaken for a cause.

People of genius have, very frequently, impaired their constitutions by study or careless inattention to their health, and the violence of their passions bearing a proportion to the vigour of their intellects, the sword's destroying the scabbard[1] has become almost proverbial, and superficial observers have inferred from thence, that men of genius have commonly weak, or, to use a more fashionable phrase, delicate constitutions. Yet the contrary, I believe, will appear to be the fact; for, on diligent inquiry, I find that strength of mind has, in most cases, been accompanied by superior strength of body, – natural soundness of constitution, – not that robust tone of nerves and vigour of muscles, which arise from bodily labour, when the mind is quiescent, or only directs the hands.

Dr Priestley has remarked, in the preface to his biographical chart, that the majority of great men have lived beyond forty-five.[2] And, considering the thoughtless manner in which they have lavished their strength, when investigating a favourite science they have wasted the lamp of life, forgetful of the mid-night hour; or, when, lost in poetic dreams, fancy has peopled the scene, and the soul has been disturbed, till it shook the constitution, by the passions that meditation had raised; whose objects, the baseless fabric of a vision, faded before the exhaus-ted eye, they must have had iron frames. Shakspeare never grasped the airy dagger with a nerveless hand, nor did Milton tremble when he led Satan far from the confines of his dreary prison. – These were not the ravings of imbecility, the sickly effusions of distempered brains; but the exuberance of fancy, that 'in a fine phrenzy'[3] wandering, was not continually reminded of its material shackles.

I am aware that this argument would carry me further than it may be supposed I wish to go; but I follow truth, and, still adhering to my first position, I will allow that bodily strength seems to give man a natural superiority over woman; and this is the only solid basis on which the superiority of the sex can be built. But I still insist, that not only the virtue, but the *knowledge* of the two sexes should be the same in nature, if not in degree, and that women, considered not only as moral, but rational creatures, ought to endeavour to acquire human virtues (or perfections) by the *same* means as men, instead of being edu-cated like a fanciful kind of *half* being – one of Rousseau's wild chimeras.*

* 'Researches into abstract and speculative truths, the principles and axioms of sciences, in short, every thing which tends to generalize our ideas, is not the proper province of women; their studies should be relative to points of practice; it belongs to them to apply those principles which men have discovered; and it is their part to make observations, which direct men to the establishment of general principles. All the ideas of women, which have not the immediate tendency to points of duty, should be directed to the study of men, and to the attainment of those agreeable accomplishments which have taste for their object; for as to works of genius, they are beyond their capacity; neither have they sufficient precision or power of attention to succeed in sciences which require accuracy: and as to physical knowledge, it belongs to those only who are most active, most inquisitive; who comprehend the greatest variety of objects; in short, it belongs to those who have the strongest powers, and who exercise them most, to judge of the relations between sensible beings and the laws of nature. A woman who is naturally weak, and does not carry her ideas to any great extent, knows how to judge and make a proper estimate of those movements which she sets to work, in order to aid her weakness; and these

But, if strength of body be, with some shew of reason, the boast of men, why are women so infatuated as to be proud of a defect? Rousseau has furnished them with a plausible excuse, which could only have occurred to a man, whose imagination had been allowed to run wild, and refine on the impressions made by exquisite senses; – that they might, forsooth, have a pretext for yielding to a natural appetite without violating a romantic species of modesty, which gratifies the pride and libertinism of man.

Women, deluded by these sentiments, sometimes boast of their weakness, cunningly obtaining power by playing on the *weakness* of men; and they may well glory in their illicit sway, for, like Turkish bashaws,[4] they have more real power than their masters: but virtue is sacrificed to temporary gratifications, and the respectability of life to the triumph of an hour.

Women, as well as despots, have now, perhaps, more power than they would have if the world, divided and subdivided into kingdoms and families, were governed by laws deduced from the exercise of reason; but in obtaining it, to carry on the comparison, their character is degraded, and licentiousness

---

movements are the passions of men. The mechanism she employs is much more powerful than ours; for all her levers move the human heart. She must have the skill to incline us to do every thing which her sex will not enable her to do herself, and which is necessary or agreeable to her; therefore she ought to study the mind of man thoroughly, not the mind of man in general, abstractedly, but the dispositions of those men to whom she is subject, either by the laws of her country or by the force of opinion. She should learn to penetrate into their real sentiments from their conversation, their actions, their looks, and gestures. She should also have the art, by her own conversation, actions, looks, and gestures, to communicate those sentiments which are agreeable to them, without seeming to intend it. Men will argue more philosophically about the human heart; but women will read the heart of man better than they. It belongs to women, if I may be allowed the expression, to form an experimental morality, and to reduce the study of man to a system. Women have most wit, men have most genius; women observe, men reason: from the concurrence of both we derive the clearest light and the most perfect knowledge, which the human mind is, of itself, capable of attaining. In one word, from hence we acquire the most intimate acquaintance, both with ourselves and others, of which our nature is capable; and it is thus that art has a constant tendency to perfect those endowments which nature has bestowed. – The world is the book of women.' *Rousseau's Emilius*.[5] I hope my readers still remember the comparison, which I have brought forward, between women and officers.

spread through the whole aggregate of society. The many become pedestal to the few. I, therefore, will venture to assert, that till women are more rationally educated, the progress of human virtue and improvement in knowledge must receive continual checks. And if it be granted that woman was not created merely to gratify the appetite of man, or to be the upper servant, who provides his meals and takes care of his linen, it must follow, that the first care of those mothers or fathers, who really attend to the education of females, should be, if not to strengthen the body, at least, not to destroy the constitution by mistaken notions of beauty and female excellence; nor should girls ever be allowed to imbibe the pernicious notion that a defect can, by any chemical process of reasoning, become an excellence. In this respect, I am happy to find, that the author of one of the most instructive books, that our country has produced for children, coincides with me in opinion; I shall quote his pertinent remarks to give the force of his respectable authority to reason.*

* A respectable old man gives the following sensible account of the method he pursued when educating his daughter: 'I endeavoured to give both to her mind and body a degree of vigour, which is seldom found in the female sex. As soon as she was sufficiently advanced in strength to be capable of the lighter labours of husbandry and gardening, I employed her as my constant companion. Selene, for that was her name, soon acquired a dexterity in all these rustic employments, which I considered with equal pleasure and admiration. If women are in general feeble both in body and mind, it arises less from nature than from education. We encourage a vicious indolence and inactivity, which we falsely call delicacy; instead of hardening their minds by the severer principles of reason and philosophy, we breed them to useless arts, which terminate in vanity and sensuality. In most of the countries which I had visited, they are taught nothing of an higher nature than a few modulations of the voice, or useless postures of the body; their time is consumed in sloth or trifles, and trifles become the only pursuits capable of interesting them. We seem to forget, that it is upon the qualities of the female sex that our own domestic comforts and the education of our children must depend. And what are the comforts or the education which a race of beings, corrupted from their infancy, and unacquainted with all the duties of life, are fitted to bestow? To touch a musical instrument with useless skill, to exhibit their natural or affected graces to the eyes of indolent and debauched young men, to dissipate their husband's patrimony in riotous and unnecessary expences, these are the only arts cultivated by women in most of the polished nations I had seen. And the consequences are uniformly such as may be expected to proceed from such polluted sources, private misery and public servitude.

But should it be proved that woman is naturally weaker than man, whence does it follow that it is natural for her to labour to become still weaker than nature intended her to be? Arguments of this cast are an insult to common sense, and favour of passion. The *divine right* of husbands, like the divine right of kings,[6] may, it is to be hoped, in this enlightened age, be contested without danger, and, though conviction may not silence many boisterous disputants, yet, when any prevailing prejudice is attacked, the wife will consider, and leave the narrow-minded to rail with thoughtless vehemence at innovation.

The mother, who wishes to give true dignity of character to her daughter, must, regardless of the sneers of ignorance, proceed on a plan diametrically opposite to that which Rousseau has recommended with all the deluding charms of eloquence and philosophical sophistry: for his eloquence renders absurdities plausible, and his dogmatic conclusions puzzle, without convincing, those who have not ability to refute them.

Throughout the whole animal kingdom every young creature requires almost continual exercise, and the infancy of children, conformable to this intimation, should be passed in harmless gambols, that exercise the feet and hands, without requiring very minute direction from the head, or the constant attention of a nurse. In fact, the care necessary for self-preservation is the first natural exercise of the understanding, as little inventions to amuse the present moment unfold the imagination. But these wise designs of nature are counteracted by mistaken fondness or blind zeal. The child is not left a moment to its own direction, particularly a girl, and thus rendered dependent – dependence is called natural.

To preserve personal beauty, woman's glory! the limbs and faculties are cramped with worse than Chinese bands,[7] and the sedentary life which they are condemned to live, whilst boys frolic in the open air, weakens the muscles and relaxes the

---

'But Selene's education was regulated by different views, and conducted upon severer principles; if that can be called severity which opens the mind to a sense of moral and religious duties, and most effectually arms it against the inevitable evils of life.'

Mr Day's Sandford and Merton, Vol. III.[8]

nerves. – As for Rousseau's remarks, which have since been echoed by several writers, that they have naturally, that is from their birth, independent of education, a fondness for dolls,[9] dressing, and talking – they are so puerile as not to merit a serious refutation. That a girl, condemned to sit for hours together listening to the idle chat of weak nurses, or to attend at her mother's toilet, will endeavour to join the conversation, is, indeed, very natural; and that she will imitate her mother or aunts, and amuse herself by adorning her lifeless doll, as they do in dressing her, poor innocent babe! is undoubtedly a most natural consequence. For men of the greatest abilities have seldom had sufficient strength to rise above the surrounding atmosphere; and, if the page of genius have always been blurred by the prejudices of the age, some allowance should be made for a sex, who, like kings, always see things through a false medium.

Pursuing these reflections, the fondness for dress, conspicuous in women, may be easily accounted for, without supposing it the result of a desire to please the sex on which they are dependent. The absurdity, in short, of supposing that a girl is naturally a coquette,[10] and that a desire connected with the impulse of nature to propagate the species, should appear even before an improper education has, by heating the imagination, called it forth prematurely, is so unphilosophical, that such a sagacious observer as Rousseau would not have adopted it, if he had not been accustomed to make reason give way to his desire of singularity, and truth to a favourite paradox.

Yet thus to give a sex to mind was not very consistent with the principles of a man who argued so warmly, and so well, for the immortality of the soul.[11] – But what a weak barrier is truth when it stands in the way of an hypothesis! Rousseau respected – almost adored virtue – and yet he allowed himself to love with sensual fondness. His imagination constantly prepared inflammable fuel for his inflammable senses;[12] but, in order to reconcile his respect for self-denial, fortitude, and those heroic virtues, which a mind like his could not coolly admire, he labours to invert the law of nature, and broaches a doctrine pregnant with mischief and derogatory to the character of supreme wisdom.

His ridiculous stories, which tend to prove that girls are *naturally* attentive to their persons, without laying any stress on daily example, are below contempt. – And that a little miss should have such a correct taste as to neglect the pleasing amusement of making O's, merely because she perceived that it was an ungraceful attitude, should be selected with the anecdotes of the learned pig. *[13]

I have, probably, had an opportunity of observing more girls in their infancy than J. J. Rousseau – I can recollect my own feelings, and I have looked steadily around me; yet, so far from coinciding with him in opinion respecting the first dawn of the female character, I will venture to affirm, that a girl, whose spirits have not been damped by inactivity, or innocence tainted by false shame, will always be a romp,[14] and the doll will never excite attention unless confinement allows her no alternative. Girls and boys, in short, would play harmlessly together, if the distinction of sex was not inculcated long before nature makes any difference. – I will go further, and affirm, as an indisputable fact, that most of the women, in the circle of my observation, who have acted like rational creatures, or shewn any vigour of intellect, have accidentally been allowed to run wild – as some of the elegant formers of the fair sex would insinuate.

The baneful consequences which flow from inattention to health during infancy, and youth, extend further than is supposed – dependence of body naturally produces dependence of mind; and how can she be a good wife or mother, the greater part of whose time is employed to guard against or endure sickness? Nor can it be expected that a woman will resolutely

---

* 'I once knew a young person who learned to write before she learned to read, and began to write with her needle before she could use a pen. At first, indeed, she took it into her head to make no other letter than the O; this letter she was constantly making of all sizes, and always the wrong way. Unluckily, one day, as she was intent on this employment, she happened to see herself in the looking-glass; when, taking a dislike to the constrained attitude in which she sat while writing, she threw away her pen, like another Pallas, and determined against making the O any more. Her brother was also equally averse to writing: it was the confinement, however, and not the constrained attitude, that most disgusted him.'

Rousseau's Emilius.[15]

endeavour to strengthen her constitution and abstain from enervating indulgencies, if artificial notions of beauty, and false
descriptions of sensibility, have been early entangled with her
motives of action. Most men are sometimes obliged to bear
with bodily inconveniencies, and to endure, occasionally, the
inclemency of the elements; but genteel women are, literally
speaking, slaves to their bodies, and glory in their subjection.

I once knew a weak woman of fashion,[16] who was more than
commonly proud of her delicacy and sensibility. She thought a
distinguishing taste and puny appetite the height of all human
perfection, and acted accordingly. – I have seen this weak sophisticated being neglect all the duties of life, yet recline with self-
complacency on a sofa, and boast of her want of appetite as a
proof of delicacy that extended to, or, perhaps, arose from, her
exquisite sensibility: for it is difficult to render intelligible such
ridiculous jargon. – Yet, at the moment, I have seen her insult a
worthy old gentlewoman, whom unexpected misfortunes had
made dependent on her ostentatious bounty, and who, in better
days, had claims on her gratitude. Is it possible that a human
creature could have become such a weak and depraved being,
if, like the Sybarites,[17] dissolved in luxury, everything like virtue
had not been worn away, or never impressed by precept, a poor
substitute, it is true, for cultivation of mind, though it serves as
a fence against vice?

Such a woman is not a more irrational monster than some of
the Roman emperors, who were depraved by lawless power.
Yet, since kings have been more under the restraint of law, and
the curb, however weak, of honour, the records of history are
not filled with such unnatural instances of folly and cruelty, nor
does the despotism that kills virtue and genius in the bud, hover
over Europe with that destructive blast which desolates Turkey,
and renders the men, as well as the soil, unfruitful.[18]

Women are every where in this deplorable state; for, in order
to preserve their innocence, as ignorance is courteously termed,
truth is hidden from them, and they are made to assume an
artificial character before their faculties have acquired any
strength. Taught from their infancy that beauty is woman's
sceptre, the mind shapes itself to the body, and, roaming round

its gilt cage, only seeks to adorn its prison. Men have various employments and pursuits which engage their attention, and give a character to the opening mind; but women, confined to one, and having their thoughts constantly directed to the most insignificant part of themselves, seldom extend their views beyond the triumph of the hour. But were their understanding once emancipated from the slavery to which the pride and sensuality of man and their short-sighted desire, like that of dominion in tyrants, of present sway, has subjected them, we should probably read of their weaknesses with surprise. I must be allowed to pursue the argument a little farther.

Perhaps, if the existence of an evil being were allowed, who, in the allegorical language of scripture, went about seeking whom he should devour,[19] he could not more effectually degrade the human character than by giving a man absolute power.

This argument branches into various ramifications. – Birth, riches, and every extrinsic advantage that exalt a man above his fellows, without any mental exertion, sink him in reality below them. In proportion to his weakness, he is played upon by designing men, till the bloated monster has lost all traces of humanity. And that tribes of men, like flocks of sheep, should quietly follow such a leader, is a solecism that only a desire of present enjoyment and narrowness of understanding can solve. Educated in slavish dependence, and enervated by luxury and sloth, where shall we find men who will stand forth to assert the rights of man; – or claim the privilege of moral beings, who should have but one road to excellence? Slavery to monarchs and ministers, which the world will be long in freeing itself from, and whose deadly grasp stops the progress of the human mind, is not yet abolished.

Let not men then in the pride of power, use the same arguments that tyrannic kings and venal ministers have used, and fallaciously assert that woman ought to be subjected because she has always been so. – But, when man, governed by reasonable laws, enjoys his natural freedom, let him despise woman, if she do not share it with him; and, till that glorious period arrives, in descanting on the folly of the sex, let him not overlook his own.

Women, it is true, obtaining power by unjust means, by practising or fostering vice, evidently lose the rank which reason would assign them, and they become either abject slaves or capricious tyrants. They lose all simplicity, all dignity of mind, in acquiring power, and act as men are observed to act when they have been exalted by the same means.

It is time to effect a revolution in female manners – time to restore to them their lost dignity – and make them, as a part of the human species, labour by reforming themselves to reform the world. It is time to separate unchangeable morals from local manners. – If men be demi-gods – why let us serve them! And if the dignity of the female soul be as disputable as that of animals – if their reason does not afford sufficient light to direct their conduct whilst unerring instinct is denied – they are surely of all creatures the most miserable! and, bent beneath the iron hand of destiny, must submit to be a *fair defect* in creation. But to justify the ways of Providence[20] respecting them, by pointing out some irrefragable reason for thus making such a large portion of mankind accountable and not accountable, would puzzle the subtilest casuist.

The only solid foundation for morality appears to be the character of the supreme Being; the harmony of which arises from a balance of attributes; – and, to speak with reverence, one attribute seems to imply the *necessity* of another. He must be just, because he is wise, he must be good, because he is omnipotent. For to exalt one attribute at the expence of another equally noble and necessary, bears the stamp of the warped reason of man – the homage of passion. Man, accustomed to bow down to power in his savage state, can seldom divest himself of this barbarous prejudice, even when civilization determines how much superior mental is to bodily strength; and his reason is clouded by these crude opinions, even when he thinks of the Deity. – His omnipotence is made to swallow up, or preside over his other attributes, and those mortals are supposed to limit his power irreverently, who think that it must be regulated by his wisdom.

I disclaim that specious humility which, after investigating nature, stops at the author. – The High and Lofty One, who inhabiteth eternity, doubtless possesses many attributes of which we can form no conception; but reason tells me that they cannot clash with those I adore – and I am compelled to listen to her voice.

It seems natural for man to search for excellence, and either to trace it in the object that he worships, or blindly to invest it with perfection, as a garment. But what good effect can the latter mode of worship have on the moral conduct of a rational being? He bends to power; he adores a dark cloud, which may open a bright prospect to him, or burst in angry, lawless fury, on his devoted head – he knows not why. And, supposing that the Deity acts from the vague impulse of an undirected will, man must also follow his own, or act according to rules, deduced from principles which he disclaims as irreverent. Into this dilemma have both enthusiasts and cooler thinkers fallen, when they laboured to free men from the wholesome restraints which a just conception of the character of God imposes.

It is not impious thus to scan the attributes of the Almighty: in fact, who can avoid it that exercises his faculties? For to love God as the fountain of wisdom, goodness, and power, appears to be the only worship useful to a being who wishes to acquire either virtue or knowledge. A blind unsettled affection may, like human passions, occupy the mind and warm the heart, whilst, to do justice, love mercy, and walk humbly with our God, is forgotten. I shall pursue this subject still further, when I consider religion in a light opposite to that recommended by Dr Gregory, who treats it as a matter of sentiment or taste.[21]

To return from this apparent digression. It were to be wished that women would cherish an affection for their husbands, founded on the same principle that devotion ought to rest upon. No other firm base is there under heaven – for let them beware of the fallacious light of sentiment; too often used as a softer phrase for sensuality. It follows then, I think, that from their infancy women should either be shut up like eastern princes, or educated in such a manner as to be able to think and act for themselves.

Why do men halt between two opinions, and expect impossibilities? Why do they expect virtue from a slave, from a being whom the constitution of civil society has rendered weak, if not vicious?

Still I know that it will require a considerable length of time to eradicate the firmly rooted prejudices which sensualists have planted; it will also require some time to convince women that they act contrary to their real interest on an enlarged scale, when they cherish or affect weakness under the name of delicacy, and to convince the world that the poisoned source of female vices and follies, if it be necessary, in compliance with custom, to use synonymous terms in a lax sense, has been the sensual homage paid to beauty: – to beauty of features; for it has been shrewdly observed by a German writer, that a pretty woman, as an object of desire, is generally allowed to be so by men of all descriptions; whilst a fine woman, who inspires more sublime emotions by displaying intellectual beauty, may be overlooked or observed with indifference, by those men who find their happiness in the gratification of their appetites. I foresee an obvious retort – whilst man remains such an imperfect being as he appears hitherto to have been, he will, more or less, be the slave of his appetites; and those women obtaining most power who gratify a predominant one, the sex is degraded by a physical, if not by a moral necessity.

This objection has, I grant, some force; but while such a sublime precept exists, as, 'be pure as your heavenly Father is pure;'[22] it would seem that the virtues of man are not limited by the Being who alone could limit them; and that he may press forward without considering whether he steps out of his sphere by indulging such a noble ambition. To the wild billows it has been said, 'thus far shalt thou go, and no further; and here shall thy proud waves be stayed.'[23] Vainly then do they beat and foam, restrained by the power that confines the struggling planets in their orbits, matter yields to the great governing Spirit. – But an immortal soul, not restrained by mechanical laws and struggling to free itself from the shackles of matter, contributes to, instead of disturbing, the order of creation, when, co-operating with the Father of spirits, it tries to govern itself by the invariable rule that, in a degree, before which our imagination faints, regulates the universe.

Besides, if women be educated for dependence; that is, to act according to the will of another fallible being, and submit, right or wrong, to power, where are we to stop? Are they to be considered as viceregents allowed to reign over a small domain, and answerable for their conduct to a higher tribunal, liable to error?

It will not be difficult to prove that such delegates will act like men subjected by fear, and make their children and servants endure their tyrannical oppression. As they submit without reason, they will, having no fixed rules to square their conduct by, be kind, or cruel, just as the whim of the moment directs; and we ought not to wonder if sometimes, galled by their heavy yoke, they take a malignant pleasure in resting it on weaker shoulders.

But, supposing a woman, trained up to obedience, be married to a sensible man, who directs her judgment without making her feel the servility of her subjection, to act with as much propriety by this reflected light as can be expected when reason is taken at second hand, yet she cannot ensure the life of her protector; he may die and leave her with a large family.

A double duty devolves on her; to educate them in the character of both father and mother; to form their principles and secure their property. But, alas! she has never thought, much less acted for herself. She has only learned to please* men, to depend

* 'In the union of the sexes, both pursue one common object, but not in the same manner. From their diversity in this particular, arises the first determinate difference between the moral relations of each. The one should be active and strong, the other passive and weak: it is necessary the one should have both the power and the will, and that the other should make little resistance.

'This principle being established, it follows that woman is expressly formed to please the man: if the obligation be reciprocal also, and the man ought to please in his turn, it is not so immediately necessary: his great merit is in his power, and he pleases merely because he is strong. This, I must confess, is not one of the refined maxims of love; it is, however, one of the laws of nature, prior to love itself.

'If woman be formed to please and be subjected to man, it is her place, doubtless, to render herself agreeable to him, instead of challenging his passion. The violence of his desires depends on her charms; it is by means of these she should urge him to the exertion of those powers which nature hath given him. The most successful method of exciting them, is, to render such exertion necessary by resistance; as, in that case, self-love is added to desire, and the one triumphs in the victory which the other obliged to acquire. Hence arise the various modes of attack and defence between the sexes; the boldness of one sex gracefully on them; yet, encumbered with children, how is she to obtain another protector – a husband to supply the place of reason? A rational man, for we are not treading on romantic ground, though he may think her a pleasing docile creature, will not choose to marry a *family* for love, when the world contains many more pretty creatures. What is then to become of her? She either falls an easy prey to some mean fortune-hunter, who defrauds her children of their paternal inheritance, and renders her miserable; or becomes the victim of discontent and blind indulgence. Unable to educate her sons, or impress them with respect; for it is not a play on words to assert, that people are never respected, though filling an important station, who are not respectable; she pines under the anguish of unavailing impotent regret. The serpent's tooth[24] enters into her very soul, and the vices of licentious youth bring her with sorrow, if not with poverty also, to the grave.

This is not an overcharged picture; on the contrary, it is a very possible case, and something similar must have fallen under every attentive eye.

I have, however, taken it for granted, that she was well-disposed, though experience shews, that the blind may as easily be led into a ditch as along the beaten road. But supposing, no very improbable conjecture, that a being only taught to please must still find her happiness in pleasing; – what an example of folly, not to say vice, will she be to her innocent daughters! The mother will be lost in the coquette, and, instead of making friends of her daughters, view them with eyes askance, for they are rivals – rivals more cruel than any other, because they invite a comparison, and drive her from the throne of beauty, who has never thought of a seat on the bench of reason.

It does not require a lively pencil, or the discriminating outline of a caricature, to sketch the domestic miseries and petty vices

---

and the timidity of the other; and, in a word, that bashfulness and modesty with which nature hath armed the weak, in order to subdue the strong.'

Rousseau's Emilius.[25]

I shall make no other comment on this ingenious passage, than just to observe, that it is the philosophy of lasciviousness.

which such a mistress of a family diffuses. Still she only acts as a woman ought to act, brought up according to Rousseau's system. She can never be reproached for being masculine, or turning out of her sphere; nay, she may observe another of his grand rules, and, cautiously preserving her reputation free from spot, be reckoned a good kind of woman. Yet in what respect can she be termed good? She abstains, it is true, without any great struggle, from committing gross crimes; but how does she fulfil her duties? Duties! – in truth she has enough to think of to adorn her body and nurse a weak constitution.

With respect to religion, she never presumed to judge for herself; but conformed, as a dependent creature should, to the ceremonies of the church which she was brought up in, piously believing that wiser heads than her own have settled that business: – and not to doubt is her point of perfection. She therefore pays her tythe of mint and cummin[26] – and thanks her God that she is not as other women are. These are the blessed effects of a good education! These the virtues of man's help-mate!*

I must relieve myself by drawing a different picture.

Let fancy now present a woman with a tolerable understanding, for I do not wish to leave the line of mediocrity, whose constitution, strengthened by exercise, has allowed her body to acquire its full vigour; her mind, at the same time, gradually expanding itself to comprehend the moral duties of life, and in what human virtue and dignity consist.

Formed thus by the discharge of the relative duties of her station, she marries from affection, without losing sight of prudence, and looking beyond matrimonial felicity, she secures her husband's respect before it is necessary to exert mean arts to please him and feed a dying flame, which nature doomed to expire

---

* 'O how lovely,' exclaims Rousseau, speaking of Sophia, 'is her ignorance! Happy is he who is destined to instruct her! She will never pretend to be the tutor of her husband, but will be content to be his pupil. Far from attempting to subject him to her taste, she will accommodate herself to his. She will be more estimable to him, than if she was learned: he will have a pleasure in instructing her.' *Rousseau's Emilius.*[27]

I shall content myself with simply asking, how friendship can subsist, when love expires, between the master and his pupil?

when the object became familiar, when friendship and for-bearance take place of a more ardent affection. – This is the natural death of love, and domestic peace is not destroyed by struggles to prevent its extinction. I also suppose the husband to be virtuous; or she is still more in want of independent principles.

Fate, however, breaks this tie. – She is left a widow, perhaps, without a sufficient provision; but she is not desolate! The pang of nature is felt; but after time has softened sorrow into melancholy resignation, her heart turns to her children with redoubled fondness, and anxious to provide for them, affection gives a sacred heroic cast to her maternal duties. She thinks that not only the eye sees her virtuous efforts from whom all her comfort now must flow, and whose approbation is life; but her imagination, a little abstracted and exalted by grief, dwells on the fond hope that the eyes which her trembling hand closed, may still see how she subdues every wayward passion to fulfil the double duty of being the father as well as the mother of her children. Raised to heroism by misfortunes, she represses the first faint dawning of a natural inclination, before it ripens into love, and in the bloom of life forgets her sex – forgets the pleasure of an awakening passion, which might again have been inspired and returned. She no longer thinks of pleasing, and conscious dignity prevents her from priding herself on account of the praise which her conduct demands. Her children have her love, and her brightest hopes are beyond the grave, where her imagination often strays.

I think I see her surrounded by her children, reaping the reward of her care. The intelligent eye meets hers, whilst health and innocence smile on their chubby cheeks, and as they grow up the cares of life are lessened by their grateful attention. She lives to see the virtues which she endeavoured to plant on principles, fixed into habits, to see her children attain a strength of character sufficient to enable them to endure adversity without forgetting their mother's example.

The task of life thus fulfilled, she calmly waits for the sleep of death, and rising from the grave, may say – Behold, thou gavest me a talent – and here are five talents.[28]

*

I wish to sum up what I have said in a few words, for I here throw down my gauntlet, and deny the existence of sexual virtues, not excepting modesty. For man and woman, truth, if I understand the meaning of the word, must be the same; yet the fanciful female character, so prettily drawn by poets and novelists, demanding the sacrifice of truth and sincerity, virtue becomes a relative idea, having no other foundation than utility, and of that utility men pretend arbitrarily to judge, shaping it to their own convenience.

Women, I allow, may have different duties to fulfil; but they are *human* duties, and the principles that should regulate the discharge of them, I sturdily maintain, must be the same.

To become respectable, the exercise of their understanding is necessary, there is no other foundation for independence of character; I mean explicity to say that they must only bow to the authority of reason, instead of being the *modest* slaves of opinion.

In the superior ranks of life how seldom do we meet with a man of superior abilities, or even common acquirements? The reason appears to me clear, the state they are born in was an unnatural one. The human character has ever been formed by the employments the individual, or class, pursues; and if the faculties are not sharpened by necessity, they must remain obtuse. The argument may fairly be extended to women; for, seldom occupied by serious business, the pursuit of pleasure gives that insignificancy to their character which renders the society of the *great* so insipid. The same want of firmness, produced by a similar cause, forces them both to fly from themselves to noisy pleasures, and artificial passions, till vanity takes place of every social affection, and the characteristics of humanity can scarcely be discerned. Such are the blessings of civil governments, as they are at present organized, that wealth and female softness equally tend to debase mankind, and are produced by the same cause; but allowing women to be rational creatures, they should be incited to acquire virtues which they may call their own, for how can a rational being be ennobled by any thing that is not obtained by its *own* exertions?

CHAP. IV

OBSERVATIONS ON THE STATE OF
DEGRADATION TO WHICH WOMAN IS
REDUCED BY VARIOUS CAUSES

That woman is naturally weak, or degraded by a concurrence of circumstances, is, I think, clear. But this position I shall simply contrast with a conclusion, which I have frequently heard fall from sensible men in favour of an aristocracy: that the mass of mankind cannot be any thing, or the obsequious slaves, who patiently allow themselves to be driven forward, would feel their own consequence, and spurn their chains. Men, they further observe, submit every where to oppression, when they have only to lift up their heads to throw off the yoke; yet, instead of asserting their birthright, they quietly lick the dust, and say, let us eat and drink, for to-morrow we die.[1] Women, I argue from analogy, are degraded by the same propensity to enjoy the present moment; and, at last, despise the freedom which they have not sufficient virtue to struggle to attain. But I must be more explicit.

With respect to the culture of the heart, it is unanimously allowed that sex is out of the question; but the line of subordination in the mental powers is never to be passed over.* Only 'absolute in loveliness,'[2] the portion of rationality granted to woman, is, indeed, very scanty; for, denying her genius and

* Into what inconsistencies do men fall when they argue without the compass of principles. Women, weak women, are compared with angels; yet, a superiour order of beings should be supposed to possess more intellect than man; or, in what does their superiority consist? In the same strain, to drop the sneer, they are allowed to possess more goodness of heart, piety, and benevolence. – I doubt the fact, though it be courteously brought forward, unless ignorance be allowed to be the mother of devotion; for I am firmly persuaded that, on an average, the proportion between virtue and knowledge, is more upon a par than is commonly granted.

judgment, it is scarcely possible to divine what remains to characterize intellect.

The stamen of immortality, if I may be allowed the phrase, is the perfectibility of human reason; for, were man created perfect, or did a flood of knowledge break in upon him, when he arrived at maturity, that precluded error, I should doubt whether his existence would be continued after the dissolution of the body. But, in the present state of things, every difficulty in morals that escapes from human discussion, and equally baffles the investigation of profound thinking, and the lightning glance of genius, is an argument on which I build my belief of the immortality of the soul. Reason is, consequentially, the simple power of improvement; or, more properly speaking, of discerning truth. Every individual is in this respect a world in itself. More or less may be conspicuous in one being than another; but the nature of reason must be the same in all, if it be an emanation of divinity, the tie that connects the creature with the Creator; for, can that soul be stamped with the heavenly image, that is not perfected by the exercise of its own reason?* Yet outwardly ornamented with elaborate care, and so adorned to delight man, 'that with honour he may love,'† the soul of woman is not allowed to have this distinction, and man, ever placed between her and reason, she is always represented as only created to see through a gross medium, and to take things on trust. But dismissing these fanciful theories, and considering woman as a whole, let it be what it will, instead of a part of man, the inquiry is whether she have reason or not. If she have, which, for a moment, I will take for granted, she was not created merely to be the solace of man, and the sexual should not destroy the human character.

Into this error men have, probably, been led by viewing education in a false light; not considering it as the first step to form a being advancing gradually towards perfection;‡ but only as a preparation for life. On this sensual error, for I must call it so, has

* 'The brutes,' says Lord Monboddo, 'remain in the state in which nature has placed them, except in so far as their natural instinct is improved by the culture *we* bestow upon them.'[3]
† Vide Milton.[4]
‡ This word is not strictly just, but I cannot find a better.

the false system of female manners been reared, which robs the whole sex of its dignity, and classes the brown and fair with the smiling flowers that only adorn the land. This has ever been the language of men, and the fear of departing from a supposed sexual character, has made even women of superiour sense adopt the same sentiments.* Thus understanding, strictly speaking, has been denied to woman; and instinct, sublimated into wit and cunning, for the purposes of life, has been substituted in its stead.

The power of generalizing ideas, of drawing comprehensive conclusions from individual observations,[5] is the only acquirement, for an immortal being, that really deserves the name of knowledge. Merely to observe, without endeavouring to account for any thing, may (in a very incomplete manner) serve as the common sense of life; but where is the store laid up that is to clothe the soul when it leaves the body?

*
     'Pleasure's the portion of th' *inferior* kind;
     But glory, virtue, Heavén for *man* design'd.

After writing these lines, how could Mrs Barbauld[6] write the following ignoble comparison?

    'To a Lady, *with some painted flowers.*'

    'Flowers to the fair: to you these flowers I bring,
    And strive to greet you with an earlier spring.
    Flowers SWEET, *and gay, and* DELICATE LIKE YOU;
    Emblems of innocence, and beauty too.
    With flowers the Graces bind their yellow hair,
    And flowery wreaths consenting lovers wear.
    Flowers, the sole luxury which nature knew,
    In Eden's pure and guiltless garden grew.
    To loftier forms are rougher tasks assign'd;
    The sheltering oak resists the stormy wind,
    The tougher yew repels invading foes,
    And the tall pine for future navies grows;
    But this soft family, to cares unknown,
    Were born for pleasure and delight ALONE.
    Gay without toil, and lovely without art,
    They spring to CHEER *the sense, and* GLAD *the heart.*
    Nor blush, my fair, to own you copy these;
    Your BEST, *your* SWEETEST *empire* is – TO PLEASE.'

So the men tell us; but virtue, says reason, must be acquired by *rough* toils, and useful struggles with worldly *cares.*

This power has not only been denied to women; but writers have insisted that it is inconsistent, with a few exceptions, with their sexual character. Let men prove this, and I shall grant that woman only exists for man. I must, however, previously remark, that the power of generalizing ideas, to any great extent, is not very common amongst men or women. But this exercise is the true cultivation of the understanding; and every thing conspires to render the cultivation of the understanding more difficult in the female than the male world.

I am naturally led by this assertion to the main subject of the present chapter, and shall now attempt to point out some of the causes that degrade the sex, and prevent women from generalizing their observations.

I shall not go back to the remote annals of antiquity to trace the history of woman; it is sufficient to allow that she has always been either a slave, or a despot, and to remark, that each of these situations equally retards the progress of reason. The grand source of female folly and vice has ever appeared to me to arise from narrowness of mind; and the very constitution of civil governments has put almost insuperable obstacles in the way to prevent the cultivation of the female understanding: – yet virtue can be built on no other foundation! The same obstacles are thrown in the way of the rich, and the same consequences ensue.

Necessity has been proverbially termed the mother of invention – the aphorism may be extended to virtue. It is an acquirement, and an acquirement to which pleasure must be sacrificed – and who sacrifices pleasure when it is within the grasp, whose mind has not been opened and strengthened by adversity, or the pursuit of knowledge goaded on by necessity? – Happy is it when people have the cares of life to struggle with; for these struggles prevent their becoming a prey to enervating vices, merely from idleness! But, if from their birth men and women be placed in a torrid zone, with the meridian sun of pleasure darting directly upon them, how can they sufficiently brace their minds to discharge the duties of life, or even to relish the affections that carry them out of themselves?

Pleasure is the business of woman's life, according to the present modification of society, and while it continues to be so, little can be expected from such weak beings. Inheriting, in a lineal descent from the first fair defect in nature, the sovereignty of beauty, they have, to maintain their power, resigned the natural rights, which the exercise of reason might have procured them, and chosen rather to be short-lived queens than labour to obtain the sober pleasures that arise from equality. Exalted by their inferiority (this sounds like a contradiction), they constantly demand homage as women, though experience should teach them that the men who pride themselves upon paying this arbitrary insolent respect to the sex, with the most scrupulous exactness, are most inclined to tyrannize over, and despise, the very weakness they cherish. Often do they repeat Mr Hume's[7] sentiments; when, comparing the French and Athenian character, he alludes to women. 'But what is more singular in this whimsical nation, say I to the Athenians, is, that a frolick of yours during the Saturnalia,[8] when the slaves are served by their masters, is seriously continued by them through the whole year, and through the whole course of their lives; accompanied too with some circumstances, which still further augment the absurdity and ridicule. Your sport only elevates for a few days those whom fortune has thrown down, and whom she too, in sport, may really elevate for ever above you. But this nation gravely exalts those, whom nature has subjected to them, and whose inferiority and infirmities are absolutely incurable. The women, though without virtue, are their masters and sovereigns.'

Ah! why do women, I write with affectionate solicitude, condescend to receive a degree of attention and respect from strangers, different from that reciprocation of civility which the dictates of humanity and the politeness of civilization authorise between man and man? And, why do they not discover, when 'in the noon of beauty's power,' that they are treated like queens only to be deluded by hollow respect, till they are led to resign, or not assume, their natural prerogatives? Confined then in cages like the feathered race, they have nothing to do but to plume themselves, and stalk with mock majesty from perch to perch. It is true they are provided with food and raiment, for which they neither toil nor spin;[9] but health, liberty, and virtue, are given in exchange. But, where, amongst mankind, has been found sufficient strength of mind to enable a being to resign these adventitious prerogatives; one who, rising with the calm dignity of reason above opinion, dared to be proud of the privileges inherent in man? And it is vain to expect it whilst hereditary power chokes the affections and nips reason in the bud.

The passions of men have thus placed women on thrones, and, till mankind become more reasonable, it is to be feared that women will avail themselves of the power which they attain with the least exertion, and which is the most indisputable. They will smile, – yes, they will smile, though told that –

> 'In beauty's empire is no mean,
> And woman, either slave or queen,
> Is quickly scorn'd when not ador'd.'[10]

But the adoration comes first, and the scorn is not anticipated.

Lewis the XIVth, in particular, spread factitious manners, and caught, in a specious way, the whole nation in his toils; for, establishing an artful chain of despotism, he made it the interest of the people at large, individually to respect his station and support his power. And women, whom he flattered by a puerile attention to the whole sex, obtained in his reign that prince-like distinction so fatal to reason and virtue.

A king is always a king – and a woman always a woman:* his authority and her sex, ever stand between them and rational converse. With a lover, I grant, she should be so, and her sensibility will naturally lead her to endeavour to excite emotion, not to gratify her vanity, but her heart. This I do not allow to be coquetry, it is the artless impulse of nature, I only exclaim against the sexual desire of conquest when the heart is out of the question.

This desire is not confined to women; 'I have endeavoured,'

---

* And a wit, always a wit, might be added; for the vain fooleries of wits and beauties to obtain attention, and make conquests, are much upon a par.

says Lord Chesterfield, 'to gain the hearts of twenty women, whose persons I would not have given a fig for.'[11] The libertine, who, in a gust of passion, takes advantage of unsuspecting tenderness, is a saint when compared with this cold-hearted rascal; for I like to use significant words. Yet only taught to please, women are always on the watch to please, and with true heroic ardour endeavour to gain hearts merely to resign or spurn them, when the victory is decided, and conspicuous.

I must descend to the minutiæ of the subject.

I lament that women are systematically degraded by receiving the trivial attentions, which men think it manly to pay to the sex, when, in fact, they are insultingly supporting their own superiority. It is not condescension to bow to an inferior. So ludicrous, in fact, do these ceremonies appear to me, that I scarcely am able to govern my muscles, when I see a man start with eager, and serious solicitude, to lift a handkerchief, or shut a door, when the *lady* could have done it herself, had she only moved a pace or two.

A wild wish has just flown from my heart to my head, and I will not stifle it though it may excite a horse-laugh. – I do earnestly wish to see the distinction of sex confounded in society, unless where love animates the behaviour. For this distinction is, I am firmly persuaded, the foundation of the weakness of character ascribed to woman; is the cause why the understanding is neglected, whilst accomplishments are acquired with sedulous care: and the same cause accounts for their preferring the graceful before the heroic virtues.

Mankind, including every description, wish to be loved and respected by *something*; and the common herd will always take the nearest road to the completion of their wishes. The respect paid to wealth and beauty is the most certain, and unequivocal; and, of course, will always attract the vulgar eye of common minds. Abilities and virtues are absolutely necessary to raise men from the middle rank of life into notice; and the natural consequence is notorious, the middle rank contains most virtue and abilities. Men have thus, in one station, at least an opportunity of exerting themselves with dignity, and of rising by the exertions which really improve a rational creature; but the whole female sex are, till their character is formed, in the same condition as the rich: for they are born, I now speak of a state of civilization, with certain sexual privileges, and whilst they are gratuitously granted them, few will ever think of works of supererogation, to obtain the esteem of a small number of superiour people.

When do we hear of women who, starting out of obscurity, boldly claim respect on account of their great abilities or daring virtues? Where are they to be found? – 'To be observed, to be attended to, to be taken notice of with sympathy, complacency, and approbation, are all the advantages which they seek.' – True! my male readers will probably exclaim; but let them, before they draw any conclusion, recollect that this was not written originally as descriptive of women, but of the rich. In Dr Smith's Theory of Moral Sentiments,[12] I have found a general character of people of rank and fortune, that, in my opinion, might with the greatest propriety be applied to the female sex. I refer the sagacious reader to the whole comparison; but must be allowed to quote a passage to enforce an argument that I mean to insist on, as the one most conclusive against a sexual character. For if, excepting warriors, no great men, of any denomination, have ever appeared amongst the nobility, may it not be fairly inferred that their local situation swallowed up the man, and produced a character similar to that of women, who are *localized*, if I may be allowed the word, by the rank they are placed in, by *courtesy*? Women, commonly called Ladies, are not to be contradicted in company, are not allowed to exert any manual strength; and from them the negative virtues only are expected, when any virtues are expected, patience, docility, good-humour, and flexibility; virtues incompatible with any vigorous exertion of intellect. Besides, by living more with each other, and being seldom absolutely alone, they are more under the influence of sentiments than passions. Solitude and reflection are necessary to give to wishes the force of passions, and to enable the imagination to enlarge the object, and make it the most desirable. The same may be said of the rich; they do not sufficiently deal in general ideas, collected by impassioned thinking, or calm investigation, to acquire that strength of character on which great resolves are built. But hear what an acute observer says of the great.

'Do the great seem insensible of the easy price at which they may acquire the publick admiration; or do they seem to imagine that to them, as to other men, it must be the purchase either of sweat or of blood? By what important accomplishments is the young nobleman instructed to support the dignity of his rank, and to render himself worthy of that superiority over his fellow-citizens, to which the virtue of his ancestors had raised them? Is it by knowledge, by industry, by patience, by self-denial, or by virtue of any kind? As all his words, as all his motions are attended to, he learns an habitual regard to every circumstance of ordinary behaviour, and studies to perform all those small duties with the most exact propriety. As he is conscious how much he is observed, and how much mankind are disposed to favour all his inclinations, he acts, upon the most indifferent occasions, with that freedom and elevation which the thought of this naturally inspires. His air, his manner, his deportment, all mark that elegant and graceful sense of his own superiority, which those who are born to inferior station can hardly ever arrive at. These are the arts by which he proposes to make mankind more easily submit to his authority, and to govern their inclinations according to his own pleasure: and in this he is seldom disappointed. These arts, supported by rank and pre-eminence, are, upon ordinary occasions, sufficient to govern the world. Lewis XIV, during the greater part of his reign, was regarded, not only in France, but over all Europe, as the most perfect model of a great prince. But what were the talents and virtues by which he acquired this great reputation? Was it by the scrupulous and inflexible justice of all his undertakings, by the immense dangers and difficulties with which they were attended, or by the unwearied and unrelenting application with which he pursued them? Was it by his extensive knowledge, by his exquisite judgment, or by his heroic valour? It was by none of these qualities. But he was, first of all, the most powerful prince in Europe, and consequently held the highest rank among kings; and then, says his historian,[13] "he surpassed all his courtiers in the gracefulness of his shape, and the majestic beauty of his features. The sound of his voice, noble and affecting, gained those hearts which his presence intimidated. He had a step and a deportment which could suit only him and his rank, and which would have been ridiculous in any other person. The embarrassment which he occasioned to those who spoke to him, flattered that secret satisfaction with which he felt his own superiority." These frivolous accomplishments, supported by his rank, and, no doubt too, by a degree of other talents and virtues, which seems, however, not to have been much above mediocrity, established this prince in the esteem of his own age, and have drawn, even from posterity, a good deal of respect for his memory. Compared with these, in his own times, and in his own presence, no other virtue, it seems, appeared to have any merit. Knowledge, industry, valour, and beneficence, trembled, were abashed, and lost all dignity before them.'[14]

Woman also thus 'in herself complete,' by possessing all these *frivolous* accomplishments, so changes the nature of things

—'That what she wills to do or say
Seems wisest, virtuousest, discreetest, best;
All higher knowledge in *her presence* falls
Degraded. Wisdom in discourse with her
Loses discountenanc'd, and, like Folly, shows;
Authority and Reason on her wait.' —[15]

And all this is built on her loveliness!

In the middle rank of life, to continue the comparison, men, in their youth, are prepared for professions, and marriage is not considered as the grand feature in their lives; whilst women, on the contrary, have no other scheme to sharpen their faculties. It is not business, extensive plans, or any of the excursive flights of ambition, that engross their attention; no, their thoughts are not employed in rearing such noble structures. To rise in the world, and have the liberty of running from pleasure to pleasure, they must marry advantageously, and to this object their time is sacrificed, and their persons often legally prostituted. A man when he enters any profession has his eye steadily fixed on some future advantage (and the mind gains great strength by having all its efforts directed to one point), and, full of his business, pleasure is considered as mere relaxation; whilst women seek for pleasure as the main purpose of existence. In fact, from the education, which they receive from society, the love of pleasure may be said to govern them all; but does this prove that there is a sex in souls? It would be just as rational to declare that the courtiers in France, when a destructive system of despotism had formed their character, were not men, because liberty, virtue, and humanity, were sacrificed to pleasure and vanity. – Fatal passions, which have ever domineered over the *whole* race!

The same love of pleasure, fostered by the whole tendency of their education, gives a trifling turn to the conduct of women in most circumstances: for instance, they are ever anxious about secondary things; and on the watch for adventures, instead of being occupied by duties.

A man, when he undertakes a journey, has, in general, the end in view; a woman thinks more of the incidental occurrences, the strange things that may possibly occur on the road; the impression that she may make on her fellow-travellers; and, above all, she is anxiously intent on the care of the finery that she carries with her, which is more than ever a part of herself, when going to figure on a new scene; when, to use an apt French turn of expression, she is going to produce a sensation. – Can dignity of mind exist with such trivial cares?

In short, women, in general, as well as the rich of both sexes, have acquired all the follies and vices of civilization, and missed the useful fruit. It is not necessary for me always to premise, that I speak of the condition of the whole sex, leaving exceptions out of the question. Their senses are inflamed, and their understandings neglected, consequently they become the prey of their senses, delicately termed sensibility, and are blown about by every momentary gust of feeling. Civilized women are, therefore, so weakened by false refinement, that, respecting morals, their condition is much below what it would be were they left in a state nearer to nature. Ever restless and anxious, their over exercised sensibility not only renders them uncomfortable themselves, but troublesome, to use a soft phrase, to others. All their thoughts turn on things calculated to excite emotion; and feeling, when they should reason, their conduct, is unstable, and their opinions are wavering – not the wavering produced by deliberation or progressive views, but by contradictory emotions. By fits and starts they are warm in many pursuits; yet this warmth, never concentrated into perseverance, soon exhausts itself; exhaled by its own heat, or meeting with some other fleeting passion, to which reason has never given any specific gravity, neutrality ensues. Miserable, indeed, must be that being whose cultivation of mind has only tended to inflame its passions! A distinction should be made between inflaming and strengthening them. The passions thus pampered, whilst the judgment is left unformed, what can be expected to ensue? – Undoubtedly, a mixture of madness and folly!

This observation should not be confined to the *fair* sex; however, at present, I only mean to apply it to them.

Novels, music, poetry, and gallantry, all tend to make women the creatures of sensation, and their character is thus formed in the mould of folly during the time they are acquiring accomplishments, the only improvement they are excited, by their station in society, to acquire. This overstretched sensibility naturally relaxes the other powers of the mind, and prevents intellect from attaining that sovereignty which it ought to attain to render a rational creature useful to others, and content with its own station: for the exercise of the understanding, as life advances, is the only method pointed out by nature to calm the passions.

Satiety has a very different effect, and I have often been forcibly struck by an emphatical description of damnation: – when the spirit is represented as continually hovering with abortive eagerness round the defiled body, unable to enjoy any thing without the organs of sense. Yet, to their senses, are women made slaves, because it is by their sensibility that they obtain present power.

And will moralists pretend to assert, that this is the condition in which one half of the human race should be encouraged to remain with listless inactivity and stupid acquiescence? Kind instructors! what were we created for? To remain, it may be said, innocent; they mean in a state of childhood. – We might as well never have been born, unless it were necessary that we should be created to enable man to acquire the noble privilege of reason, the power of discerning good from evil, whilst we lie down in the dust from whence we were taken, never to rise again. –

It would be an endless task to trace the variety of meannesses, cares, and sorrows, into which women are plunged by the prevailing opinion, that they were created rather to feel than reason, and that all the power they obtain, must be obtained by their charms and weakness:

'Fine by defect, and amiably weak!'[16]

And, made by this amiable weakness entirely dependent, excepting what they gain by illicit sway, on man, not only for protection, but advice, is it surprising that, neglecting the duties that reason alone points out, and shrinking from trials calculated to strengthen their minds, they only exert themselves to give their defects a graceful covering, which may serve to heighten their charms in the eye of the voluptuary, though it sink them below the scale of moral excellence?

Fragile in every sense of the word, they are obliged to look up to man for every comfort. In the most trifling dangers they cling to their support, with parasitical tenacity, piteously demanding succour; and their *natural* protector extends his arm, or lifts up his voice, to guard the lovely trembler – from what? Perhaps the frown of an old cow, or the jump of a mouse; a rat, would be a serious danger. In the name of reason, and even common sense, what can save such beings from contempt; even though they be soft and fair?

These fears, when not affected, may produce some pretty attitudes; but they shew a degree of imbecility which degrades a rational creature in a way women are not aware of – for love and esteem are very distinct things.

I am fully persuaded that we should hear of none of these infantine airs, if girls were allowed to take sufficient exercise, and not confined in close rooms till their muscles are relaxed, and their powers of digestion destroyed. To carry the remark still further, if fear in girls, instead of being cherished, perhaps, created, were treated in the same manner as cowardice in boys, we should quickly see women with more dignified aspects. It is true, they could not then with equal propriety be termed the sweet flowers that smile in the walk of man; but they would be more respectable members of society, and discharge the important duties of life by the light of their own reason. 'Educate women like men,' says Rousseau, 'and the more they resemble our sex the less power will they have over us.'[17] This is the very point I aim at. I do not wish them to have power over men; but over themselves.

In the same strain have I heard men argue against instructing the poor; for many are the forms that aristocracy assumes. 'Teach them to read and write,' say they, 'and you take them out of the station assigned them by nature.' An eloquent Frenchman has answered them, I will borrow his sentiments. But they know not, when they make man a brute, that they may expect every instant to see him transformed into a ferocious beast. Without knowledge there can be no morality!

Ignorance is a frail base for virtue! Yet, that it is the condition for which woman was organized, has been insisted upon by the writers who have most vehemently argued in favour of the superiority of man; a superiority not in degree, but essence; though, to soften the argument, they have laboured to prove, with chivalrous generosity, that the sexes ought not to be compared; man was made to reason, woman to feel: and that together, flesh and spirit, they make the most perfect whole, by blending happily reason and sensibility into one character.

And what is sensibility? 'Quickness of sensation; quickness of perception; delicacy.' Thus is it defined by Dr Johnson;[18] and the definition gives me no other idea than of the most exquisitely polished instinct. I discern not a trace of the image of God in either sensation or matter. Refined seventy times seven,[19] they are still material; intellect dwells not there; nor will fire ever make lead gold!

I come round to my old argument; if woman be allowed to have an immortal soul, she must have, as the employment of life, an understanding to improve. And when, to render the present state more complete, though every thing proves it to be but a fraction of a mighty sum, she is incited by present gratification to forget her grand destination, nature is counteracted, or she was born only to procreate and rot. Or, granting brutes, of every description, a soul, though not a reasonable one, the exercise of instinct and sensibility may be the step, which they are to take, in this life, towards the attainment of reason in the next; so that through all eternity they will lag behind man, who, why we cannot tell, had the power given him of attaining reason in his first mode of existence.

When I treat of the peculiar duties of women, as I should treat of the peculiar duties of a citizen or father, it will be found that I do not mean to insinuate that they should be taken out of their families, speaking of the majority. 'He that hath wife and children,' says Lord Bacon, 'hath given hostages to fortune; for they are impediments to great enterprises, either of virtue or mischief. Certainly the best works, and of greatest merit for the public, have proceeded from the unmarried or childless men.'[20] I say the same of women. But, the welfare of society is not built on extraordinary exertions; and were it more reasonably organized, there would be still less need of great abilities, or heroic virtues.

In the regulation of a family, in the education of children, understanding, in an unsophisticated sense, is particularly required: strength both of body and mind; yet the men who, by their writings, have most earnestly laboured to domesticate women, have endeavoured, by arguments dictated by a gross appetite, which satiety had rendered fastidious, to weaken their bodies and cramp their minds. But, if even by these sinister methods they really *persuaded* women, by working on their feelings, to stay at home, and fulfil the duties of a mother and mistress of a family, I should cautiously oppose opinions that led women to right conduct, by prevailing on them to make the discharge of such important duties the main business of life, though reason were insulted. Yet, and I appeal to experience, if by neglecting the understanding they be as much, nay, more detached from these domestic employments, than they could be by the most serious intellectual pursuit, though it may be observed, that the mass of mankind will never vigorously pursue an intellectual object,* I

---

* The mass of mankind are rather the slaves of their appetites than of their passions.

may be allowed to infer that reason is absolutely necessary to enable a woman to perform any duty properly, and I must again repeat, that sensibility is not reason.

The comparison with the rich still occurs to me; for, when men neglect the duties of humanity, women will follow their example; a common stream hurries them both along with thoughtless celerity. Riches and honours prevent a man from enlarging his understanding, and enervate all his powers by reversing the order of nature, which has ever made true pleasure the reward of labour. Pleasure – enervating pleasure is, likewise, within women's reach without earning it. But, till hereditary possessions are spread abroad, how can we expect men to be proud of virtue? And, till they are, women will govern them by the most direct means, neglecting their dull domestic duties to catch the pleasure that sits lightly on the wing of time.

'The power of the woman,' says some author, 'is her sensibility;' and men, not aware of the consequence, do all they can to make this power swallow up every other. Those who constantly employ their sensibility will have most: for example, poets, painters, and composers.* Yet, when the sensibility is thus increased at the expence of reason, and even the imagination, why do philosophical men complain of their fickleness? The sexual attention of man particularly acts on female sensibility, and this sympathy has been exercised from their youth up. A husband cannot long pay those attentions with the passion necessary to excite lively emotions, and the heart, accustomed to lively emotions, turns to a new lover, or pines in secret, the prey of virtue or prudence. I mean when the heart has really been rendered susceptible, and the taste formed; for I am apt to conclude, from what I have seen in fashionable life, that vanity is oftener fostered than sensibility by the mode of education, and the intercourse between the sexes, which I have reprobated; and that coquetry more frequently proceeds from vanity than from that inconstancy, which overstrained sensibility naturally produces.

---

* Men of these descriptions pour it into their compositions, to amalgamate the gross materials; and, moulding them with passion, give to the inert body a soul; but, in woman's imagination, love alone concentrates these ethereal beams.

Another argument that has had great weight with me, must, I think, have some force with every considerate benevolent heart. Girls who have been thus weakly educated, are often cruelly left by their parents without any provision; and, of course, are dependent on, not only the reason, but the bounty of their brothers.[21] These brothers are, to view the fairest side of the question, good sort of men, and give as a favour, what children of the same parents had an equal right to. In this equivocal humiliating situation, a docile female may remain some time, with a tolerable degree of comfort. But, when the brother marries, a probable circumstance, from being considered as the mistress of the family, she is viewed with averted looks as an intruder, an unnecessary burden on the benevolence of the master of the house, and his new partner.

Who can recount the misery, which many unfortunate beings, whose minds and bodies are equally weak, suffer in such situations – unable to work, and ashamed to beg? The wife, a cold-hearted, narrow-minded, woman, and this is not an unfair supposition; for the present mode of education does not tend to enlarge the heart any more than the understanding, is jealous of the little kindness which her husband shews to his relations; and her sensibility not rising to humanity, she is displeased at seeing the property of *her* children lavished on an helpless sister.

These are matters of fact, which have come under my eye again and again. The consequence is obvious, the wife has recourse to cunning to undermine the habitual affection, which she is afraid openly to oppose; and neither tears not caresses are spared till the spy is worked out of her home, and thrown on the world, unprepared for its difficulties; or sent, as a great effort of generosity, or from some regard to propriety, with a small stipend, and an uncultivated mind, into joyless solitude.

These two women may be much upon a par, with respect to reason and humanity; and changing situations, might have acted just the same selfish part; but had they been differently educated, the case would also have been very different. The wife would not have had that sensibility, of which self is the centre, and reason might have taught her not to expect, and not even to be flattered by, the affection of her husband, if it led him to violate prior duties. She would wish not to love him merely because he loved her, but on account of his virtues; and the sister might have been able to struggle for herself instead of eating the bitter bread of dependence.

I am, indeed, persuaded that the heart, as well as the understanding, is opened by cultivation; and by, which may not appear so clear, strengthening the organs; I am not now talking of momentary flashes of sensibility, but of affections. And, perhaps, in the education of both sexes, the most difficult task is so to adjust instruction as not to narrow the understanding, whilst the heart is warmed by the generous juices of spring, just raised by the electric fermentation of the season; nor to dry up the feelings by employing the mind in investigations remote from life.

With respect to women, when they receive a careful education, they are either made fine ladies, brimful of sensibility, and teeming with capricious fancies; or mere notable women. The latter are often friendly, honest creatures, and have a shrewd kind of good sense joined with worldly prudence, that often render them more useful members of society than the fine sentimental lady, though they possess neither greatness of mind nor taste. The intellectual world is shut against them; take them out of their family or neighbourhood, and they stand still; the mind finding no employment, for literature affords a fund of amusement which they have never sought to relish, but frequently to despise. The sentiments and taste of more cultivated minds appear ridiculous, even in those whom chance and family connections have led them to love; but in mere acquaintance they think it all affectation.

A man of sense can only love such a woman on account of her sex, and respect her, because she is a trusty servant. He lets her, to preserve his own peace, scold the servants, and go to church in clothes made of the very best materials. A man of her own size of understanding would, probably, not agree so well with her; for he might wish to encroach on her prerogative, and manage some domestic concerns himself. Yet women, whose minds are not enlarged by cultivation, or the natural selfishness of sensibility expanded by reflection, are very unfit to manage a family; for, by an undue stretch of power, they are always

tyrannizing to support a superiority that only rests on the arbitrary distinction of fortune. The evil is sometimes more serious,
and domestics are deprived of innocent indulgences, and made
to work beyond their strength, in order to enable the notable
woman to keep a better table, and outshine her neighbours in
finery and parade. If she attend to her children, it is, in general,
to dress them in a costly manner – and, whether this attention
arise from vanity or fondness, it is equally pernicious.

Besides, how many women of this description pass their days;
or, at least, their evenings, discontentedly. Their husbands
acknowledge that they are good managers, and chaste wives;
but leave home to seek for more agreeable, may I be allowed to
use a significant French word, *piquant* society; and the patient
drudge, who fulfils her task, like a blind horse in a mill, is
defrauded of her just reward; for the wages due to her are the
caresses of her husband; and women who have so few resources
in themselves, do not very patiently bear this privation of a
natural right.

A fine lady, on the contrary, has been taught to look down
with contempt on the vulgar employments of life; though she
has only been incited to acquire accomplishments that rise a
degree above sense; for even corporeal accomplishments cannot
be acquired with any degree of precision unless the understanding has been strengthened by exercise. Without a foundation of
principles taste is superficial, grace must arise from something
deeper than imitation. The imagination, however, is heated,
and the feelings rendered fastidious, if not sophisticated; or, a
counterpoise of judgment is not acquired, when the heart still
remains artless, though it becomes too tender.

These women are often amiable; and their hearts are really
more sensible to general benevolence, more alive to the sentiments that civilize life, than the square-elbowed family drudge;
but, wanting a due proportion of reflection and self-government,
they only inspire love; and are the mistresses of their husbands,
whilst they have any hold on their affections; and the platonic
friends of his male acquaintance. These are the fair defects in
nature; the women who appear to be created not to enjoy the
fellowship of man, but to save him from sinking into absolute

brutality, by rubbing off the rough angles of his character; and by playful dalliance to give some dignity to the appetite that draws him to them. – Gracious Creator of the whole human race! hast thou created such a being as woman, who can trace thy wisdom in thy works, and feel that thou alone art by thy nature exalted above her, – for no better purpose? – Can she believe that she was only made to submit to man, her equal, a being, who, like her, was sent into the world to acquire virtue? – Can she consent to be occupied merely to please him; merely to adorn the earth, when her soul is capable of rising to thee? – And can she rest supinely dependent on man for reason, when she ought to mount with him the arduous steeps of knowledge? –

Yet, if love be the supreme good, let women be only educated to inspire it, and let every charm be polished to intoxicate the senses; but, if they be moral beings, let them have a chance to become intelligent; and let love to man be only a part of that glowing flame of universal love, which, after encircling humanity, mounts in grateful incense to God.

To fulfil domestic duties much resolution is necessary, and a serious kind of perseverance that requires a more firm support than emotions, however lively and true to nature. To give an example of order, the soul of virtue, some austerity of behaviour must be adopted, scarcely to be expected from a being who, from its infancy, has been made the weathercock of its own sensations. Whoever rationally means to be useful must have a plan of conduct; and, in the discharge of the simplest duty, we are often obliged to act contrary to the present impulse of tenderness or compassion. Severity is frequently the most certain, as well as the most sublime proof of affection; and the want of this power over the feelings, and of that lofty, dignified affection, which makes a person prefer the future good of the beloved object to a present gratification, is the reason why so many fond mothers spoil their children, and has made it questionable whether negligence or indulgence be most hurtful: but I am inclined to think, that the latter has done most harm.

Mankind seem to agree that children should be left under the management of women during their childhood. Now, from all the observation that I have been able to make, women of sensibility are the most unfit for this task, because they will infallibly, carried away by their feelings, spoil a child's temper. The management of the temper, the first, and most important branch of education, requires the sober steady eye of reason; a plan of conduct equally distant from tyranny and indulgence: yet these are the extremes that people of sensibility alternately fall into; always shooting beyond the mark. I have followed this train of reasoning much further, till I have concluded, that a person of genius is the most improper person to be employed in education, public or private. Minds of this rare species see things too much in masses, and seldom, if ever, have a good temper. That habitual cheerfulness, termed good-humour, is, perhaps, as seldom united with great mental powers, as with strong feelings. And those people who follow, with interest and admiration, the flights of genius; or, with cooler approbation suck in the instruction which has been elaborately prepared for them by the profound thinker, ought not to be disgusted, if they find the former choleric, and the latter morose; because liveliness of fancy, and a tenacious comprehension of mind, are scarcely compatible with that pliant urbanity which leads a man, at least, to bend to the opinions and prejudices of others, instead of roughly confronting them.

But, treating of education or manners, minds of a superior class are not to be considered, they may be left to chance; it is the multitude, with moderate abilities, who call for instruction, and catch the colour of the atmosphere they breathe. This respectable concourse, I contend, men and women, should not have their sensations heightened in the hot-bed of luxurious indolence, at the expence of their understanding; for, unless there be a ballast of understanding, they will never become either virtuous or free: an aristocracy, founded on property, or sterling talents, will ever sweep before it, the alternately timid, and ferocious, slaves of feeling.

Numberless are the arguments, to take another view of the subject, brought forward with a shew of reason, because supposed to be deduced from nature, that men have used morally and physically, to degrade the sex. I must notice a few.

The female understanding has often been spoken of with

contempt, as arriving sooner at maturity than the male. I shall not answer this argument by alluding to the early proofs of reason, as well as genius, in Cowley,[22] Milton, and Pope,* but only appeal to experience to decide whether young men, who are early introduced into company (and examples now abound), do not acquire the same precocity. So notorious is this fact, that the bare mentioning of it must bring before people, who at all mix in the world, the idea of a number of swaggering apes of men, whose understandings are narrowed by being brought into the society of men when they ought to have been spinning a top or twirling a hoop.

It has also been asserted, by some naturalists, that men do not attain their full growth and strength till thirty; but that women arrive at maturity by twenty. I apprehend that they reason on false ground, led astray by the male prejudice, which deems beauty the perfection of woman – mere beauty of features and complexion, the vulgar acceptation of the word, whilst male beauty is allowed to have some connection with the mind. Strength of body, and that character of countenance, which the French term a *physionomie*, women do not acquire before thirty, any more than men. The little artless tricks of children, it is true, are particularly pleasing and attractive; yet, when the pretty freshness of youth is worn off, these artless graces become studied airs, and disgust every person of taste. In the countenance of girls we only look for vivacity and bashful modesty; but, the springtide of life over, we look for soberer sense in the face, and for traces of passion, instead of the dimples of animal spirits; expecting to see individuality of character, the only fastener of the affections.† We then wish to converse, not to fondle; to give scope to our imaginations as well as to the sensations of our hearts.

At twenty the beauty of both sexes is equal; but the libertinism of man leads him to make the distinction, and superannuated coquettes are commonly of the same opinion; for, when they

---

* Many other names might be added.

† The strength of an affection is, generally, in the same proportion as the character of the species in the object beloved, is lost in that of the individual.

can no longer inspire love, they pay for the vigour and vivacity of youth. The French, who admit more of mind into their notions of beauty, give the preference to women of thirty. I mean to say that they allow women to be in their most perfect state, when vivacity gives place to reason, and to that majestic seriousness of character, which marks maturity; – or, the resting point. In youth, till twenty, the body shoots out, till thirty the solids are attaining a degree of density; and the flexible muscles, growing daily more rigid, give character to the countenance; that is, they trace the operations of the mind with the iron pen of fate, and tell us not only what powers are within, but how they have been employed.

It is proper to observe, that animals who arrive slowly at maturity, are the longest lived, and of the noblest species. Men cannot, however, claim any natural superiority from the grandeur of longevity; for in this respect nature has not distinguished the male.

Polygamy is another physical degradation; and a plausible argument for a custom, that blasts every domestic virtue, is drawn from the well-attested fact, that in the countries where it is established, more females are born than males. This appears to be an indication of nature, and to nature, apparently reasonable speculations must yield. A further conclusion obviously presented itself; if polygamy be necessary, woman must be inferior to man, and made for him.

With respect to the formation of the fetus in the womb, we are very ignorant; but it appears to me probable, that an accidental physical cause may account for this phenomenon, and prove it not to be a law of nature. I have met with some pertinent observations on the subject in Forster's Account of the Isles of the South-Sea,[23] that will explain my meaning. After observing that of the two sexes amongst animals, the most vigorous and hottest constitution always prevails, and produces its kind; he adds, – 'If this be applied to the inhabitants of Africa, it is evident that the men there, accustomed to polygamy, are enervated by the use of so many women, and therefore less vigorous; the women, on the contrary, are of a hotter constitution, not only on account of their more irritable nerves, more sensible organization, and more lively fancy; but likewise because they are deprived in their matrimony of that share of physical love which, in a monogamous condition, would all be theirs; and thus, for the above reasons, the generality of children are born females.

'In the greater part of Europe it has been proved by the most accurate lists of mortality, that the proportion of men to women is nearly equal, or, if any difference takes place, the males born are more numerous, in the proportion of 105 to 100.'

The necessity of polygamy, therefore, does not appear; yet when a man seduces a woman, it should, I think, be termed a *left-handed* marriage, and the man should be *legally* obliged to maintain the woman and her children, unless adultery, a natural divorcement, abrogated the law. And this law should remain in force as long as the weakness of women caused the word seduction to be used as an excuse for their frailty and want of principle; nay, while they depend on man for a subsistence, instead of earning it by the exertion of their own hands or heads. But these women should not, in the full meaning of the relationship, be termed wives, or the very purpose of marriage would be subverted, and all those endearing charities that flow from personal fidelity, and give a sanctity to the tie, when neither love nor friendship unites the hearts, would melt into selfishness. The woman who is faithful to the father of her children demands respect, and should not be treated like a prostitute; though I readily grant that if it be necessary for a man and woman to live together in order to bring up their offspring, nature never intended that a man should have more than one wife.

Still, highly as I respect marriage, as the foundation of almost every social virtue, I cannot avoid feeling the most lively compassion for those unfortunate females who are broken off from society, and by one error torn from all those affections and relationships that improve the heart and mind. It does not frequently even deserve the name of error; for many innocent girls become the dupes of a sincere, affectionate heart, and still more are, as it may emphatically be termed, *ruined* before they know the difference between virtue and vice: – and thus prepared by their education for infamy, they become infamous. Asylums and Magdalens[24] are not the proper remedies for these abuses. It is justice, not charity, that is wanting in the world!

A woman who has lost her honour, imagines that she cannot fall lower, and as for recovering her former station, it is impossible; no exertion can wash this stain away. Losing thus every spur, and having no other means of support, prostitution becomes her only refuge, and the character is quickly depraved by circumstances over which the poor wretch has little power, unless she possesses an uncommon portion of sense and loftiness of spirit. Necessity never makes prostitution the business of men's lives; though numberless are the women who are thus rendered systematically vicious. This, however, arises, in a great degree, from the state of idleness in which women are educated, who are always taught to look up to man for a maintenance, and to consider their persons as the proper return for his exertions to support them. Meretricious airs, and the whole science of wantonness, have then a more powerful stimulus than either appetite or vanity; and this remark gives force to the prevailing opinion, that with chastity all is lost that is respectable in woman. Her character depends on the observance of one virtue, though the only passion fostered in her heart – is love. Nay, the honour of a woman is not made even to depend on her will.

When Richardson* makes Clarissa tell Lovelace[25] that he had robbed her of her honour, he must have had strange notions of honour and virtue. For, miserable beyond all names of misery is the condition of a being, who could be degraded without its own consent! This excess of strictness I have heard vindicated as a salutary error. I shall answer in the words of Leibnitz – 'Errors are often useful; but it is commonly to remedy other errors.'[26]

Most of the evils of life arise from a desire of present enjoyment that outruns itself. The obedience required of women in the marriage state comes under this description; the mind, naturally weakened by depending on authority, never exerts its own powers, and the obedient wife is thus rendered a weak

---

* Dr Young supports the same opinion, in his plays, when he talks of the misfortune that shunned the light of day.[27]

indolent mother. Or, supposing that this is not always the consequence, a future state of existence is scarcely taken into the reckoning when only negative virtues are cultivated. For, in treating of morals, particularly when women are alluded to, writers have too often considered virtue in a very limited sense, and made the foundation of it *solely* worldly utility; nay, a still more fragile base has been given to this stupendous fabric, and the wayward fluctuating feelings of men have been made the standard of virtue. Yes, virtue as well as religion, has been subjected to the decisions of taste.

It would almost provoke a smile of contempt, if the vain absurdities of man did not strike us on all sides, to observe, how eager men are to degrade the sex from whom they pretend to receive the chief pleasure of life; and I have frequently with full conviction retorted Pope's sarcasm on them; or, to speak explicitly, it has appeared to me applicable to the whole human race. A love of pleasure or sway seems to divide mankind,[28] and the husband who lords it in his little haram thinks only of his pleasure or his convenience. To such lengths, indeed, does an intemperate love of pleasure carry some prudent men, or worn out libertines, who marry to have a safe bed-fellow, that they seduce their own wives. – Hymen banishes modesty, and chaste love takes its flight.

Love, considered as an animal appetite, cannot long feed on itself without expiring. And this extinction in its own flame, may be termed the violent death of love. But the wife who has thus been rendered licentious, will probably endeavour to fill the void left by the loss of her husband's attentions; for she cannot contentedly become merely an upper servant after having been treated like a goddess. She is still handsome, and, instead of transferring her fondness to her children, she only dreams of enjoying the sunshine of life. Besides, there are many husbands so devoid of sense and parental affection, that during the first effervescence of voluptuous fondness they refuse to let their wives suckle their children. They are only to dress and live to please them: and love – even innocent love, soon sinks into lasciviousness when the exercise of a duty is sacrificed to its indulgence.

Personal attachment is a very happy foundation for friendship; yet, when even two virtuous young people marry, it would, perhaps, be happy if some circumstances checked their passion; if the recollection of some prior attachment, or disappointed affection, made it on one side, at least, rather a match founded on esteem. In that case they would look beyond the present moment, and try to render the whole of life respectable, by forming a plan to regulate a friendship which only death ought to dissolve.

Friendship is a serious affection; the most sublime of all affections, because it is founded on principle, and cemented by time. The very reverse may be said of love. In a great degree, love and friendship cannot subsist in the same bosom; even when inspired by different objects they weaken or destroy each other, and for the same object can only be felt in succession. The vain fears and fond jealousies, the winds which fan the flame of love, when judiciously or artfully tempered, are both incompatible with the tender confidence and sincere respect of friendship.

Love, such as the glowing pen of genius has traced, exists not on earth, or only resides in those exalted, fervid imaginations that have sketched such dangerous pictures. Dangerous, because they not only afford a plausible excuse, to the voluptuary who disguises sheer sensuality under a sentimental veil; but as they spread affectation, and take from the dignity of virtue. Virtue, as the very word imports, should have an appearance of seriousness, if not of austerity; and to endeavour to trick her out in the garb of pleasure, because the epithet has been used as another name for beauty, is to exalt her on a quicksand; a most insidious attempt to hasten her fall by apparent respect. Virtue and pleasure are not, in fact, so nearly allied in this life as some eloquent writers have laboured to prove. Pleasure prepares the fading wreath, and mixes the intoxicating cup; but the fruit which virtue gives, is the recompence of toil: and, gradually seen as it ripens, only affords calm satisfaction; nay, appearing to be the result of the natural tendency of things, it is scarcely observed. Bread, the common food of life, seldom thought of as a blessing, supports the constitution and preserves health; still feasts delight the heart of man, though disease and even death lurk in the cup of dainty that elevates the spirits or tickles the palate. The lively heated imagination likewise, to apply the comparison, draws the picture of love, as it draws every other picture, with those glowing colours, which the daring hand will steal from the rainbow that is directed by a mind, condemned in a world like this, to prove its noble origin by panting after unattainable perfection; ever pursuing what it acknowledges to be a fleeting dream. An imagination of this vigorous cast can give existence to insubstantial forms, and stability to the shadowy reveries which the mind naturally falls into when realities are found vapid. It can then depict love with celestial charms, and dote on the grand ideal object – it can imagine a degree of mutual affection that shall refine the soul, and not expire when it has served as a 'scale to heavenly;'[29] and, like devotion, make it absorb every meaner affection and desire. In each other's arms, as in a temple, with its summit lost in the clouds, the world is to be shut out, and every thought and wish, that do not nurture pure affection and permanent virtue. – Permanent virtue! alas! Rousseau, respectable visionary! thy paradise would soon be violated by the entrance of some unexpected guest. Like Milton's it would only contain angels, or men sunk below the dignity of rational creatures. Happiness is not material, it cannot be seen or felt! Yet the eager pursuit of the good which every one shapes to his own fancy, proclaims man the lord of this lower world, and to be an intelligential creature, who is not to receive, but acquire happiness. They, therefore, who complain of the delusions of passion, do not recollect that they are exclaiming against a strong proof of the immortality of the soul.

But leaving superior minds to correct themselves, and pay dearly for their experience, it is necessary to observe, that it is not against strong, persevering passions, but romantic wavering feelings that I wish to guard the female heart by exercising the understanding: for these paradisiacal reveries are oftener the effect of idleness than of a lively fancy.

Women have seldom sufficient serious employment to silence their feelings; a round of little cares, or vain pursuits frittering away all strength of mind and organs, they become naturally only objects of sense. – In short, the whole tenour of female education (the education of society) tends to render the best disposed romantic and inconstant; and the remainder vain and mean. In the present state of society this evil can scarcely be remedied, I am afraid, in the slightest degree; should a more laudable ambition ever gain ground they may be brought nearer to nature and reason, and become more virtuous and useful as they grow more respectable.

But, I will venture to assert that their reason will never acquire sufficient strength to enable it to regulate their conduct, whilst the making an appearance in the world is the first wish of the majority of mankind. To this weak with the natural affections, and the most useful virtues are sacrificed. Girls marry merely to *better themselves*, to borrow a significant vulgar phrase, and have such perfect power over their hearts as not to permit themselves to *fall in love* till a man with a superiour fortune offers. On this subject I mean to enlarge in a future chapter; it is only necessary to drop a hint at present, because women are so often degraded by suffering the selfish prudence of age to chill the ardour of youth.

From the same source flows an opinion that young girls ought to dedicate great part of their time to needle-work;[30] yet, this employment contracts their faculties more than any other that could have been chosen for them, by confining their thoughts to their persons. Men order their clothes to be made, and have done with the subject; women make their own clothes, necessary or ornamental, and are continually talking about them; and their thoughts follow their hands. It is not indeed the making of necessaries that weakens the mind; but the frippery of dress. For when a woman in the lower rank of life makes her husband's and children's clothes, she does her duty, this is her part of the family business; but when women work only to dress better than they could otherwise afford, it is worse than sheer loss of time. To render the poor virtuous they must be employed, and women in the middle rank of life, did they not ape the fashions of the nobility, without catching their ease, might employ them, whilst they themselves managed their families, instructed their children, and exercised their own minds. Gardening, experimental philosophy, and literature, would afford them subjects to think of and matter for conversation, that in some degree would exercise their understandings. The conversation of French women, who are not so rigidly nailed to their chairs to twist lappets, and knot ribands,[31] is frequently superficial; but, I contend, that it is not half so insipid as that of those English women whose time is spent in making caps, bonnets, and the whole mischief of trimmings, not to mention shopping, bargain-hunting, &c. &c.: and it is the decent, prudent women, who are most degraded by these practices; for their motive is simply vanity. The wanton who exercises her taste to render her passion alluring, has something more in view.

These observations all branch out of a general one, which I have before made, and which cannot be too often insisted upon, for, speaking of men, women, or professions, it will be found that the employment of the thoughts shapes the character both generally and individually. The thoughts of women ever hover round their persons, and is it surprising that their persons are reckoned most valuable? Yet some degree of liberty of mind is necessary even to form the person; and this may be one reason why some gentle wives have so few attractions beside that of sex. Add to this, sedentary employments render the majority of women sickly – and false notions of female excellence make them proud of this delicacy, though it be another fetter, that by calling the attention continually to the body, cramps the activity of the mind.

Women of quality seldom do any of the manual part of their dress, consequently only their taste is exercised, and they acquire, by thinking less of the finery, when the business of their toilet is over, that ease, which seldom appears in the deportment of women, who dress merely for the sake of dressing. In fact, the observation with respect to the middle rank, the one in which talents thrive best, extends not to women; for those of the superior class, by catching, at least, a smattering of literature, and conversing more with men, on general topics, acquire more knowledge than the women who ape their fashions and faults without sharing their advantages. With respect to virtue, to use the word in a comprehensive sense, I have seen most in low life.

Many poor women maintain their children by the sweat of their brow, and keep together families that the vices of the fathers would have scattered abroad; but gentlewomen are too indolent to be actively virtuous, and are softened rather than refined by civilization. Indeed, the good sense which I have met with, among the poor women who have had few advantages of education, and yet have acted heroically, strongly confirmed me in the opinion that trifling employments have rendered woman a trifler. Man, taking her* body, the mind is left to rust; so that while physical love enervates man, as being his favourite recreation, he will endeavour to enslave woman: – and, who can tell, how many generations may be necessary to give vigour to the virtue and talents of the freed posterity of abject slaves?†

In tracing the causes that, in my opinion, have degraded woman, I have confined my observations to such as universally act upon the morals and manners of the whole sex, and to me it appears clear that they all spring from want of understanding. Whether this arise from a physical or accidental weakness of faculties, time alone can determine; for I shall not lay any great stress on the example of a few women‡ who, from having received a masculine education, have acquired courage and resolution; I only contend that the men who have been placed in similar situations, have acquired a similar character – I speak of bodies of men, and that men of genius and talents have started out of a class, in which women have never yet been placed.

* 'I take her body,' says Ranger.[32]
† 'Supposing that women are voluntary slaves – slavery of any kind is unfavourable to human happiness and improvement.' *Knox's Essays*.[33]
‡ Sappho, Eloisa, Mrs Macaulay, the Empress of Russia, Madame d'Eon,[34] &c. These, and many more, may be reckoned exceptions; and, are not all heroes, as well as heroines, exceptions to general rules? I wish to see women neither heroines nor brutes; but reasonable creatures.

CHAP. V

ANIMADVERSIONS ON SOME OF THE WRITERS WHO HAVE RENDERED WOMEN OBJECTS OF PITY, BORDERING ON CONTEMPT

The opinions speciously supported, in some modern publications on the female character and education, which have given the tone to most of the observations made, in a more cursory manner, on the sex, remain now to be examined.

SECT. I

I shall begin with Rousseau, and give a sketch of his character of woman, in his own words, interspersing comments and reflections. My comments, it is true, will all spring from a few simple principles, and might have been deduced from what I have already said; but the artificial structure has been raised with so much ingenuity, that it seems necessary to attack it in a more circumstantial manner, and make the application myself.

Sophia, says Rousseau, should be as perfect a woman as Emilius is a man, and to render her so, it is necessary to examine the character which nature has given to the sex.

He then proceeds to prove that woman ought to be weak and passive, because she has less bodily strength than man; and hence infers, that she was formed to please and to be subject to him; and that it is her duty to render herself *agreeable* to her master – this being the grand end of her existence.* Still, however, to give a little mock dignity to lust, he insists that man should not exert his strength, but depend on the will of the woman, when he seeks for pleasure with her.

* I have already inserted the passage, page 63.

'Hence we deduce a third consequence from the different constitutions of the sexes; which is, that the strongest should be master in appearance, and be dependent in fact on the weakest; and that not from any frivolous practice of gallantry or vanity of protectorship, but from an invariable law of nature, which, furnishing woman with a greater facility to excite desires than she has given man to satisfy them, makes the latter dependent on the good pleasure of the former, and compels him to endeavour to please in his turn, *in order to obtain her consent that he should be strongest.** On these occasions, the most delightful circumstance a man finds in his victory is, to doubt whether it was the woman's weakness that yielded to his superior strength, or whether her inclinations spoke in his favour: the females are also generally artful enough to leave this matter in doubt. The understanding of women answers in this respect perfectly to their constitution: so far from being ashamed of their weakness, they glory in it; their tender muscles make no resistance; they affect to be incapable of lifting the smallest burthens, and would blush to be thought robust and strong. To what purpose is all this? Not merely for the sake of appearing delicate, but through an artful precaution: it is thus they provide an excuse beforehand, and a right to be feeble when they think it expedient.'[1]

I have quoted this passage, lest my readers should suspect that I warped the author's reasoning to support my own arguments. I have already asserted that in educating women these fundamental principles lead to a system of cunning and lasciviousness.

Supposing woman to have been formed only to please, and be subject to man, the conclusion is just, she ought to sacrifice every other consideration to render herself agreeable to him: and let this brutal desire of self-preservation be the grand spring of all her actions, when it is proved to be the iron bed of fate, to fit which her character should be stretched or contracted, regardless of all moral or physical distinctions. But, if, as I think, may be demonstrated, the purposes, of even this life, viewing the whole, be subverted by practical rules built upon this ignoble base, I may be allowed to doubt whether woman were created

---

* What nonsense!

for man: and, though the cry of irreligion, or even atheism, be raised against me, I will simply declare, that were an angel from heaven to tell me that Moses's beautiful, poetical cosmogony, and the account of the fall of man, were literally true, I could not believe what my reason told me was derogatory to the character of the Supreme Being: and, having no fear of the devil before mine eyes, I venture to call this a suggestion of reason, instead of resting my weakness on the broad shoulders of the first seducer of my frail sex.

'It being once demonstrated,' continues Rousseau, 'that man and woman are not, nor ought to be, constituted alike in temperament and character, it follows of course that they should not be educated in the same manner. In pursuing the directions of nature, they ought indeed to act in concert, but they should not be engaged in the same employments: the end of their pursuits should be the same, but the means they should take to accomplish them, and of consequence their tastes and inclinations, should be different.'

. . . .

'Whether I consider the peculiar destination of the sex, observe their inclinations, or remark their duties, all things equally concur to point out the peculiar method of education best adapted to them. Woman and man were made for each other; but their mutual dependence is not the same. The men depend on the women only on account of their desires; the women on the men both on account of their desires and their necessities: we could subsist better without them than they without us.'

. . . .

'For this reason, the education of the women should be always relative to the men. To please, to be useful to us, to make us love and esteem them, to educate us when young, and take care of us when grown up, to advise, to console us, to render our lives easy and agreeable: these are the duties of women at all times, and what they should be taught in their infancy. So long as we fail to recur to this principle, we run wide of the mark, and all the precepts which are given them contribute neither to their happiness nor our own.'

. . . .

'Girls are from their earliest infancy fond of dress. Not content with being pretty, they are desirous of being thought so; we see, by all their little airs, that this thought engages their attention; and they are hardly capable of understanding what is said to them, before they are to be governed by talking to them of what people will think of their behaviour. The same motive, however, indiscreetly made use of with boys, has not the same effect: provided they are let pursue their amusements at pleasure, they care very little what people think of them. Time and pains are necessary to subject boys to this motive.

'Whencesoever girls derive this first lesson, it is a very good one. As the body is born, in a manner, before the soul, our first concern should be to cultivate the former; this order is common to both sexes, but the object of that cultivation is different. In the one sex it is the development of corporeal powers; in the other, that of personal charms: not that either the quality of strength or beauty ought to be confined exclusively to one sex; but only that the order of the cultivation of both is in that respect reversed. Women certainly require as much strength as to enable them to move and act gracefully, and men as much address as to qualify them to act with ease.'

. . . .

'Children of both sexes have a great many amusements in common; and so they ought; have they not also many such when they are grown up? Each sex has also its peculiar taste to distinguish in this particular. Boys love sports of noise and activity; to beat the drum, to whip the top, and to drag about their little carts: girls, on the other hand, are fonder of things of show and ornament; such as mirrours, trinkets, and dolls: the doll is the peculiar amusement of the females; from whence we see their taste plainly adapted to their destination. The physical part of the art of pleasing lies in dress; and this is all which children are capacitated to cultivate of that art.'

. . . .

'Here then we see a primary propensity firmly established, which you need only to pursue and regulate. The little creature will doubtless be very desirous to know how to dress up her doll, to make its sleeve-knots, its flounces, its head-dress, &c.

she is obliged to have so much recourse to the people about her, for their assistance in these articles, that it would be much more agreeable to her to owe them all to her own industry. Hence we have a good reason for the first lessons that are usually taught these young females: in which we do not appear to be setting them a task, but obliging them, by instructing them in what is immediately useful to themselves. And, in fact, almost all of them learn with reluctance to read and write; but very readily apply themselves to the use of their needles. They imagine themselves already grown up, and think with pleasure that such qualifications will enable them to decorate themselves.'[2]

This is certainly only an education of the body; but Rousseau is not the only man who has indirectly said that merely the person of a *young* woman, without any mind, unless animal spirits come under that description, is very pleasing. To render it weak, and what some may call beautiful, the understanding is neglected, and girls forced to sit still, play with dolls and listen to foolish conversations; – the effect of habit is insisted upon as an undoubted indication of nature. I know it was Rousseau's opinion that the first years of youth should be employed to form the body, though in educating Emilius he deviates from this plan; yet, the difference between strengthening the body, on which strength of mind in a great measure depends, and only giving it an easy motion, is very wide.

Rousseau's observations, it is proper to remark, were made in a country where the art of pleasing was refined only to extract the grossness of vice. He did not go back to nature, or his ruling appetite disturbed the operations of reason, else he would not have drawn these crude inferences.

In France boys and girls, particularly the latter, are only educated to please, to manage their persons, and regulate their exterior behaviour; and their minds are corrupted, at a very early age, by the worldly and pious cautions they receive to guard them against immodesty. I speak of past times. The very confessions which mere children were obliged to make, and the questions asked by the holy men, I assert these facts on good authority, were sufficient to impress a sexual character; and the education of society was a school of coquetry and art. At the age of ten or eleven; nay, often much sooner, girls began to coquet, and talked, unreproved, of establishing themselves in the world by marriage.

In short, they were treated like women, almost from their very birth, and compliments were listened to instead of instruction. These, weakening the mind, Nature was supposed to have acted like a step-mother, when she formed this after-thought of creation.

Not allowing them understanding, however, it was but consistent to subject them to authority independent of reason; and to prepare them for this subjection, he gives the following advice:

'Girls ought to be active and diligent; nor is that all; they should also be early subjected to restraint. This misfortune, if it really be one, is inseparable from their sex; nor do they ever throw it off but to suffer more cruel evils. They must be subject, all their lives, to the most constant and severe restraint, which is that of decorum: it is, therefore, necessary to accustom them early to such confinement, that it may not afterwards cost them too dear; and to the suppression of their caprices, that they may the more readily submit to the will of others. If, indeed, they be fond of being always at work, they should be sometimes compelled to lay it aside. Dissipation, levity, and inconstancy, are faults that readily spring up from their first propensities, when corrupted or perverted by too much indulgence. To prevent this abuse, we should teach them, above all things, to lay a due restraint on themselves. The life of a modest woman is reduced, by our absurd institutions, to a perpetual conflict with herself: not but it is just that this sex should partake of the sufferings which arise from those evils it hath caused us.'[3]

And why is the life of a modest woman a perpetual conflict? I should answer, that this very system of education makes it so. Modesty, temperance, and self-denial, are the sober offspring of reason; but when sensibility is nurtured at the expence of the understanding, such weak beings must be restrained by arbitrary means, and be subjected to continual conflicts; but give their activity of mind a wider range, and nobler passions and motives will govern their appetites and sentiments.

'The common attachment and regard of a mother, nay, mere habit, will make her beloved by her children, if she do nothing to incur their hate. Even the constraint she lays them under, if well directed, will increase their affection, instead of lessening it; because a state of dependence being natural to the sex, they perceive themselves formed for obedience.'[4]

This is begging the question; for servitude not only debases the individual, but its effects seem to be transmitted to posterity. Considering the length of time that women have been dependent, is it surprising that some of them hug their chains, and fawn like the spaniel? 'These dogs,' observes a naturalist, 'at first kept their ears erect; but custom has superseded nature, and a token of fear is become a beauty.'

'For the same reason,' adds Rousseau, 'women have, or ought to have, but little liberty; they are apt to indulge themselves excessively in what is allowed them. Addicted in every thing to extremes, they are even more transported at their diversions than boys.'[5]

The answer to this is very simple. Slaves and mobs have always indulged themselves in the same excesses, when once they broke loose from authority. – The bent bow recoils with violence, when the hand is suddenly relaxed that forcibly held it; and sensibility, the play-thing of outward circumstances, must be subjected to authority, or moderated by reason.

'There results,' he continues, 'from this habitual restraint a tractableness which women have occasion for during their whole lives, as they constantly remain either under subjection to the men, or to the opinions of mankind; and are never permitted to set themselves above those opinions. The first and most important qualification in a woman is good-nature or sweetness of temper: formed to obey a being so imperfect as man, often full of vices, and always full of faults, she ought to learn betimes even to suffer injustice, and to bear the insults of a husband without complaint; it is not for his sake, but her own, that she should be of a mild disposition. The perverseness and ill-nature of the women only serve to aggravate their own misfortunes, and the misconduct of their husbands; they might plainly perceive that such are not the arms by which they gain the superiority.'[6]

Formed to live with such an imperfect being as man, they ought to learn from the exercise of their faculties the necessity of forbearance; but all the sacred rights of humanity are violated by insisting on blind obedience; or, the most sacred rights belong *only* to man.

The being who patiently endures injustice, and silently bears insults, will soon become unjust, or unable to discern right from wrong. Besides, I deny the fact, this is not the true way to form or meliorate the temper; for, as a sex, men have better tempers than women, because they are occupied by pursuits that interest the head as well as the heart; and the steadiness of the head gives a healthy temperature to the heart. People of sensibility have seldom good tempers. The formation of the temper is the cool work of reason, when, as life advances, she mixes with happy art, jarring elements. I never knew a weak or ignorant person who had a good temper, though that constitutional good humour, and that docility, which fear stamps on the behaviour, often obtains the name. I say behaviour, for genuine meekness never reached the heart or mind, unless as the effect of reflection; and that simple restraint produces a number of peccant humours in domestic life, many sensible men will allow, who find some of these gentle irritable creatures, very troublesome companions.

'Each sex,' he further argues, 'should preserve its peculiar tone and manner; a meek husband may make a wife impertinent; but mildness of disposition on the woman's side will always bring a man back to reason, at least if he be not absolutely a brute, and will sooner or later triumph over him.'[7] Perhaps the mildness of reason might sometimes have this effect; but abject fear always inspires contempt; and tears are only eloquent when they flow down fair cheeks.

Of what materials can that heart be composed, which can melt when insulted, and instead of revolting at injustice, kiss the rod? Is it unfair to infer that her virtue is built on narrow views and selfishness, who can caress a man, with true feminine softness, the very moment when he treats her tyrannically? Nature never dictated such insincerity; – and, though prudence of this sort be termed a virtue, morality becomes vague when any part is supposed to rest on falsehood. These are mere expedients, and expedients are only useful for the moment.

Let the husband beware of trusting too implicitly to this servile obedience; for if his wife can with winning sweetness caress him when angry, and when she ought to be angry, unless contempt had stifled a natural effervescence, she may do the same after parting with a lover. These are all preparations for adultery; or, should the fear of the world, or of hell, restrain her desire of pleasing other men, when she can no longer please her husband, what substitute can be found by a being who was only formed, by nature and art, to please man? what can make her amends for this privation, or where is she to seek for a fresh employment? where find sufficient strength of mind to determine to begin the search, when her habits are fixed, and vanity has long ruled her chaotic mind?

But this partial moralist recommends cunning systematically and plausibly.

'Daughters should be always submissive; their mothers, however, should not be inexorable. To make a young person tractable, she ought not to be made unhappy, to make her modest she ought not to be rendered stupid. On the contrary, I should not be displeased at her being permitted to use some art, not to elude punishment in case of disobedience, but to exempt herself from the necessity of obeying. It is not necessary to make her dependence burdensome, but only to let her feel it. Subtilty is a talent natural to the sex; and, as I am persuaded, all our natural inclinations are right and good in themselves, I am of opinion this should be cultivated as well as the others: it is requisite for us only to prevent its abuse.'

'Whatever is, is right,'[8] he then proceeds triumphantly to infer. Granted; – yet, perhaps, no aphorism ever contained a more paradoxical assertion. It is a solemn truth with respect to God. He, reverentially I speak, sees the whole at once, and saw its just proportions in the womb of time; but man, who can only inspect disjointed parts, finds many things wrong; and it is a part of the system, and therefore right, that he should endeavour to alter what appears to him to be so, even while he bows to the Wisdom of his Creator, and respects the darkness he labours to disperse.

The inference that follows is just, supposing the principle to be sound. 'The superiority of address, peculiar to the female sex, is a very equitable indemnification for their inferiority in point of strength: without this, woman would not be the companion of man; but his slave: it is by her superiour art and ingenuity that she preserves her equality, and governs him while she affects to obey. Woman has every thing against her, as well our faults, as her own timidity and weakness; she has nothing in her favour, but her subtilty and her beauty. Is it not very reasonable, therefore, she should cultivate both?'⁹ Greatness of mind can never dwell with cunning, or address; for I shall not boggle about words, when their direct signification is insincerity and falsehood, but content myself with observing, that if any class of mankind be so created that it must necessarily be educated by rules not strictly deducible from truth, virtue is an affair of convention. How could Rousseau dare to assert, after giving this advice, that in the grand end of existence the object of both sexes should be the same, when he well knew that the mind, formed by its pursuits, is expanded by great views swallowing up little ones, or that it becomes itself little?

Men have superiour strength of body; but were it not for mistaken notions of beauty, women would acquire sufficient to enable them to earn their own subsistence, the true definition of independence; and to bear those bodily inconveniencies and exertions that are requisite to strengthen the mind.

Let us then, by being allowed to take the same exercise as boys, not only during infancy, but youth, arrive at perfection of body, that we may know how far the natural superiority of man extends. For what reason or virtue can be expected from a creature when the seed-time of life is neglected? None – did not the winds of heaven casually scatter many useful seeds in the fallow ground.

'Beauty cannot be acquired by dress, and coquetry is an art not so early and speedily attained. While girls are yet young, however, they are in a capacity to study agreeable gesture, a pleasing modulation of voice, an easy carriage and behaviour; as well as to take the advantage of gracefully adapting their looks and attitudes to time, place and occasion. Their application, therefore, should not be solely confined to the arts of industry and the needle, when they come to display other talents, whose utility is already apparent.

'For my part, I would have a young English woman cultivate her agreeable talents, in order to please her future husband, with as much care and assiduity as a young Circassian cultivates hers, to fit her for the Haram of an Eastern bashaw.'[10]

To render women completely insignificant, he adds – 'The tongues of women are very voluble; they speak earlier, more readily, and more agreeably, than the men; they are accused also of speaking much more: but so it ought to be, and I should be very ready to convert this reproach into a compliment; their lips and eyes have the same activity, and for the same reason. A man speaks of what he knows, a woman of what pleases her; the one requires knowledge, the other taste; the principal object of a man's discourse should be what is useful, that of a woman's what is agreeable. There ought to be nothing in common between their different conversation but truth.

'We ought not, therefore, to restrain the prattle of girls, in the same manner as we should that of boys, with that severe question; *To what purpose are you talking?* but by another, which is no less difficult to answer, *How will your discourse be received?* In infancy, while they are as yet incapable to discern good from evil, they ought to observe it, as a law, never to say any thing disagreeable to those whom they are speaking to: what will render the practice of this rule also the more difficult, is, that it must ever be subordinate to the former, of never speaking falsely or telling an untruth.'[11] To govern the tongue in this manner must require great address indeed; and it is too much practised both by men and women. – Out of the abundance of the heart how few speak! So few, that I, who love simplicity, would gladly give up politeness for a quarter of the virtue that has been sacrificed to an equivocal quality which at best should only be the polish of virtue.

But, to complete the sketch. 'It is easy to be conceived, that if male children be not in a capacity to form any true notions of religion, those ideas must be greatly above the conception of the females: it is for this very reason, I would begin to speak to them the earlier on this subject; for if we were to wait till they were in a capacity to discuss methodically such profound questions, we should run a risk of never speaking to them on this subject as long as they lived. Reason in women is a practical reason, capacitating them artfully to discover the means of attaining a known end, but which would never enable them to discover that end itself. The social relations of the sexes are indeed truly admirable: from their union there results a moral person, of which woman may be termed the eyes, and man the hand, with this dependence on each other, that it is from the man that the woman is to learn what she is to see, and it is of the woman that man is to learn what he ought to do. If woman could recur to the first principles of things as well as man, and man was capacitated to enter into their *minutiæ* as well as woman, always independent of each other, they would live in perpetual discord, and their union could not subsist. But in the present harmony which naturally subsists between them, their different faculties tend to one common end; it is difficult to say which of them conduces the most to it: each follows the impulse of the other; each is obedient, and both are masters.

'As the conduct of a woman is subservient to the public opinion, her faith in matters of religion should, for that very reason, be subject to authority. *Every daughter ought to be of the same religion as her mother, and every wife to be of the same religion as her husband: for, though such religion should be false, that docility which induces the mother and daughter to submit to the order of nature, takes away, in the sight of God, the criminality of their error.'* As they are not in a capacity to judge for themselves, they ought to abide by the decision of their fathers and husbands as confidently as by that of the church.

'As authority ought to regulate the religion of the women, it

---

* What is to be the consequence, if the mother's and husband's opinion should *chance* not to agree? An ignorant person cannot be reasoned out of an error – and when *persuaded* to give up one prejudice for another the mind is unsettled. Indeed, the husband may not have any religion to teach her, though in such a situation she will be in great want of a support to her virtue, independent of worldly considerations.

is not so needful to explain to them the reasons for their belief, as to lay down precisely the tenets they are to believe: for the creed, which presents only obscure ideas to the mind, is the source of fanaticism; and that which presents absurdities, leads to infidelity.'[12]

Absolute, uncontroverted authority, it seems, must subsist somewhere: but is not this a direct and exclusive appropriation of reason? The *rights* of humanity have been thus confined to the male line from Adam downwards. Rousseau would carry his male aristocracy still further, for he insinuates, that he should not blame those, who contend for leaving woman in a state of the most profound ignorance, if it were not necessary in order to preserve her chastity and justify the man's choice, in the eyes of the world, to give her a little knowledge of men, and the customs produced by human passions; else she might propagate at home without being rendered less voluptuous and innocent by the exercise of her understanding: excepting, indeed, during the first year of marriage, when she might employ it to dress like Sophia. 'Her dress is extremely modest in appearance, and yet very coquettish in fact: she does not make a display of her charms, she conceals them; but in concealing them, she knows how to affect your imagination. Every one who sees her will say, There is a modest and discreet girl; but while you are near her, your eyes and affections wander all over her person, so that you cannot withdraw them; and you would conclude, that every part of her dress, simple as it seems, was only put in its proper order to be taken to pieces by the imagination.'[13] Is this modesty? Is this a preparation for immortality? Again. – What opinion are we to form of a system of education, when the author says of his heroine, 'that with her, doing things well, is but a *secondary* concern; her principal concern is to do them *neatly*.'[14]

Secondary, in fact, are all her virtues and qualities, for, respecting religion, he makes her parents thus address her, accustomed to submission – 'Your husband will instruct you in *good time*.'[15]

After thus cramping a woman's mind, if, in order to keep it fair, he have not made it quite a blank, he advises her to reflect, that a reflecting man may not yawn in her company, when he is tired of caressing her. – What has she to reflect about who must obey? and would it not be a refinement on cruelty only to open her mind to make the darkness and misery of her fate *visible*? Yet, these are his sensible remarks, how consistent with what I have already been obliged to quote, to give a fair view of the subject, the reader may determine.

'They who pass their whole lives in working for their daily bread, have no ideas beyond their business or their interest, and all their understanding seems to lie in their fingers' ends. This ignorance is neither prejudicial to their integrity nor their morals; it is often of service to them. Sometimes, by means of reflection, we are led to compound with our duty, and we conclude by substituting a jargon of words, in the room of things. Our own conscience is the most enlightened philosopher. There is no need to be acquainted with Tully's offices,[16] to make a man of probity; and perhaps the most virtuous woman in the world, is the least acquainted with the definition of virtue. But it is no less true, that an improved understanding only can render society agreeable; and it is a melancholy thing for a father of a family, who is fond of home, to be obliged to be always wrapped up in himself, and to have nobody about him to whom he can impart his sentiments.

'Besides, how should a woman void of reflection be capable of educating her children? How should she discern what is proper for them? How should she incline them to those virtues she is unacquainted with, or to that merit of which she has no idea? She can only sooth or chide them; render them insolent or timid; she will make them formal coxcombs, or ignorant blockheads; but will never make them sensible or amiable.'[17] How indeed should she, when her husband is not always at hand to lend her his reason? – when they both together make but one moral being. A blind will, 'eyes without hands,' would go a very little way; and perchance his abstract reason, that should concentrate the scattered beams of her practical reason, may be employed in judging of the flavour of wine, descanting on the sauces most proper for turtle; or, more profoundly intent at a card-table, he may be generalizing his ideas as he bets away his fortune, leaving all the *minutiæ* of education to his helpmate, or to chance.

But, granting that woman ought to be beautiful, innocent, and silly, to render her a more alluring and indulgent companion; – what is her understanding sacrificed for? And why is all this preparation necessary only, according to Rousseau's own account, to make her the mistress of her husband, a very short time? For no man ever insisted more on the transient nature of love. Thus speaks the philosopher. 'Sensual pleasures are transient. The habitual state of the affections always loses by their gratification. The imagination, which decks the object of our desires, is lost in fruition. Excepting the Supreme Being, who is self-existent, there is nothing beautiful but what is ideal.'[18]

But he returns to his unintelligible paradoxes again, when he thus addresses Sophia. 'Emilius, in becoming your husband, is become your master; and claims your obedience. Such is the order of nature. When a man is married, however, to such a wife as Sophia, it is proper he should be directed by her: this is also agreeable to the order of nature: it is, therefore, to give you as much authority over his heart as his sex gives him over your person, that I have made you the arbiter of his pleasures. It may cost you, perhaps, some disagreeable self-denial; but you will be certain of maintaining your empire over him, if you can preserve it over yourself – what I have already observed, also, shows me, that this difficult attempt does not surpass your courage.

'Would you have your husband constantly at your feet? keep him at some distance from your person. You will long maintain the authority in love, if you know but how to render your favours rare and valuable. It is thus you may employ even the arts of coquetry in the service of virtue, and those of love in that of reason.'[19]

I shall close my extracts with a just description of a comfortable couple. 'And yet you must not imagine, that even such management will always suffice. Whatever precaution be taken, enjoyment will, by degrees, take off the edge of passion. But when love hath lasted as long as possible, a pleasing habitude supplies its place, and the attachment of a mutual confidence succeeds to the transports of passion. Children often form a more agreeable and permanent connection between married people than even love itself. When you cease to be the mistress of Emilius, you will continue to be his wife and friend, you will be the mother of his children.'*[20]

Children, he truly observes, form a much more permanent connexion between married people than love. Beauty, he declares, will not be valued, or even seen after a couple have lived six months together; artificial graces and coquetry will likewise pall on the senses: why then does he say that a girl should be educated for her husband with the same care as for an eastern haram?

I now appeal from the reveries of fancy and refined licentiousness to the good sense of mankind, whether, if the object of education be to prepare women to become chaste wives and sensible mothers, the method so plausibly recommended in the foregoing sketch, be the one best calculated to produce those ends? Will it be allowed that the surest way to make a wife chaste, is to teach her to practise the wanton arts of a mistress, termed virtuous coquetry, by the sensualist who can no longer relish the artless charms of sincerity, or taste the pleasure arising from a tender intimacy, when confidence is unchecked by suspicion, and rendered interesting by sense?

The man who can be contented to live with a pretty, useful companion, without a mind, has lost in voluptuous gratifications a taste for more refined enjoyments; he has never felt the calm satisfaction, that refreshes the parched heart, like the silent dew of heaven, – of being beloved by one who could understand him. – In the society of his wife he is still alone, unless when the man is sunk in the brute. 'The charm of life,' says a grave philosophical reasoner, is 'sympathy; nothing pleases us more than to observe in other men a fellow-feeling with all the emotions of our own breast.'[21]

But, according to the tenour of reasoning, by which women are kept from the tree of knowledge, the important years of youth, the usefulness of age, and the rational hopes of futurity, are all to be sacrificed to render women an object of desire for a *short* time. Besides, how could Rousseau expect them to be

* Rousseau's Emilius.

virtuous and constant when reason is neither allowed to be the foundation of their virtue, nor truth the object of their inquiries?

But all Rousseau's errors in reasoning arose from sensibility, and sensibility to their charms women are very ready to forgive! When he should have reasoned he became impassioned, and reflection inflamed his imagination instead of enlightening his understanding. Even his virtues also led him farther astray; for, born with a warm constitution and lively fancy, nature carried him toward the other sex with such eager fondness, that he soon became lascivious. Had he given way to these desires, the fire would have extinguished itself in a natural manner; but virtue, and a romantic kind of delicacy, made him practise self-denial; yet, when fear, delicacy, or virtue, restrained him, he debauched his imagination, and reflecting on the sensations to which fancy gave force, he traced them in the most glowing colours, and sunk them deep into his soul.

He then sought for solitude, not to sleep with the man of nature; or calmly investigate the causes of things under the shade where Sir Isaac Newton indulged contemplation,[22] but merely to indulge his feelings. And so warmly has he painted, what he forcibly felt, that, interesting the heart and inflaming the imagination of his readers; in proportion to the strength of their fancy, they imagine that their understanding is convinced when they only sympathize with a poetic writer, who skilfully exhibits the objects of sense, most voluptuously shadowed or gracefully veiled – And thus making us feel whilst dreaming that we reason, erroneous conclusions are left in the mind.

Why was Rousseau's life divided between ecstasy and misery? Can any other answer be given than this, that the effervescence of his imagination produced both; but, had his fancy been allowed to cool, it is possible that he might have acquired more strength of mind. Still, if the purpose of life be to educate the intellectual part of man, all with respect to him was right; yet, had not death led to a nobler scene of action, it is probable that he would have enjoyed more equal happiness on earth, and have felt the calm sensations of the man of nature instead of being prepared for another stage of existence by nourishing the passions which agitate the civilized man.

But peace to his manes! I war not with his ashes, but his opinions. I war only with the sensibility that led him to degrade woman by making her the slave of love.

> —'Curs'd vassalage,
> First idoliz'd till love's hot fire be o'er,
> Then slaves to those who courted us before.'
> *Dryden*.[23]

The pernicious tendency of those books, in which the writers insidiously degrade the sex whilst they are prostrate before their personal charms, cannot be too often or too severely exposed.

Let us, my dear contemporaries, arise above such narrow prejudices! If wisdom be desirable on its own account, if virtue, to deserve the name, must be founded on knowledge; let us endeavour to strengthen our minds by reflection, till our heads become a balance for our hearts; let us not confine all our thoughts to the petty occurrences of the day, or our knowledge to an acquaintance with our lovers' or husbands' hearts; but let the practice of every duty be subordinate to the grand one of improving our minds, and preparing our affections for a more exalted state!

Beware then, my friends, of suffering the heart to be moved by every trivial incident: the reed is shaken by a breeze, and annually dies, but the oak stands firm, and for ages braves the storm!

Were we, indeed, only created to flutter our hour out and die[24] – why let us then indulge sensibility, and laugh at the severity of reason. – Yet, alas! even then we should want strength of body and mind, and life would be lost in feverish pleasures or wearisome languor.

But the system of education, which I earnestly wish to see exploded, seems to presuppose what ought never to be taken for granted, that virtue shields us from the casualties of life; and that fortune, slipping off her bandage, will smile on a well-educated female, and bring in her hand an Emilius or a Telemachus.[25] Whilst, on the contrary, the reward which virtue promises to her votaries is confined, it seems clear, to their own bosoms; and often must they contend with the most vexatious worldly cares, and bear with the vices and humours of relations for whom they can never feel a friendship.

There have been many women in the world who, instead of being supported by the reason and virtue of their fathers and brothers, have strengthened their own minds by struggling with their vices and follies; yet have never met with a hero, in the shape of a husband; who, paying the debt that mankind owed them, might chance to bring back their reason to its natural dependent state, and restore the usurped prerogative, of rising above opinion, to man.

SECT. II

Dr Fordyce's sermons[26] have long made a part of a young woman's library; nay, girls at school are allowed to read them; but I should instantly dismiss them from my pupil's, if I wished to strengthen her understanding, by leading her to form sound principles on a broad basis; or, were I only anxious to cultivate her taste; though they must be allowed to contain many sensible observations.

Dr Fordyce may have had a very laudable end in view; but these discourses are written in such an affected style, that were it only on that account, and had I nothing to object against his *mellifluous* precepts, I should not allow girls to peruse them, unless I designed to hunt every spark of nature out of their composition, melting every human quality into female meekness and artificial grace. I say artificial, for true grace arises from some kind of independence of mind.

Children, careless of pleasing, and only anxious to amuse themselves, are often very graceful; and the nobility who have mostly lived with inferiours, and always had the command of money, acquire a graceful ease of deportment, which should rather be termed habitual grace of body, than that superiour gracefulness which is truly the expression of the mind. This mental grace, not noticed by vulgar eyes, often flashes across a rough countenance, and irradiating every feature, shows simplicity and independence of mind. – It is then we read characters of immortality in the eye, and see the soul in every gesture, though when at rest, neither the face nor limbs may have much beauty to recommend them; or the behaviour, any thing peculiar to attract universal attention. The mass of mankind, however, look for more *tangible* beauty; yet simplicity is, in general, admired, when people do not consider what they admire; and can there be simplicity without sincerity? But, to have done with remarks that are in some measure desultory, though naturally excited by the subject –

In declamatory periods Dr Fordyce spins out Rousseau's eloquence; and in most sentimental rant, details his opinions respecting the female character, and the behaviour which woman ought to assume to render her lovely.

He shall speak for himself, for thus he makes Nature address man. 'Behold these smiling innocents, whom I have graced with my fairest gifts, and committed to your protection; behold them with love and respect; treat them with tenderness and honour. They are timid and want to be defended. They are frail; O do not take advantage of their weakness! Let their fears and blushes endear them. Let their confidence in you never be abused. – But is it possible, that any of you can be such barbarians, so supremely wicked, as to abuse it? Can you find in your hearts* to despoil the gentle, trusting creatures of their treasure, or do any thing to strip them of their native robe of virtue? Curst be the impious hand that would dare to violate the unblemished form of Chastity! Thou wretch! thou ruffian! forbear; nor venture to provoke heaven's fiercest vengeance.'27 I know not any comment that can be made seriously on this curious passage, and I could produce many similar ones; and some, so very sentimental, that I have heard rational men use the word indecent, when they mentioned them with disgust.

Throughout there is a display of cold artificial feelings, and that parade of sensibility which boys and girls should be taught

---

* Can you? – Can you? would be the most emphatical comment, were it drawled out in a whining voice.

to despise as the sure mark of a little vain mind. Florid appeals are made to heaven, and to the *beauteous innocents*, the fairest images of heaven here below, whilst sober sense is left far behind. – This is not the language of the heart, nor will it ever reach it, though the ear may be tickled.

I shall be told, perhaps, that the public have been pleased with these volumes. – True – and Hervey's Meditations[28] are still read, though he equally sinned against sense and taste.

I particularly object to the lover-like phrases of pumped up passion, which are every where interspersed. If women be ever allowed to walk without leading-strings,[29] why must they be cajoled into virtue by artful flattery and sexual compliments? – Speak to them the language of truth and soberness, and away with the lullaby strains of condescending endearment! Let them be taught to respect themselves as rational creatures, and not led to have a passion for their own insipid persons. It moves my gall to hear a preacher descanting on dress and needle-work; and still more, to hear him address the *British fair, the fairest of the fair*, as if they had only feelings.

Even recommending piety he uses the following argument. 'Never, perhaps, does a fine woman strike more deeply, than when, composed into pious recollection, and possessed with the noblest considerations, she assumes, without knowing it, superiour dignity and new graces; so that the beauties of holiness seem to radiate about her, and the by-standers are almost induced to fancy her already worshipping amongst her kindred angels!'[30] Why are women to be thus bred up with a desire of conquest? the very word, used in this sense, gives me a sickly qualm! Do religion and virtue offer no stronger motives, no brighter reward? Must they always be debased by being made to consider the sex of their companions? Must they be taught always to be pleasing? And when levelling their small artillery at the heart of man, is it necessary to tell them that a little sense is sufficient to render their attention *incredibly soothing*? 'As a small degree of knowledge entertains in a woman, so from a woman, though for a different reason, a small expression of kindness delights, particularly if she have beauty!'[31] I should have supposed for the same reason.

Why are girls to be told that they resemble angels; but to sink them below women? Or, that a gentle innocent female is an object that comes nearer to the idea which we have formed of angels than any other. Yet they are told, at the same time, that they are only like angels when they are young and beautiful; consequently, it is their persons, not their virtues, that procure them this homage.

Idle empty words! What can such delusive flattery lead to, but vanity and folly? The lover, it is true, has a poetical licence to exalt his mistress; his reason is the bubble of his passion, and he does not utter a falsehood when he borrows the language of adoration. His imagination may raise the idol of his heart, unblamed, above humanity; and happy would it be for women, if they were only flattered by the men who loved them; I mean, who love the individual, not the sex; but should a grave preacher interlard his discourses with such fooleries?

In sermons or novels, however, voluptuousness is always true to its text. Men are allowed by moralists to cultivate, as Nature directs, different qualities, and assume the different characters, that the same passions, modified almost to infinity, give to each individual. A virtuous man may have a choleric or a sanguine constitution, be gay or grave, unreproved; be firm till he is almost overbearing, or, weakly submissive, have no will or opinion of his own; but all women are to be levelled, by meekness and docility, into one character of yielding softness and gentle compliance.

I will use the preacher's own words. 'Let it be observed, that in your sex manly exercises are never graceful; that in them a tone and figure, as well as an air and deportment, of the masculine kind, are always forbidding; and that men of sensibility desire in every woman soft features, and a flowing voice, a form, not robust, and demeanour delicate and gentle.'[32]

Is not the following portrait – the portrait of a house slave? 'I am astonished at the folly of many women, who are still reproaching their husbands for leaving them alone, for preferring this or that company to theirs, for treating them with this and the other mark of disregard or indifference; when, to speak the truth, they have themselves in a great measure to blame. Not that I would justify the men in any thing wrong on their part. But had you behaved to them with more *respectful observance*, and a more *equal tenderness; studying their humours, over- looking their mistakes, submitting to their opinions* in matters indifferent, passing by little instances of unevenness, caprice, or passion, giving *soft* answers to hasty words, complaining as seldom as possible, and making it your daily care to relieve their anxieties and prevent their wishes, to enliven the hour of dulness, and call up the ideas of felicity: had you pursued this conduct, I doubt not but you would have maintained and even increased their esteem, so far as to have secured every degree of influence that could conduce to their virtue, or your mutual satisfaction; and your house might at this day have been the abode of dom- estic bliss.'[33] Such a woman ought to be an angel – or she is an ass – for I discern not a trace of the human character, neither reason nor passion in this domestic drudge, whose being is absorbed in that of a tyrant's.

Still Dr Fordyce must have very little acquaintance with the human heart, if he really supposed that such conduct would bring back wandering love, instead of exciting contempt. No, beauty, gentleness, &c. &c. may gain a heart; but esteem, the only lasting affection, can alone be obtained by virtue supported by reason. It is respect for the understanding that keeps alive tenderness for the person.

As these volumes are so frequently put into the hands of young people, I have taken more notice of them than, strictly speaking, they deserve; but as they have contributed to vitiate the taste, and enervate the understanding of many of my fellow- creatures, I could not pass them silently over.

SECT. III

Such paternal solicitude pervades Dr Gregory's Legacy to his Daughters, that I enter on the task of criticism with affectionate respect; but as this little volume has many attractions to rec- ommend it to the notice of the most respectable part of my sex, I cannot silently pass over arguments that so speciously support opinions which, I think, have had the most baneful effect on the morals and manners of the female world.

His easy familiar style is particularly suited to the tenor of his advice, and the melancholy tenderness which his respect for the memory of a beloved wife, diffuses through the whole work, renders it very interesting; yet there is a degree of concise elegance conspicuous in many passages that disturbs this sympathy; and we pop on the author, when we only expected to meet the – father.

Besides, having two objects in view, he seldom adhered steadily to either; for wishing to make his daughters amiable, and fearing lest unhappiness should only be the consequence, of instilling sentiments that might draw them out of the track of common life without enabling them to act with consonant independence and dignity, he checks the natural flow of his thoughts, and neither advises one thing nor the other.

In the preface he tells them a mournful truth, 'that they will hear, at least once in their lives, the genuine sentiments of a man who has no interest in deceiving them.'[34]

Hapless woman! what can be expected from thee when the beings on whom thou art said naturally to depend for reason and support, have all an interest in deceiving thee! This is the root of the evil that has shed a corroding mildew on all thy virtues; and blighting in the bud thy opening faculties, has rendered thee the weak thing thou art! It is this separate interest – this insidious state of warfare, that undermines morality, and divides mankind!

If love have made some women wretched – how many more has the cold unmeaning intercourse of gallantry rendered vain and useless! yet this heartless attention to the sex is reckoned so manly, so polite that, till society is very differently organized, I fear, this vestige of gothic manners will not be done away by a more reasonable and affectionate mode of conduct. Besides, to strip it of its imaginary dignity, I must observe, that in the most uncivilized European states this lip-service prevails in a very great degree, accompanied with extreme dissoluteness of morals. In Portugal,[35] the country that I particularly allude to, it takes place of the most serious moral obligations; for a man is seldom assassinated when in the company of a woman. The savage hand of rapine is unnerved by this chivalrous spirit; and, if the stroke of vengeance cannot be stayed – the lady is entreated to pardon the rudeness and depart in peace, though sprinkled, perhaps, with her husband's or brother's blood.

I shall pass over his strictures on religion, because I mean to discuss that subject in a separate chapter.

The remarks relative to behaviour, though many of them very sensible, I entirely disapprove of, because it appears to me to be beginning, as it were, at the wrong end. A cultivated understanding, and an affectionate heart, will never want starched rules of decorum – something more substantial than seemliness will be the result; and, without understanding the behaviour here recommended, would be rank affectation. Decorum, indeed, is the one thing needful! – decorum is to supplant nature, and banish all simplicity and variety of character out of the female world. Yet what good end can all this superficial counsel produce? It is, however, much easier to point out this or that mode of behaviour, than to set the reason to work; but, when the mind has been stored with useful knowledge, and strengthened by being employed, the regulation of the behaviour may safely be left to its guidance.

Why, for instance, should the following caution be given when art of every kind must contaminate the mind; and why entangle the grand motives of action, which reason and religion equally combine to enforce, with pitiful worldly shifts and slight of hand tricks to gain the applause of gaping tasteless fools? 'Be even cautious in displaying your good sense.* It will be thought you assume a superiority over the rest of the company – But if you happen to have any learning, keep it a profound secret, especially from the men who generally look with a jealous and malignant eye on a woman of great parts, and a cultivated understanding.'[36] If men of real merit, as he afterwards observes, be superior to this meanness, where is the necessity that the behaviour of the whole sex should be modulated to please fools,

---

* Let women once acquire good sense – and if it deserve the name, it will teach them; or, of what use will it be? how to employ it.

or men, who having little claim to respect as individuals, choose to keep close in their phalanx. Men, indeed, who insist on their common superiority, having only this sexual superiority, are certainly very excusable.

There would be no end to rules for behaviour, if it be proper always to adopt the tone of the company; for thus, for ever varying the key, a *flat* would often pass for a *natural* note.

Surely it would have been wiser to have advised women to improve themselves till they rose above the fumes of vanity; and then to let the public opinion come round – for where are rules of accommodation to stop? The narrow path of truth and virtue inclines neither to the right nor left – it is a straightforward business, and they who are earnestly pursuing their road, may bound over many decorous prejudices, without leaving modesty behind. Make the heart clean, and give the head employment, and I will venture to predict that there will be nothing offensive in the behaviour.

The air of fashion, which many young people are so eager to attain, always strikes me like the studied attitudes of some modern pictures, copied with tasteless servility after the antiques; – the soul is left out, and none of the parts are tied together by what may properly be termed character. This varnish of fashion, which seldom sticks very close to sense, may dazzle the weak; but leave nature to itself, and it will seldom disgust the wise. Besides, when a woman has sufficient sense not to pretend to any thing which she does not understand in some degree, there is no need of determining to hide her talents under a bushel.[37] Let things take their natural course, and all will be well.

It is this system of dissimulation, throughout the volume, that I despise. Women are always to *seem* to be this and that – yet virtue might apostrophize them, in the words of Hamlet – Seems! I know not seems! – Have that within that passeth show![38] –

Still the same tone occurs; for in another place, after recommending, without sufficiently discriminating delicacy, he adds, 'The men will complain of your reserve. They will assure you that a franker behaviour would make you more amiable. But, trust me, they are not sincere when they tell you so. – I acknowledge that on some occasions it might render you more agreeable as companions, but it would make you less amiable as women: an important distinction, which many of your sex are not aware of.'[39] –

This desire of being always women, is the very consciousness that degrades the sex. Excepting with a lover, I must repeat with emphasis, a former observation, – it would be well if they were only agreeable or rational companions. – But in this respect his advice is even inconsistent with a passage which I mean to quote with the most marked approbation.

'The sentiment, that a woman may allow all innocent free-doms, provided her virtue is secure, is both grossly indelicate and dangerous, and has proved fatal to many of your sex.'[40] With this opinion I perfectly coincide. A man, or a woman, of any feeling, must always wish to convince a beloved object that it is the caresses of the individual, not the sex, that are received and returned with pleasure; and, that the heart, rather than the senses, is moved. Without this natural delicacy, love becomes a selfish personal gratification that soon degrades the character.

I carry this sentiment still further. Affection, when love is out of the question, authorises many personal endearments, that naturally flowing from an innocent heart, give life to the behaviour; but the personal intercourse of appetite, gallantry, or vanity, is despicable. When a man squeezes the hand of a pretty woman, handing her to a carriage, whom he has never seen before, she will consider such an impertinent freedom in the light of an insult, if she have any true delicacy, instead of being flattered by this unmeaning homage to beauty. These are the privileges of friendship, or the momentary homage which the heart pays to virtue, when it flashes suddenly on the notice – mere animal spirits have no claim to the kindnesses of affection!

Wishing to feed the affections with what is now the food of vanity, I would fain persuade my sex to act from simpler principles. Let them merit love, and they will obtain it, though they may never be told that – 'The power of a fine woman over the hearts of men, of men of the finest parts, is even beyond what she conceives.'[41]

I have already noticed the narrow cautions with respect to

duplicity, female softness, delicacy of constitution; for these are the changes which he rings round without ceasing – in a more decorous manner, it is true, than Rousseau; but it all comes home to the same point, and whoever is at the trouble to analyze these sentiments, will find the first principles not quite so delicate as the superstructure.

The subject of amusements is treated in too cursory a manner; but with the same spirit.

When I treat of friendship, love, and marriage, it will be found that we materially differ in opinion; I shall not then forestall what I have to observe on these important subjects; but confine my remarks to the general tenor of them, to that cautious family prudence, to those confined views of partial unenlightened affection, which exclude pleasure and improvement, by vainly wishing to ward off sorrow and error – and by thus guarding the heart and mind, destroy also all their energy. – It is far better to be often deceived than never to trust; to be disappointed in love than never to love; to lose a husband's fondness than forfeit his esteem.

Happy would it be for the world, and for individuals, of course, if all this unavailing solicitude to attain worldly happiness, on a confined plan, were turned into an anxious desire to improve the understanding. – 'Wisdom is the principal thing: *therefore* get wisdom; and with all thy gettings get understanding.' – 'How long, ye simple ones, will ye love simplicity, and hate knowledge?'[42] Saith Wisdom to the daughters of men! –

SECT. IV

I do not mean to allude to all the writers who have written on the subject of female manners – it would, in fact, be only beating over the old ground, for they have, in general, written in the same strain; but attacking the boasted prerogative of man – the prerogative that may emphatically be called the iron sccptre of tyranny, the original sin of tyrants, I declare against all power built on prejudices, however hoary.

If the submission demanded be founded on justice – there is no appealing to a higher power – for God is Justice itself. Let us then, as children of the same parent, if not bastardized by being the younger born, reason together, and learn to submit to the authority of reason – when her voice is distinctly heard. But, if it be proved, that this throne of prerogative only rests on a chaotic mass of prejudices, that have no inherent principle of order to keep them together, or on an elephant, tortoise, or even the mighty shoulders of a son of the earth,[43] they may escape, who dare to brave the consequence, without any breach of duty, without sinning against the order of things.

Whilst reason raises man above the brutal herd, and death is big with promises, they alone are subject to blind authority who have no reliance on their own strength. They are free – who will be free!'*–

The being who can govern itself has nothing to fear in life; but if any thing be dearer than its own respect, the price must be paid to the last farthing. Virtue, like every thing valuable, must be loved for herself alone; or she will not take up her abode with us. She will not impart that peace, 'which passeth understanding,'[44] when she is merely made the stilts of reputation; and respected, with pharisaical exactness, because 'honesty is the best policy.'

That the plan of life which enables us to carry some knowledge and virtue into another world, is the one best calculated to ensure content in this, cannot be denied; yet few people act according to this principle, though it be universally allowed that it admits not of dispute. Present pleasure, or present power, carry before it these sober convictions; and it is for the day, not for life, that man bargains with happiness. How few! – how very few! have sufficient foresight, or resolution, to endure a small evil at the moment, to avoid a greater hereafter.

Woman in particular, whose virtue† is built on mutable prejudices, seldom attains to this greatness of mind; so that, becoming the slave of her own feelings, she is easily subjugated by those of others. Thus degraded, her reason, her misty reason! is employed rather to burnish than to snap her chains.

---

* 'He is the free man, whom the *truth* makes free!'
                                    Cowper.[45]
† I mean to use a word that comprehends more than chastity the sexual virtue.

Indignantly have I heard women argue in the same track as men, and adopt the sentiments that brutalize them, with all the pertinacity of ignorance.

I must illustrate my assertion by a few examples. Mrs Piozzi, who often repeated by rote, what she did not understand, comes forward with Johnsonian periods.

'Seek not for happiness in singularity; and dread a refinement of wisdom as a deviation into folly.' Thus she dogmatically addresses a new married man; and to elucidate this pompous exordium, she adds, 'I said that the person of your lady would not grow more pleasing to you, but pray let her never suspect that it grows less so: that a woman will pardon an affront to her understanding much sooner than one to her person, is well known; nor will any of us contradict the assertion. All our attainments, all our arts, are employed to gain and keep the heart of man; and what mortification can exceed the disappointment, if the end be not obtained? There is no reproof however pointed, no punishment however severe, that a woman of spirit will not prefer to neglect; and if she can endure it without complaint, it only proves that she means to make herself amends by the attention of others for the slights of her husband!'[46]

These are truly masculine sentiments. – 'All our *arts* are employed to gain and keep the heart of man:' – and what is the inference? – if her person, and was there ever a person, though formed with Medicean symmetry,[47] that was not slighted? be neglected, she will make herself amends by endeavouring to please other men. Noble morality! But thus is the understanding of the whole sex affronted, and their virtue deprived of the common basis of virtue. A woman must know, that her person cannot be as pleasing to her husband as it was to her lover, and if she be offended with him for being a human creature, she may as well whine about the loss of his heart as about any other foolish thing. – And this very want of discernment or unreasonable anger, proves that he could not change his fondness for her person into affection for her virtues or respect for her understanding.

Whilst women avow, and act up to such opinions, their understandings, at least, deserve the contempt and obloquy that men, *who never* insult their persons, have pointedly levelled at the female mind. And it is the sentiments of these polite men, who do not wish to be encumbered with mind, that vain women thoughtlessly adopt. Yet they should know, that insulted reason alone can spread that *sacred* reserve about the person, which renders human affections, for human affections have always some base alloy, as permanent as is consistent with the grand end of existence – the attainment of virtue.

The Baroness de Stael speaks the same language as the lady just cited, with more enthusiasm. Her eulogium on Rousseau was accidentally put into my hands, and her sentiments, the sentiments of too many of my sex, may serve as the text for a few comments. 'Though Rousseau,' she observes, 'has endeavoured to prevent women from interfering in public affairs, and acting a brilliant part in the theatre of politics; yet in speaking of them, how much has he done it to their satisfaction! If he wished to deprive them of some rights foreign to their sex, how has he for ever restored to them all those to which it has a claim! And in attempting to diminish their influence over the deliberations of men, how sacredly has he established the empire they have over their happiness! In aiding them to descend from an usurped throne, he has firmly seated them upon that to which they were destined by nature; and though he be full of indignation against them when they endeavour to resemble men, yet when they come before him with all the *charms, weaknesses, virtues* and *errors*, of their sex, his respect for their *persons* amounts almost to adoration.'[48] True! – For never was there a sensualist who paid more fervent adoration at the shrine of beauty. So devout, indeed, was his respect for the person, that excepting the virtue of chastity, for obvious reasons, he only wished to see it embellished by charms, weaknesses, and errors. He was afraid lest the austerity of reason should disturb the soft playfulness of love. The master wished to have a meretricious slave to fondle, entirely dependent on his reason and bounty; he did not want a companion, whom he should be compelled to esteem, or a friend to whom he could confide the care of his children's education, should death deprive them of their father, before he had fulfilled the sacred task. He denies woman reason, shuts her out from knowledge, and turns her aside from truth; yet his pardon is granted, because 'he admits the passion of love.'[49] It would require some ingenuity to shew why women were to be under such an obligation to him for thus admitting love; when it is clear that he admits it only for the relaxation of men, and to perpetuate the species; but he talked with passion, and that powerful spell worked on the sensibility of a young encomiast. 'What signifies it,' pursues this rhapsodist, 'to women, that his reason disputes with them the empire, when his heart is devotedly theirs.'[50] It is not empire, – but equality, that they should contend for. Yet, if they only wished to lengthen out their sway, they should not entirely trust to their persons, for though beauty may gain a heart, it cannot keep it, even while the beauty is in full bloom, unless the mind lend, at least, some graces.

When women are once sufficiently enlightened to discover their real interest, on a grand scale, they will, I am persuaded, be very ready to resign all the prerogatives of love, that are not mutual, speaking of them as lasting prerogatives, for the calm satisfaction of friendship, and the tender confidence of habitual esteem. Before marriage they will not assume any insolent airs, or afterwards abjectly submit; but endeavouring to act like reasonable creatures, in both situations, they will not be tumbled from a throne to a stool.

Madame Genlis has written several entertaining books for children; and her Letters on Education[51] afford many useful hints, that sensible parents will certainly avail themselves of; but her views are narrow, and her prejudices as unreasonable as strong.

I shall pass over her vehement argument in favour of the eternity of future punishments, because I blush to think that a human being should ever argue vehemently in such a cause, and only make a few remarks on her absurd manner of making the parental authority supplant reason. For every where does she inculcate not only *blind* submission to parents; but to the opinion of the world.*

* A person is not to act in this or that way, though convinced they are right in so doing, because some equivocal circumstances may lead the world to *suspect* that they acted from different motives. – This is sacrificing the substance for a shadow. Let people but watch their own hearts, and act rightly, as far as they can judge, and they may patiently wait till the opinion of the world comes

She tells a story of a young man engaged by his father's express desire to a girl of fortune. Before the marriage could take place, she is deprived of her fortune, and thrown friendless on the world. The father practises the most infamous arts to separate his son from her, and when the son detects his villany, and following the dictates of honour marries the girl, nothing but misery ensues, because forsooth he married *without* his father's consent.[52] On what ground can religion or morality rest when justice is thus set at defiance? With the same view she represents an accomplished young woman, as ready to marry any body that her *mamma* pleased to recommend; and, as actually marrying the young man of her own choice, without feeling any emotions of passion, because that a well educated girl had not time to be in love. Is it possible to have much respect for a system of education that thus insults reason and nature?

Many similar opinions occur in her writings, mixed with sentiments that do honour to her head and heart. Yet so much superstition is mixed with her religion, and so much worldly wisdom with her morality, that I should not let a young person read her works, unless I could afterwards converse on the subjects, and point out the contradictions.

Mrs Chapone's Letters[53] are written with such good sense, and unaffected humility, and contain so many useful observations, that I only mention them to pay the worthy writer this tribute of respect. I cannot, it is true, always coincide in opinion with her; but I always respect her.

The very word respect brings Mrs Macaulay[54] to my remembrance. The woman of the greatest abilities, undoubtedly, that this country has ever produced. – And yet this woman has been suffered to die without sufficient respect being paid to her memory.

Posterity, however, will be more just; and remember that Catharine Macaulay was an example of intellectual acquirements supposed to be incompatible with the weakness of her sex. In her style of writing, indeed, no sex appears, for it is like the sense it conveys, strong and clear.

---

round. It is best to be directed by a simple motive – for justice has too often been sacrificed to propriety; – another word for convenience.

I will not call hers a masculine understanding, because I admit
not of such an arrogant assumption of reason; but I contend that
it was a sound one, and that her judgment, the matured fruit
of profound thinking, was a proof that a woman can acquire
judgment, in the full extent of the word. Possessing more pen-
etration than sagacity, more understanding than fancy, she writes
with sober energy and argumentative closeness; yet sympathy
and benevolence give an interest to her sentiments, and that vital
heat to arguments, which forces the reader to weigh them.*

When I first thought of writing these strictures I anticipated
Mrs Macaulay's approbation, with a little of that sanguine
ardour, which it has been the business of my life to depress; but
soon heard with the sickly qualm of disappointed hope; and the
still seriousness of regret – that she was no more!

SECT. V

Taking a view of the different works which have been written
on education, Lord Chesterfield's Letters must not be silently
passed over. Not that I mean to analyze his unmanly, immoral
system, or even to cull any of the useful, shrewd remarks which
occur in his epistles – No, I only mean to make a few reflections
on the avowed tendency of them – the art of acquiring an early
knowledge of the world. An art, I will venture to assert, that
preys secretly, like the worm in the bud, on the expanding
powers, and turns to poison the generous juices which should
mount with vigour in the youthful frame, inspiring warm affections and great resolves.†

For every thing, saith the wise man, there is a season;[55] – and

---

* Coinciding in opinion with Mrs Macaulay relative to many branches of
education, I refer to her valuable work, instead of quoting her sentiments to
support my own.
† That children ought to be constantly guarded against the vices and follies of
the world, appears, to me, a very mistaken opinion; for in the course of my
experience, and my eyes have looked abroad, I never knew a youth educated in
this manner, who had early imbibed these chilling suspicions, and repeated by
rote the hesitating *if* of age, that did not prove a selfish character.

who would look for the fruits of autumn during the genial months of spring? But this is mere declamation, and I mean to reason with those worldly-wise instructors, who, instead of cultivating the judgment, instill prejudices, and render hard the heart that gradual experience would only have cooled. An early acquaintance with human infirmities; or, what is termed know-ledge of the world, is the surest way, in my opinion, to contract the heart and damp the natural youthful ardour which produces not only great talents, but great virtues. For the vain attempt to bring forth the fruit of experience, before the sapling has thrown out its leaves, only exhausts its strength, and prevents its assum-ing a natural form; just as the form and strength of subsiding metals are injured when the attraction of cohesion is disturbed.

Tell me, ye who have studied the human mind, is it not a strange way to fix principles by showing young people that they are seldom stable? And how can they be fortified by habits when they are proved to be fallacious by example? Why is the ardour of youth thus to be damped, and the luxuriancy of fancy cut to the quick? This dry caution may, it is true, guard a character from worldly mischances; but will infallibly preclude excellence in either virtue or knowledge.* The stumbling-block thrown across every path by suspicion, will prevent any vigorous exer-tions of genius or benevolence, and life will be stripped of its most alluring charm long before its calm evening, when man should retire to contemplation for comfort and support.

A young man who has been bred up with domestic friends, and led to store his mind with as much speculative knowledge as can be acquired by reading and the natural reflections which youthful ebullitions of animal spirits and instinctive feelings inspire, will enter the world with warm and erroneous expec-tations. But this appears to be the course of nature; and in morals, as well as in works of taste, we should be observant of her sacred indications, and not presume to lead when we ought obsequiously to follow.

---

* I have already observed that an early knowledge of the world, obtained in a natural way, by mixing in the world, has the same effect: instancing officers and women.

In the world few people act from principle; present feelings, and early habits, are the grand springs: but how would the former be deadened, and the latter rendered iron corroding fetters, if the world were shewn to young people just as it is; when no knowledge of mankind or their own hearts, slowly obtained by experience, rendered them forbearing? Their fellow creatures would not then be viewed as frail beings; like themselves, condemned to struggle with human infirmities, and sometimes displaying the light, and sometimes the dark side of their character; extorting alternate feelings of love and disgust; but guarded against as beasts of prey, till every enlarged social feeling, in a word, – humanity, was eradicated.

In life, on the contrary, as we gradually discover the imperfections of our nature, we discover virtues, and various circumstances attach us to our fellow creatures, when we mix with them, and view the same objects, that are never thought of in acquiring a hasty unnatural knowledge of the world. We see a folly swell into a vice, by almost imperceptible degrees, and pity while we blame; but, if the hideous monster burst suddenly on our sight, fear and disgust rendering us more severe than man ought to be, might lead us with blind zeal to usurp the character of omnipotence, and denounce damnation on our fellow mortals, forgetting that we cannot read the heart, and that we have seeds of the same vices lurking in our own.

I have already remarked that we expect more from instruction, than mere instruction can produce: for, instead of preparing young people to encounter the evils of life with dignity, and to acquire wisdom and virtue by the exercise of their own faculties, precepts are heaped upon precepts, and blind obedience required, when conviction should be brought home to reason.

Suppose, for instance, that a young person in the first ardour of friendship deifies the beloved object – what harm can arise from this mistaken enthusiastic attachment? Perhaps it is necessary for virtue first to appear in a human form to impress youthful hearts; the ideal model, which a more matured and exalted mind looks up to, and shapes for itself, would elude their sight. He who loves not his brother whom he hath seen, how can he love God?[56] asked the wisest of men.

It is natural for youth to adorn the first object of its affection with every good quality, and the emulation produced by ignorance, or, to speak with more propriety, by inexperience, brings forward the mind capable of forming such an affection, and when, in the lapse of time, perfection is found not to be within the reach of mortals, virtue, abstractedly, is thought beautiful, and wisdom sublime. Admiration then gives place to friendship, properly so called, because it is cemented by esteem; and the being walks alone only dependent on heaven for that emulous panting after perfection which ever glows in a noble mind. But this knowledge a man must gain by the exertion of his own faculties; and this is surely the blessed fruit of disappointed hope! for He who delighteth to diffuse happiness and shew mercy to the weak creatures, who are learning to know him, never implanted a good propensity to be a tormenting ignis fatuus.[57]

Our trees are now allowed to spread with wild luxuriance, nor do we expect by force to combine the majestic marks of time with youthful graces; but wait patiently till they have struck deep their root, and braved many a storm. – Is the mind then, which, in proportion to its dignity, advances more slowly towards perfection, to be treated with less respect? To argue from analogy, every thing around us is in a progressive state; and when an unwelcome knowledge of life produces almost a satiety of life, and we discover by the natural course of things that all that is done under the sun is vanity,[58] we are drawing near the awful close of the drama. The days of activity and hope are over, and the opportunities which the first stage of existence has afforded of advancing in the scale of intelligence, must soon be summed up. – A knowledge at this period of the futility of life, or earlier, if obtained by experience, is very useful, because it is natural; but when a frail being is shewn the follies and vices of man, that he may be taught prudently to guard against the common casualties of life by sacrificing his heart – surely it is not speaking harshly to call it the wisdom of this world, contrasted with the nobler fruit of piety and experience.

I will venture a paradox, and deliver my opinion without reserve; if men were only born to form a circle of life and death, it would be wise to take every step that foresight could suggest to render life happy. Moderation in every pursuit would then be supreme wisdom; and the prudent voluptuary might enjoy a degree of content, though he neither cultivated his understanding nor kept his heart pure. Prudence, supposing we were mortal, would be true wisdom, or, to be more explicit, would procure the greatest portion of happiness, considering the whole of life, but knowledge beyond the conveniences of life would be a curse.

Why should we injure our health by close study? The exalted pleasure which intellectual pursuits afford would scarcely be equivalent to the hours of languor that follow; especially, if it be necessary to take into the reckoning the doubts and disappointments that cloud our researches. Vanity and vexation close every inquiry: for the cause which we particularly wished to discover flies like the horizon before us as we advance. The ignorant, on the contrary, resemble children, and suppose, that if they could walk straight forward they should at last arrive where the earth and clouds meet. Yet, disappointed as we are in our researches, the mind gains strength by the exercise, sufficient, perhaps, to comprehend the answers which, in another step of existence, it may receive to the anxious questions it asked, when the understanding with feeble wing was fluttering round the visible effects to dive into the hidden cause.

The passions also, the winds of life, would be useless, if not injurious, did the substance which composes our thinking being, after we have thought in vain, only become the support of vegetable life, and invigorate a cabbage, or blush in a rose. The appetites would answer every earthly purpose, and produce more moderate and permanent happiness. But the powers of the soul that are of little use here, and, probably, disturb our animal enjoyments, even while conscious dignity makes us glory in possessing them, prove that life is merely an education, a state of infancy, to which the only hopes worth cherishing should not be sacrificed. I mean, therefore, to infer, that we ought to have a precise idea of what we wish to attain by education, for the immortality of the soul is contradicted by the actions of many people who firmly profess the belief.

If you mean to secure ease and prosperity on earth as the first consideration, and leave futurity to provide for itself; you act prudently in giving your child an early insight into the weak-nesses of his nature. You may not, it is true, make an Inkle[59] of him; but do not imagine that he will stick to more than the letter of the law, who has very early imbibed a mean opinion of human nature; nor will he think it necessary to rise much above the common standard. He may avoid gross vices, because honesty is the best policy; but he will never aim at attaining great virtues. The example of writers and artists will illustrate this remark.

I must therefore venture to doubt whether what has been thought an axiom in morals may not have been a dogmatical assertion made by men who have coolly seen mankind through the medium of books, and say, in direct contradiction to them, that the regulation of the passions is not, always, wisdom. – On the contrary, it should seem, that one reason why men have superiour judgment, and more fortitude than women, is un-doubtedly this, that they give a freer scope to the grand passions, and by more frequently going astray enlarge their minds. If then by the exercise of their own* reason they fix on some stable principle, they have probably to thank the force of their pas-sions, nourished by *false* views of life, and permitted to overleap the boundary that secures content. But if, in the dawn of life, we could soberly survey the scenes before as in perspective, and see every thing in its true colours, how could the passions gain sufficient strength to unfold the faculties?

Let me now as from an eminence survey the world stripped of all its false delusive charms. The clear atmosphere enables me to see each object in its true point of view, while my heart is still. I am calm as the prospect in a morning when the mists, slowly dispersing, silently unveil the beauties of nature, refreshed by rest.

In what light will the world now appear? – I rub my eyes and think, perchance, that I am just awaking from a lively dream.

I see the sons and daughters of men, pursuing shadows, and anxiously wasting their powers to feed passions which have no adequate object – if the very excess of these blind impulses, pampered by that lying, yet constantly trusted guide, the imagin-ation, did not, by preparing them for some other state, render

* 'I find that all is but lip-wisdom which wants experience,' says Sidney.[60]

short-sighted mortals wiser without their own concurrence or, what comes to the same thing, when they were pursuing some imaginary present good.

After viewing objects in this light, it would not be very fanciful to imagine that this world was a stage on which a pantomime is daily performed for the amusement of superiour beings. How would they be diverted to see the ambitious man consuming himself by running after a phantom, and, 'pursuing the bubble fame in the cannon's mouth'[61] that was to blow him to nothing: for when consciousness is lost, it matters not whether we mount in a whirlwind or descend in rain. And should they compassionately invigorate his sight and shew him the thorny path which led to eminence, that like a quicksand sinks as he ascends, disappointing his hopes when almost within his grasp, would he not leave to others the honour of amusing them, and labour to secure the present moment, though from the constitution of his nature he would not find it very easy to catch the flying stream? Such slaves are we to hope and fear!

But, vain as the ambitious man's pursuits would be, he is often striving for something more substantial than fame – that indeed would be the veriest meteor, the wildest fire that could lure a man to ruin. – What! renounce the most trifling gratification to be applauded when he should be no more! Wherefore this struggle, whether man be mortal or immortal, if that noble passion did not really raise the being above his fellows? –

And love! What diverting scenes would it produce – Pantaloon's[62] tricks must yield to more egregious folly. To see a mortal adorn an object with imaginary charms, and then fall down and worship the idol which he had himself set up – how ridiculous! But what serious consequences ensue to rob man of that portion of happiness, which the Deity by calling him into existence has (or, on what can his attributes rest?) indubitably promised: would not all the purposes of life have been much better fulfilled if he had only felt what has been termed physical love? And, would not the sight of the object, not seen through the medium of the imagination, soon reduce the passion to an appetite, if reflection, the noble distinction of man, did not give it force, and make it an instrument to raise him above this earthy dross, by teaching him to love the centre of all perfection; whose wisdom appears clearer and clearer in the works of nature, in proportion as reason is illuminated and exalted by contemplation, and by acquiring that love of order which the struggles of passion produce?

The habit of reflection, and the knowledge attained by fostering any passion, might be shewn to be equally useful, though the object be proved equally fallacious; for they would all appear in the same light, if they were not magnified by the governing passion implanted in us by the Author of all good, to call forth and strengthen the faculties of each individual, and enable it to attain all the experience that an infant can obtain, who does certain things, it cannot tell why.

I descend from my height, and mixing with my fellow-creatures, feel myself hurried along the common stream; ambition, love, hope, and fear, exert their wonted power, though we be convinced by reason that their present and most attractive promises are only lying dreams; but had the cold hand of circumspection damped each generous feeling before it had left any permanent character, or fixed some habit, what could be expected, but selfish prudence and reason just rising above instinct? Who that has read Dean Swift's disgusting description of the Yahoos, and insipid one of Houyhnhnm[63] with a philosophical eye, can avoid seeing the futility of degrading the passions, or making man rest in contentment?

The youth should *act*; for had he the experience of a grey head he would be fitter for death than life, though his virtues, rather residing in his head than his heart, could produce nothing great, and his understanding, prepared for this world, would not, by its noble flights, prove that it had a title to a better.

Besides, it is not possible to give a young person a just view of life; he must have struggled with his own passions before he can estimate the force of the temptation which betrayed his brother into vice. Those who are entering life, and those who are departing, see the world from such very different points of view, that they can seldom think alike, unless the unfledged reason of the former never attempted a solitary flight.

When we hear of some daring crime – it comes full on us in

the deepest shade of turpitude, and raises indignation; but the eye that gradually saw the darkness thicken, must observe it with more compassionate forbearance. The world cannot be seen by an unmoved spectator, we must mix in the throng, and feel as men feel before we can judge of their feelings. If we mean, in short, to live in the world to grow wiser and better, and not merely to enjoy the good things of life, we must attain a knowledge of others at the same time that we become acquainted with ourselves – knowledge acquired any other way only hardens the heart and perplexes the understanding.

I may be told, that the knowledge thus acquired, is sometimes purchased at too dear a rate. I can only answer that I very much doubt whether any knowledge can be attained without labour and sorrow; and those who wish to spare their children both, should not complain, if they are neither wise nor virtuous. They only aimed at making them prudent; and prudence, early in life, is but the cautious craft of ignorant self-love.

I have observed that young people, to whose education particular attention has been paid, have, in general, been very superficial and conceited, and far from pleasing in any respect, because they had neither the unsuspecting warmth of youth, nor the cool depth of age. I cannot help imputing this unnatural appearance principally to that hasty premature instruction, which leads them presumptuously to repeat all the crude notions they have taken upon trust, so that the careful education which they received, makes them all their lives the slaves of prejudices.

Mental as well as bodily exertion is, at first, irksome; so much so, that the many would fain let others both work and think for them. An observation which I have often made will illustrate my meaning. When in a circle of strangers, or acquaintances, a person of moderate abilities asserts an opinion with heat, I will venture to affirm, for I have traced this fact home, very often, that it is a prejudice. These echoes have a high respect for the understanding of some relation or friend, and without fully comprehending the opinions, which they are so eager to retail, they maintain them with a degree of obstinacy, that would surprise even the person who concocted them.

I know that a kind of fashion now prevails of respecting

prejudices; and when any one dares to face them, though actuated by humanity and armed by reason, he is superciliously asked whether his ancestors were fools. No, I should reply; opinions, at first, of every description, were all, probably, considered, and therefore were founded on some reason; yet not unfrequently, of course, it was rather a local expedient than a fundamental principle, that would be reasonable at all times. But, moss-covered opinions assume the disproportioned form of prejudices, when they are indolently adopted only because age has given them a venerable aspect, though the reason on which they were built ceases to be a reason, or cannot be traced. Why are we to love prejudices, merely because they are prejudices?* A prejudice is a fond obstinate persuasion for which we can give no reason; for the moment a reason can be given for an opinion, it ceases to be a prejudice, though it may be an error in judgment: and are we then advised to cherish opinions only to set reason at defiance? This mode of arguing, if arguing it may be called, reminds me of what is vulgarly termed a woman's reason. For women sometimes declare that they love, or believe, certain things, *because* they love, or believe them.

It is impossible to converse with people to any purpose, who only use affirmatives and negatives. Before you can bring them to a point, to start fairly from, you must go back to the simple principles that were antecedent to the prejudices broached by power; and it is ten to one but you are stopped by the philosophical assertion, that certain principles are as practically false as they are abstractly true.† Nay, it may be inferred, that reason has whispered some doubts, for it generally happens that people assert their opinions with the greatest heat when they begin to waver; striving to drive out their own doubts by convincing their opponent, they grow angry when those gnawing doubts are thrown back to prey on themselves.

The fact is, that men expect from education, what education cannot give. A sagacious parent or tutor may strengthen the

* Vide Mr Burke.[64]
† 'Convince a man against his will,
   He's of the same opinion still.'[65]

body and sharpen the instruments by which the child is to gather knowledge; but the honey must be the reward of the individual's own industry. It is almost as absurd to attempt to make a youth wise by the experience of another, as to expect the body to grow strong by the exercise which is only talked of, or seen.* Many of those children whose conduct has been most narrowly watched, become the weakest men, because their instructors only instill certain notions into their minds, that have no other foundation than their authority; and if they be loved or respected, the mind is cramped in its exertions and wavering in its advances. The business of education in this case, is only to conduct the shooting tendrils to a proper pole; yet after laying precept upon precept, without allowing a child to acquire judgment itself, parents expect them to act in the same manner by this borrowed fallacious light, as if they had illuminated it themselves; and be, when they enter life, what their parents are at the close. They do not consider that the tree, and even the human body, does not strengthen its fibres till it has reached its full growth.

There appears to be something analogous in the mind. The senses and the imagination give a form to the character, during childhood and youth; and the understanding, as life advances, gives firmness to the first fair purposes of sensibility – till virtue, arising rather from the clear conviction of reason than the impulse of the heart, morality is made to rest on a rock against which the storms of passion vainly beat.

I hope I shall not be misunderstood when I say, that religion will not have this condensing energy, unless it be founded on reason. If it be merely the refuge of weakness or wild fanaticism, and not a governing principle of conduct, drawn from self-knowledge, and a rational opinion respecting the attributes of God, what can it be expected to produce? The religion which consists in warming the affections, and exalting the imagination, is only the poetical part, and may afford the individual pleasure without rendering it a more moral being. It may be a substitute for worldly pursuits; yet narrow, instead of enlarging the heart:

---

* 'One sees nothing when one is content to contemplate only; it is necessary to act oneself to be able to see how others act.' *Rousseau.*

but virtue must be loved as in itself sublime and excellent, and not for the advantages it procures or the evils it averts, if any great degree of excellence be expected. Men will not become moral when they only build airy castles in a future world to compensate for the disappointments which they meet with in this; if they turn their thoughts from relative duties to religious reveries.

Most prospects in life are marred by the shuffling worldly wisdom of men, who, forgetting that they cannot serve God and mammon,[66] endeavour to blend contradictory things. – If you wish to make your son rich, pursue one course – if you are only anxious to make him virtuous, you must take another; but do not imagine that you can bound from one road to the other without losing your way.*

* See an excellent essay on this subject by Mrs Barbauld, in *Miscellaneous Pieces in Prose*.[67]

THE EFFECT WHICH AN EARLY ASSOCIATION
OF IDEAS HAS UPON THE CHARACTER

Educated in the enervating style recommended by the writers on whom I have been animadverting; and not having a chance, from their subordinate state in society, to recover their lost ground, is it surprising that women every where appear a defect in nature? Is it surprising, when we consider what a determinate effect an early association of ideas[1] has on the character, that they neglect their understandings, and turn all their attention to their persons?

The great advantages which naturally result from storing the mind with knowledge, are obvious from the following considerations. The association of our ideas is either habitual or instantaneous; and the latter mode seems rather to depend on the original temperature of the mind than on the will. When the ideas, and matters of fact, are once taken in, they lie by for use, till some fortuitous circumstance makes the information dart into the mind with illustrative force, that has been received at very different periods of our lives. Like the lightning's flash are many recollections; one idea assimilating and explaining another, with astonishing rapidity. I do not now allude to that quick perception of truth, which is so intuitive that it baffles research, and makes us at a loss to determine whether it is reminiscence or ratiocination, lost sight of in its celerity, that opens the dark cloud. Over those instantaneous associations we have little power; for when the mind is once enlarged by excursive flights, or profound reflection, the raw materials will, in some degree, arrange themselves. The understanding, it is true, may keep us from going out of drawing when we group our thoughts, or transcribe from the imagination the warm sketches of fancy; but the animal spirits, the individual character, give the colouring. Over this subtile electric fluid,* how little power do we possess, and over it how little power can reason obtain! These fine intractable spirits appear to be the essence of genius, and beaming in its eagle eye, produce in the most eminent degree the happy energy of associating thoughts that surprise, delight, and instruct. These are the glowing minds that concentrate pictures for their fellow-creatures; forcing them to view with interest the objects reflected from the impassioned imagination, which they passed over in nature.

I must be allowed to explain myself. The generality of people cannot see or feel poetically, they want fancy, and therefore fly from solitude in search of sensible objects; but when an author lends them his eyes they can see as he saw, and be amused by images they could not select, though lying before them.

Education thus only supplies the man of genius with knowledge to give variety and contrast to his associations; but there is an habitual association of ideas, that grows 'with our growth,'² which has a great effect on the moral character of mankind; and by which a turn is given to the mind that commonly remains throughout life. So ductile is the understanding, and yet so stubborn, that the associations which depend on adventitious circumstances, during the period that the body takes to arrive at maturity, can seldom be disentangled by reason. One idea calls up another, its old associate, and memory, faithful to the first impressions, particularly when the intellectual powers are not employed to cool our sensations, retraces them with mechanical exactness.

This habitual slavery, to first impressions, has a more baneful effect on the female than the male character, because business and other dry employments of the understanding, tend to deaden the feelings and break associations that do violence to reason. But females, who are made women of when they are mere children, and brought back to childhood when they ought to

---

* I have sometimes, when inclined to laugh at materialists,³ asked whether, as the most powerful effects in nature are apparently produced by fluids, the magnetic, &c. the passions might not be fine volatile fluids that embraced humanity, keeping the more refractory elementary parts together – or whether they were simply a liquid fire that pervaded the more sluggish materials, giving them life and heat?

leave the go-cart for ever, have not sufficient strength of mind to efface the superinductions of art that have smothered nature.

Every thing that they see or hear serves to fix impressions, call forth emotions, and associate ideas, that give a sexual character to the mind. False notions of beauty and delicacy stop the growth of their limbs and produce a sickly soreness, rather than delicacy of organs; and thus weakened by being employed in unfolding instead of examining the first associations, forced on them by every surrounding object, how can they attain the vigour necessary to enable them to throw off their factitious character? – where find strength to recur to reason and rise superiour to a system of oppression, that blasts the fair promises of spring? This cruel association of ideas, which every thing conspires to twist into all their habits of thinking, or, to speak with more precision, of feeling, receives new force when they begin to act a little for themselves; for they then perceive that it is only through their address to excite emotions in men, that pleasure and power are to be obtained. Besides, the books professedly written for their instruction, which make the first impression on their minds, all inculcate the same opinions. Educated then in worse than Egyptian bondage,[4] it is unreasonable, as well as cruel, to upbraid them with faults that can scarcely be avoided, unless a degree of native vigour be supposed, that falls to the lot of very few amongst mankind.

For instance, the severest sarcasms have been levelled against the sex, and they have been ridiculed for repeating 'a set of phrases learnt by rote,' when nothing could be more natural, considering the education they receive, and that their 'highest praise is to obey, unargued'[5] – the will of man. If they be not allowed to have reason sufficient to govern their own conduct – why, all they learn – must be learned by rote! And when all their ingenuity is called forth to adjust their dress, 'a passion for a scarlet coat,' is so natural, that it never surprised me; and, allowing Pope's summary of their character to be just, 'that every woman is at heart a rake,'[6] why should they be bitterly censured for seeking a congenial mind, and preferring a rake to a man of sense?

Rakes know how to work on their sensibility, whilst the modest merit of reasonable men has, of course, less effect on their feelings, and they cannot reach the heart by the way of the understanding, because they have few sentiments in common.

It seems a little absurd to expect women to be more reasonable than men in their *likings*, and still to deny them the uncontrouled use of reason. When do men *fall-in-love* with sense? When do they, with their superiour powers and advantages, turn from the person to the mind? And how can they then expect women, who are only taught to observe behaviour, and acquire manners rather than morals, to despise what they have been all their lives labouring to attain? Where are they suddenly to find judgment enough to weigh patiently the sense of an awkward virtuous man, when his manners, of which they are made critical judges, are rebuffing, and his conversation cold and dull, because it does not consist of pretty repartees, or well turned compliments? In order to admire or esteem any thing for a continuance, we must, at least, have our curiosity excited by knowing, in some degree, what we admire; for we are unable to estimate the value of qualities and virtues above our comprehension. Such a respect, when it is felt, may be very sublime; and the confused consciousness of humility may render the dependent creature an interesting object, in some points of view; but human love must have grosser ingredients; and the person very naturally will come in for its share – and, an ample share it mostly has!

Love is, in a great degree, an arbitrary passion, and will reign, like some other stalking mischiefs, by its own authority, without deigning to reason; and it may also be easily distinguished from esteem, the foundation of friendship, because it is often excited by evanescent beauties and graces, though, to give an energy to the sentiment, something more solid must deepen their impression and set the imagination to work, to make the most fair – the first good.

Common passions are excited by common qualities. – Men look for beauty and the simper of good-humoured docility: women are captivated by easy manners; a gentleman-like man seldom fails to please them, and their thirsty ears eagerly drink the insinuating nothings of politeness, whilst they turn from the unintelligible sounds of the charmer – reason, charm he never so wisely. With respect to superficial accomplishments, the rake certainly has the advantage; and of these females can form an opinion, for it is their own ground. Rendered gay and giddy by the whole tenor of their lives, the very aspect of wisdom, or the severe graces of virtue, must have a lugubrious appearance to them; and produce a kind of restraint from which they and love, sportive child, naturally revolt. Without taste, excepting of the lighter kind, for taste is the offspring of judgment, how can they discover that true beauty and grace must arise from the play of the mind? and how can they be expected to relish in a lover what they do not, or very imperfectly, possess themselves? The sympathy that unites hearts, and invites to confidence, in them is so very faint, that it cannot take fire, and thus mount to passion. No, I repeat it, the love cherished by such minds, must have grosser fuel!

The inference is obvious; till women are led to exercise their understandings, they should not be satirized for their attachment to rakes; or even for being rakes at heart, when it appears to be the inevitable consequence of their education. They who live to please – must find their enjoyments, their happiness, in pleasure! It is a trite, yet true remark, that we never do any thing well, unless we love it for its own sake.

Supposing, however, for a moment, that women were, in some future revolution of time, to become, what I sincerely wish them to be, even love would acquire more serious dignity, and be purified in its own fires; and virtue giving true delicacy to their affections, they would turn with disgust from a rake. Reasoning then, as well as feeling, the only province of woman, at present, they might easily guard against exteriour graces, and quickly learn to despise the sensibility that had been excited and hackneyed in the ways of women, whose trade was vice; and allurements, wanton airs. They would recollect that the flame, one must use appropriated expressions, which they wished to light up, had been exhausted by lust, and that the sated appetite, losing all relish for pure and simple pleasures, could only be roused by licentious arts or variety. What satisfaction could a woman of delicacy promise herself in a union with such a man, when the very artlessness of her affection might appear insipid? Thus does Dryden describe the situation,

> —'Where love is duty, on the female side,
> On theirs mere sensual gust, and sought with surly pride.'[7]

But one grand truth women have yet to learn, though much it imports them to act accordingly. In the choice of a husband, they should not be led astray by the qualities of a lover – for a lover the husband, even supposing him to be wise and virtuous, cannot long remain.

Were women more rationally educated, could they take a more comprehensive view of things, they would be contented to love but once in their lives; and after marriage calmly let passion subside into friendship – into that tender intimacy, which is the best refuge from care; yet is built on such pure, still affections, that idle jealousies would not be allowed to disturb the discharge of the sober duties of life, or to engross the thoughts that ought to be otherwise employed. This is a state in which many men live; but few, very few women. And the difference may easily be accounted for, without recurring to a sexual character. Men, for whom we are told women were made, have too much occupied the thoughts of women; and this association has so entangled love with all their motives of action; and, to harp a little on an old string, having been solely employed either to prepare themselves to excite love, or actually putting their lessons in practice, they cannot live without love. But, when a sense of duty, or fear of shame, obliges them to restrain this pampered desire of pleasing beyond certain lengths, too far for delicacy, it is true, though far from criminality, they obstinately determine to love, I speak of the passion, their husbands to the end of the chapter – and then acting the part which they foolishly exacted from their lovers, they become abject wooers, and fond slaves.

Men of wit and fancy are often rakes; and fancy is the food of love. Such men will inspire passion. Half the sex, in its present infantine state, would pine for a Lovelace; a man so witty, so graceful, and so valiant: and can they *deserve* blame for acting according to principles so constantly inculcated? They want a lover, and protector; and behold him kneeling before them – bravery prostrate to beauty! The virtues of a husband are thus thrown by love into the back ground, and gay hopes, or lively emotions, banish reflection till the day of reckoning come; and come it surely will, to turn the sprightly lover into a surly suspicious tyrant, who contemptuously insults the very weakness he fostered. Or, supposing the rake reformed, he cannot quickly get rid of old habits. When a man of abilities is first carried away by his passions, it is necessary that sentiment and taste varnish the enormities of vice, and give a zest to brutal indulgences; but when the gloss of novelty is worn off, and pleasure palls upon the sense, lasciviousness becomes barefaced, and enjoyment only the desperate effort of weakness flying from reflection as from a legion of devils. Oh! virtue, thou art not an empty name! All that life can give – thou givest!

If much comfort cannot be expected from the friendship of a reformed rake of superiour abilities, what is the consequence when he lacketh sense, as well as principles? Verily misery, in its most hideous shape. When the habits of weak people are consolidated by time, a reformation is barely possible; and actually makes the beings miserable who have not sufficient mind to be amused by innocent pleasure; like the tradesman who retires from the hurry of business, nature presents to them only a universal blank; and the restless thoughts prey on the damped spirits.* Their reformation, as well as his retirement, actually makes them wretched because it deprives them of all employment, by quenching the hopes and fears that set in motion their sluggish minds.

If such be the force of habit; if such be the bondage of folly, how carefully ought we to guard the mind from storing up vicious associations; and equally careful should we be to cultivate the understanding, to save the poor wight from the weak dependent state of even harmless ignorance. For it is the right use of reason alone which makes us independent of every thing – excepting the unclouded Reason – 'Whose service is perfect freedom.'[8]

---

* I have frequently seen this exemplified in women whose beauty could no longer be repaired. They have retired from the noisy scenes of dissipation; but, unless they became methodists, the solitude of the select society of their family connections or acquaintance, has presented only a fearful void; consequently, nervous complaints, and all the vapourish train of idleness, rendered them quite as useless, and far more unhappy, than when they joined the giddy throng.

CHAP. VII

MODESTY. – COMPREHENSIVELY CONSIDERED, AND NOT AS A SEXUAL VIRTUE

Modesty! Sacred offspring of sensibility and reason! – true delicacy of mind! – may I unblamed presume to investigate thy nature, and trace to its covert the mild charm, that mellowing each harsh feature of a character, renders what would otherwise only inspire cold admiration – lovely! – Thou that smoothest the wrinkles of wisdom, and softenest the tone of the sublimest virtues till they all melt into humanity; – thou that spreadest the ethereal cloud that, surrounding love, heightens every beauty, it half shades, breathing those coy sweets that steal into the heart, and charm the senses – modulate for me the language of persuasive reason, till I rouse my sex from the flowery bed, on which they supinely sleep life away!

In speaking of the association of our ideas, I have noticed two distinct modes; and in defining modesty, it appears to me equally proper to discriminate that purity of mind, which is the effect of chastity, from a simplicity of character that leads us to form a just opinion of ourselves, equally distant from vanity or presumption, though by no means incompatible with a lofty consciousness of our own dignity. Modesty, in the latter signification of the term, is, that soberness of mind which teaches a man not to think more highly of himself than he ought to think, and should be distinguished from humility, because humility is a kind of self-abasement.

A modest man often conceives a great plan, and tenaciously adheres to it, conscious of his own strength, till success gives it a sanction that determines its character. Milton was not arrogant when he suffered a suggestion of judgment to escape him that proved a prophecy; nor was General Washington when he

accepted of the command of the American forces.[1] The latter
has always been characterized as a modest man; but had he been
merely humble, he would probably have shrunk back irresolute,
afraid of trusting to himself the direction of an enterprise, on
which so much depended.

A modest man is steady, an humble man timid, and a vain
one presumptuous: – this is the judgment, which the observation
of many characters, has led me to form. Jesus Christ was modest,
Moses was humble, and Peter vain.[2]

Thus, discriminating modesty from humility in one case, I
do not mean to confound it with bashfulness in the other.
Bashfulness, in fact, is so distinct from modesty, that the most
bashful lass, or raw country lout, often become the most impudent; for their bashfulness being merely the instinctive timidity
of ignorance, custom soon changes it into assurance.*

The shameless behaviour of the prostitutes, who infest the
streets of this metropolis, raising alternate emotions of pity and
disgust, may serve to illustrate this remark. They trample on
virgin bashfulness with a sort of bravado, and glorying in their
shame, become more audaciously lewd than men, however
depraved, to whom this sexual quality has not been gratuitously
granted, ever appear to be. But these poor ignorant wretches
never had any modesty to lose, when they consigned themselves
to infamy; for modesty is a virtue, not a quality. No, they were
only bashful, shame-faced innocents; and losing their innocence,
their shame-facedness was rudely brushed off; a virtue would
have left some vestiges in the mind, had it been sacrificed to
passion, to make us respect the grand ruin.

*   'Such is the country-maiden's fright,
                    When first a red-coat is in sight;
                    Behind the door she hides her face;
                    Next time at distance eyes the lace:
                    She now can all his terrors stand,
                    Nor from his squeeze withdraws her hand.
                    She plays familiar in his arms,
                    And ev'ry soldier hath his charms;
                    From tent to tent she spreads her flame;
                    For custom conquers fear and shame.'

                                                Gay.[3]

Purity of mind, or that genuine delicacy, which is the only virtuous support of chastity, is near akin to that refinement of humanity, which never resides in any but cultivated minds. It is something nobler than innocence, it is the delicacy of reflection, and not the coyness of ignorance. The reserve of reason, which, like habitual cleanliness, is seldom seen in any great degree, unless the soul is active, may easily be distinguished from rustic shyness or wanton skittishness; and, so far from being incompatible with knowledge, it is its fairest fruit. What a gross idea of modesty had the writer of the following remark! 'The lady who asked the question whether women may be instructed in the modern system of botany, consistently with female delicacy? – was accused of ridiculous prudery: nevertheless, if she had proposed the question to me, I should certainly have answered – They cannot.'[4] Thus is the fair book of knowledge to be shut with an everlasting seal! On reading similar passages I have reverentially lifted up my eyes and heart to Him who liveth for ever and ever, and said, O my Father, hast Thou by the very constitution of her nature forbid Thy child to seek Thee in the fair forms of truth? And, can her soul be sullied by the knowledge that awfully calls her to Thee?

I have then philosophically pursued these reflections till I inferred that those women who have most improved their reason must have the most modesty – though a dignified sedateness of deportment may have succeeded the playful, bewitching bashfulness of youth.*

And thus have I argued. To render chastity the virtue from which unsophisticated modesty will naturally flow, the attention should be called away from employments which only exercise the sensibility; and the heart made to beat time to humanity, rather than to throb with love. The woman who has dedicated a considerable portion of her time to pursuits purely intellectual, and whose affections have been exercised by humane plans of usefulness, must have more purity of mind, as a natural consequence, than the ignorant beings whose time and thoughts

---

* Modesty is the graceful calm virtue of maturity; bashfulness, the charm of vivacious youth.

have been occupied by gay pleasures or schemes to conquer hearts.* The regulation of the behaviour is not modesty, though those who study rules of decorum are, in general, termed modest women. Make the heart clean, let it expand and feel for all that is human, instead of being narrowed by selfish passions; and let the mind frequently contemplate subjects that exercise the understanding, without heating the imagination, and artless modesty will give the finishing touches to the picture.

She who can discern the dawn of immortality, in the streaks that shoot athwart the misty night of ignorance, promising a clearer day, will respect, as a sacred temple, the body that enshrines such an improvable soul. True love, likewise, spreads this kind of mysterious sanctity round the beloved object, making the lover most modest when in her presence.† So reserved is affection that, receiving or returning personal endearments, it wishes, not only to shun the human eye, as a kind of profanation; but to diffuse an encircling cloudy obscurity to shut out even the saucy sparkling sunbeams. Yet, that affection does not deserve the epithet of chaste, which does not receive a sublime gloom of tender melancholy, that allows the mind for a moment to stand still and enjoy the present satisfaction, when a consciousness of the Divine presence is felt – for this must ever be the food of joy!

As I have always been fond of tracing to its source in nature any prevailing custom, I have frequently thought that it was a sentiment of affection for whatever had touched the person of

---

* I have conversed, as man with man, with medical men, on anatomical subjects; and compared the proportions of the human body with artists – yet such modesty did I meet with, that I was never reminded by word or look of my sex, of the absurd rules which make modesty a pharisaical cloak[5] of weakness. And I am persuaded that in the pursuit of knowledge women would never be insulted by sensible men, and rarely by men of any description, if they did not by mock modesty remind them that they were women: actuated by the same spirit as the Portugueze ladies, who would think their charms insulted, if, when left alone with a man, he did not, at least, attempt to be grossly familiar with their persons. Men are not always men in the company of women, nor would women always remember that they are women, if they were allowed to acquire more understanding.

† Male or female; for the world contains many modest men.

an absent or lost friend, which gave birth to that respect for relicks, so much abused by selfish priests. Devotion, or love, may be allowed to hallow the garments as well as the person; for the lover must want fancy who has not a sort of sacred respect for the glove or slipper of his mistress. He could not confound them with vulgar things of the same kind. This fine sentiment, perhaps, would not bear to be analyzed by the experimental philosopher – but of such stuff is human rapture made up! – A shadowy phantom glides before us, obscuring every other object; yet when the soft cloud is grasped, the form melts into common air, leaving a solitary void, or sweet perfume, stolen from the violet, that memory long holds dear. But, I have tripped unawares on fairy ground, feeling the balmy gale of spring stealing on me, though November frowns.

As a sex, women are more chaste than men, and as modesty is the effect of chastity, they may deserve to have this virtue ascribed to them in rather an appropriated sense; yet, I must be allowed to add an hesitating if: – for I doubt whether chastity will produce modesty, though it may propriety of conduct, when it is merely a respect for the opinion of the world,* and when coquetry and the lovelorn tales of novelists employ the thoughts. Nay, from experience, and reason, I should be led to expect to meet with more modesty amongst men than women, simply because men exercise their understandings more than women.

But, with respect to propriety of behaviour, excepting one class of females, women have evidently the advantage. What can be more disgusting than that impudent dross of gallantry, thought so manly, which makes many men stare insultingly at every female they meet? Can it be termed respect for the sex? No, this loose behaviour shews such habitual depravity, such weakness of mind, that it is vain to expect much public or private virtue, till both men and women grow more modest – till men, curbing a sensual fondness for the sex, or an affectation of manly assurance, more properly speaking, impudence, treat

---

* The immodest behaviour of many married women, who are nevertheless faithful to their husbands' beds, will illustrate this remark.

each other with respect – unless appetite or passion give the
tone, peculiar to it, to their behaviour. I mean even personal
respect – the modest respect of humanity, and fellow-feeling
– not the libidinous mockery of gallantry, nor the insolent
condescension of protectorship.

To carry the observation still further, modesty must heartily
disclaim, and refuse to dwell with that debauchery of mind,
which leads a man coolly to bring forward, without a blush,
indecent allusions, or obscene witticisms, in the presence of a
fellow creature; women are now out of the question, for then it
is brutality. Respect for man, as man, is the foundation of every
noble sentiment. How much more modest is the libertine who
obeys the call of appetite or fancy, than the lewd joker who sets
the table in a roar!

This is one of the many instances in which the sexual distinction respecting modesty has proved fatal to virtue and happiness.
It is, however, carried still further, and woman, weak woman!
made by her education the slave of sensibility, is required, on
the most trying occasions, to resist that sensibility. 'Can any
thing,' says Knox, 'be more absurd than keeping women in a
state of ignorance, and yet so vehemently to insist on their
resisting temptation?'[6] – Thus when virtue or honour make it
proper to check a passion, the burden is thrown on the weaker
shoulders, contrary to reason and true modesty, which, at least,
should render the self-denial mutual, to say nothing of the
generosity of bravery, supposed to be a manly virtue.

In the same strain runs Rousseau's and Dr Gregory's advice
respecting modesty, strangely miscalled! for they both desire a
wife to leave it in doubt whether sensibility or weakness led her
to her husband's arms. – The woman is immodest who can let
the shadow of such a doubt remain in her husband's mind a
moment.

But to state the subject in a different light. – The want of
modesty, which I principally deplore as subversive of morality,
arises from the state of warfare so strenuously supported by
voluptuous men as the very essence of modesty, though, in fact,
its bane; because it is a refinement on lust, that men fall into
who have not sufficient virtue to relish the innocent pleasures

of love. A man of delicacy carries his notions of modesty still further, for neither weakness nor sensibility will gratify him – he looks for affection.

Again; men boast of their triumphs over women, what do they boast of? Truly the creature of sensibility was surprised by her sensibility into folly – into vice;* and the dreadful reckoning falls heavily on her own weak head, when reason wakes. For where art thou to find comfort, forlorn and disconsolate one? He who ought to have directed thy reason, and supported thy weakness, has betrayed thee! In a dream of passion thou consented to wander through flowery lawns, and heedlessly stepping over the precipice to which thy guide, instead of guarding, lured thee, thou startest from thy dream only to face a sneering, frowning world, and to find thyself alone in a waste, for he that triumphed in thy weakness is now pursuing new conquests; but for thee – there is no redemption on this side the grave! – And what resource hast thou in an enervated mind to raise a sinking heart?

But, if the sexes be really to live in a state of warfare, if nature have pointed it out, let them act nobly, or let pride whisper to them, that the victory is mean when they merely vanquish sensibility. The real conquest is that over affection not taken by surprise – when, like Heloisa, a woman gives up all the world, deliberately, for love. I do not now consider the wisdom or virtue of such a sacrifice, I only contend that it was a sacrifice to affection, and not merely to sensibility, though she had her share. – And I must be allowed to call her a modest woman, before I dismiss this part of the subject, by saying, that till men are more chaste women will be immodest. Where, indeed, could modest women find husbands from whom they would not continually turn with disgust? Modesty must be equally cultivated by both sexes, or it will ever remain a sickly hot-house plant, whilst the affectation of it, the fig leaf borrowed by wantonness, may give a zest to voluptuous enjoyments.

Men will probably still insist that woman ought to have more modesty than man; but it is not dispassionate reasoners who

---

* The poor moth fluttering round a candle, burns its wings.

will most earnestly oppose my opinion. No, they are the men of fancy, the favourites of the sex, who outwardly respect and inwardly despise the weak creatures whom they thus sport with. They cannot submit to resign the highest sensual gratification, nor even to relish the epicurism of virtue – self-denial.

To take another view of the subject, confining my remarks to women.

The ridiculous falsities* which are told to children, from mistaken notions of modesty, tend very early to inflame their imaginations and set their little minds to work, respecting subjects, which nature never intended they should think of till the body arrived at some degree of maturity; then the passions naturally begin to take place of the senses, as instruments to unfold the understanding, and form the moral character.

In nurseries, and boarding-schools, I fear, girls are first spoiled; particularly in the latter. A number of girls sleep in the same room, and wash together. And, though I should be sorry to contaminate an innocent creature's mind by instilling false delicacy, or those indecent prudish notions, which early cautions respecting the other sex naturally engender, I should be very anxious to prevent their acquiring nasty, or immodest habits; and as many girls have learned very nasty tricks, from ignorant servants, the mixing them thus indiscriminately together, is very improper.

To say the truth women are, in general, too familiar with each other, which leads to that gross degree of familiarity that so frequently renders the marriage state unhappy. Why in the name of decency are sisters, female intimates, or ladies and their waiting-women, to be so grossly familiar as to forget the respect

* Children very early see cats with their kittens, birds with their young ones, &c. Why then are they not to be told that their mothers carry and nourish them in the same way? As there would then be no appearance of mystery they would never think of the subject more. Truth may always be told to children, if it be told gravely; but it is the immodesty of affected modesty, that does all the mischief; and this smoke heats the imagination by vainly endeavouring to obscure certain objects. If, indeed, children could be kept entirely from improper company, we should never allude to any such subjects; but as this is impossible, it is best to tell them the truth, especially as such information, not interesting them, will make no impression on their imagination.

which one human creature owes to another? That squeamish delicacy which shrinks from the most disgusting offices when affection* or humanity lead us to watch at a sick pillow, is despicable. But, why women in health should be more familiar with each other than men are, when they boast of their superior delicacy, is a solecism in manners which I could never solve.

In order to preserve health and beauty, I should earnestly recommend frequent ablutions, to dignify my advice that it may not offend the fastidious ear; and, by example, girls ought to be taught to wash and dress alone, without any distinction of rank; and if custom should make them require some little assistance, let them not require it till that part of the business is over which ought never to be done before a fellow-creature; because it is an insult to the majesty of human nature. Not on the score of modesty, but decency; for the care which some modest women take, making at the same time a display of that care, not to let their legs be seen, is as childish as immodest.†

I could proceed still further, till I animadverted on some still more nasty customs, which men never fall into. Secrets are told – where silence ought to reign; and that regard to cleanliness, which some religious sects have, perhaps, carried too far, especially the Essenes,[7] amongst the Jews, by making that an insult to God which is only an insult to humanity, is violated in a beastly manner. How can *delicate* women obtrude on notice that part of the animal œconomy, which is so very disgusting? And is it not very rational to conclude, that the women who have not been taught to respect the human nature of their own sex, in these particulars, will not long respect the mere difference of sex in their husbands? After their maidenish bashfulness is once lost, I, in fact, have generally observed, that women fall into old habits; and treat their husbands as they did their sisters or female acquaintance.

---

* Affection would rather make one choose to perform these offices, to spare the delicacy of a friend, by still keeping a veil over them, for the personal helplessness, produced by sickness, is of an humbling nature.

† I remember to have met with a sentence, in a book of education, that made me smile. 'It would be needless to caution you against putting your hand, by chance, under your neck-handkerchief; for a modest woman never did so!'

Besides, women from necessity, because their minds are not cultivated, have recourse very often to what I familiarly term bodily wit; and their intimacies are of the same kind. In short, with respect to both mind and body, they are too intimate. That decent personal reserve which is the foundation of dignity of character, must be kept up between woman and woman, or their minds will never gain strength or modesty.

On this account also, I object to many females being shut up together in nurseries, schools, or convents. I cannot recollect without indignation, the jokes and hoiden tricks, which knots of young women indulge themselves in, when in my youth[8] accident threw me, an awkward rustic, in their way. They were almost on a par with the double meanings, which shake the convivial table when the glass has circulated freely. But, it is vain to attempt to keep the heart pure, unless the head is furnished with ideas, and set to work to compare them, in order to acquire judgment, by generalizing simple ones; and modesty, by making the understanding damp the sensibility.

It may be thought that I lay too great a stress on personal reserve; but it is ever the handmaid of modesty. So that were I to name the graces that ought to adorn beauty, I should instantly exclaim, cleanliness, neatness, and personal reserve. It is obvious, I suppose, that the reserve I mean has nothing sexual in it, and that I think it *equally* necessary in both sexes. So necessary, indeed, is that reserve and cleanliness which indolent women too often neglect, that I will venture to affirm that when two or three women live in the same house, the one will be most respected by the male part of the family, who reside with them, leaving love entirely out of the question, who pays this kind of habitual respect to her person.

When domestic friends meet in a morning, there will naturally prevail an affectionate seriousness, especially, if each look forward to the discharge of daily duties; and it may be reckoned fanciful, but this sentiment has frequently risen spontaneously in my mind, I have been pleased after breathing the sweet-bracing morning air, to see the same kind of freshness in the countenances I particularly loved; I was glad to see them braced, as it were, for the day, and ready to run their course with the sun.

The greetings of affection in the morning are by these means more respectful than the familiar tenderness which frequently prolongs the evening talk. Nay, I have often felt hurt, not to say disgusted, when a friend has appeared, whom I parted with full dressed the evening before, with her clothes huddled on, because she chose to indulge herself in bed till the last moment.

Domestic affection can only be kept alive by these neglected attentions; yet if men and women took half as much pains to dress habitually neat, as they do to ornament, or rather to disfigure, their persons, much would be done towards the attainment of purity of mind. But women only dress to gratify men of gallantry; for the lover is always best pleased with the simple garb that fits close to the shape. There is an impertinence in ornaments that rebuffs affection; because love always clings round the idea of home.

As a sex, women are habitually indolent; and every thing tends to make them so. I do not forget the spurts of activity which sensibility produces; but as these flights of feelings only increase the evil, they are not to be confounded with the slow, orderly walk of reason. So great in reality is their mental and bodily indolence, that till their body be strengthened and their understanding enlarged by active exertions, there is little reason to expect that modesty will take place of bashfulness. They may find it prudent to assume its semblance; but the fair veil will only be worn on gala days.

Perhaps, there is not a virtue that mixes so kindly with every other as modesty. – It is the pale moon-beam that renders more interesting every virtue it softens, giving mild grandeur to the contracted horizon. Nothing can be more beautiful than the poetical fiction, which makes Diana with her silver crescent, the goddess of chastity.[9] I have sometimes thought, that wandering with sedate step in some lonely recess, a modest dame of antiquity must have felt a glow of conscious dignity when, after contemplating the soft shadowy landscape, she has invited with placid fervour the mild reflection of her sister's beams to turn to her chaste bosom.

A Christian has still nobler motives to incite her to preserve her chastity and acquire modesty, for her body has been called the Temple of the living God;[10] of that God who requires more than modesty of mien. His eye searcheth the heart; and let her remember, that if she hope to find favour in the sight of purity itself, her chastity must be founded on modesty, and not on worldly prudence; or verily a good reputation will be her only reward; for that awful intercourse, that sacred communication, which virtue establishes between man and his Maker, must give rise to the wish of being pure as he is pure!

After the foregoing remarks, it is almost superfluous to add, that I consider all those feminine airs of maturity, which succeed bashfulness, to which truth is sacrificed, to secure the heart of a husband, or rather to force him to be still a lover when nature would, had she not been interrupted in her operations, have made love give place to friendship, as immodest. The tenderness which a man will feel for the mother of his children is an excellent substitute for the ardour of unsatisfied passion; but to prolong that ardour it is indelicate, not to say immodest, for women to feign an unnatural coldness of constitution. Women as well as men ought to have the common appetites and passions of their nature, they are only brutal when unchecked by reason: but the obligation to check them is the duty of mankind, not a sexual duty. Nature, in these respects, may safely be left to herself; let women only acquire knowledge and humanity, and love will teach them modesty.* There is no need of falsehoods, disgusting as futile, for studied rules of behaviour only impose on shallow observers; a man of sense soon sees through, and despises the affectation.

The behaviour of young people, to each other, as men and women, is the last thing that should be thought of in education. In fact, behaviour in most circumstances is now so much thought of, that simplicity of character is rarely to be seen: yet, if men were only anxious to cultivate each virtue, and let it take root firmly in the mind, the grace resulting from it, its natural exteri-

---

* The behaviour of many newly married women has often disgusted me. They seem anxious never to let their husbands forget the privilege of marriage; and to find no pleasure in his society unless he is acting the lover. Short, indeed, must be the reign of love, when the flame is thus constantly blown up, without its receiving any solid fuel!

our mark, would soon strip affectation of its flaunting plumes; because, fallacious as unstable, is the conduct that is not founded upon truth!

Would ye, O my sisters, really possess modesty, ye must remember that the possession of virtue, of any denomination, is incompatible with ignorance and vanity! ye must acquire that soberness of mind, which the exercise of duties, and the pursuit of knowledge, alone inspire, or ye will still remain in a doubtful dependent situation, and only be loved whilst ye are fair! The downcast eye, the rosy blush, the retiring grace, are all proper in their season; but modesty, being the child of reason, cannot long exist with the sensibility that is not tempered by reflection. Besides, when love, even innocent love, is the whole employ of your lives, your hearts will be too soft to afford modesty that tranquil retreat, where she delights to dwell, in close union with humanity.

It has long since occurred to me that advice respecting behaviour, and all the various modes of preserving a good reputation, which have been so strenuously inculcated on the female
world, were specious poisons, that incrusting morality eat away
the substance. And, that this measuring of shadows produced a
false calculation, because their length depends so much on the
height of the sun, and other adventitious circumstances.

Whence arises the easy fallacious behaviour of a courtier? From
his situation, undoubtedly: for standing in need of dependents,
he is obliged to learn the art of denying without giving offence,
and, of evasively feeding hope with the chameleon's food:[1] thus
does politeness sport with truth, and eating away the sincerity and
humanity natural to man, produce the fine gentleman.

Women likewise acquire, from a supposed necessity, an
equally artificial mode of behaviour. Yet truth is not with impunity to be sported with, for the practised dissembler, at last,
become the dupe of his own arts, loses that sagacity, which has
been justly termed common sense; namely, a quick perception
of common truths: which are constantly received as such by the
unsophisticated mind, though it might not have had sufficient
energy to discover them itself, when obscured by local prejudices. The greater number of people take their opinions on trust
to avoid the trouble of exercising their own minds, and these
indolent beings naturally adhere to the letter, rather than the
spirit of a law, divine or human. 'Women,' says some author, I
cannot recollect who, 'mind not what only heaven sees.' Why,
indeed, should they? it is the eye of man that they have been
taught to dread – and if they can lull their Argus to sleep,[2] they

seldom think of heaven or themselves, because their reputation is safe; and it is reputation, not chastity and all its fair train, that they are employed to keep free from spot, not as a virtue, but to preserve their station in the world.

To prove the truth of this remark, I need only advert to the intrigues of married women, particularly in high life, and in countries where women are suitably married, according to their respective ranks, by their parents. If an innocent girl become a prey to love, she is degraded for ever, though her mind was not polluted by the arts which married women, under the convenient cloke of marriage, practise; nor has she violated any duty – but the duty of respecting herself. The married woman, on the contrary, breaks a most sacred engagement, and becomes a cruel mother when she is a false and faithless wife. If her husband have still an affection for her, the arts which she must practise to deceive him, will render her the most contemptible of human beings; and, at any rate, the contrivances necessary to preserve appearances, will keep her mind in that childish, or vicious, tumult, which destroys all its energy. Besides, in time, like those people who habitually take cordials to raise their spirits, she will want an intrigue to give life to her thoughts, having lost all relish for pleasures that are not highly seasoned by hope or fear.

Sometimes married women act still more audaciously; I will mention an instance.

A woman of quality, notorious for her gallantries, though as she still lived with her husband, nobody chose to place her in the class where she ought to have been placed, made a point of treating with the most insulting contempt a poor timid creature, abashed by a sense of her former weakness, whom a neighbouring gentleman had seduced and afterwards married. This woman had actually confounded virtue with reputation; and, I do believe, valued herself on the propriety of her behaviour before marriage, though when once settled to the satisfaction of her family, she and her lord were equally faithless, – so that the half alive heir to an immense estate came from heaven knows where![3]

To view this subject in another light.

I have known a number of women who, if they did not love their husbands, loved nobody else, give themselves entirely up to vanity and dissipation, neglecting every domestic duty; nay, even squandering away all the money which should have been saved for their helpless younger children, yet have plumed themselves on their unsullied reputation, as if the whole compass of their duty as wives and mothers was only to preserve it. Whilst other indolent women, neglecting every personal duty, have thought that they deserved their husbands' affection, because, forsooth, they acted in this respect with propriety.

Weak minds are always fond of resting in the ceremonials of duty, but morality offers much simpler motives; and it were to be wished that superficial moralists had said less respecting behaviour, and outward observances, for unless virtue, of any kind, be built on knowledge, it will only produce a kind of insipid decency. Respect for the opinion of the world, has, however, been termed the principal duty of woman in the most express words, for Rousseau declares, 'that reputation is no less indispensable than chastity.' 'A man,' adds he, 'secure in his own good conduct, depends only on himself, and may brave the public opinion: but a woman, in behaving well, performs but half her duty; as what is thought of her, is as important to her as what she really is. It follows hence, that the system of a woman's education should, in this respect, be directly contrary to that of ours. Opinion is the grave of virtue among the men; but its throne among women.'[4] It is strictly logical to infer that the virtue that rests on opinion is merely worldly, and that it is the virtue of a being to whom reason has been denied. But, even with respect to the opinion of the world, I am convinced that this class of reasoners are mistaken.

This regard for reputation, independent of its being one of the natural rewards of virtue, however, took its rise from a cause that I have already deplored as the grand source of female depravity, the impossibility of regaining respectability by a return to virtue, though men preserve theirs during the indulgence of vice. It was natural for women then to endeavour to preserve what once lost – was lost for ever, till this care swallowing up every other care, reputation for chastity, became the one thing needful to the sex. But vain is the scrupulosity of ignorance, for neither religion nor virtue, when they reside in the heart, require such a puerile attention to mere ceremonies, because the behaviour must, upon the whole, be proper, when the motive is pure.

To support my opinion I can produce very respectable authority; and the authority of a cool reasoner ought to have weight to enforce consideration, though not to establish a sentiment. Speaking of the general laws of morality, Dr Smith observes, – 'That by some very extraordinary and unlucky circumstance, a good man may come to be suspected of a crime of which he was altogether incapable, and upon that account be most unjustly exposed for the remaining part of his life to the horror and aversion of mankind. By an accident of this kind he may be said to lose his all, notwithstanding his integrity and justice, in the same manner as a cautious man, notwithstanding his utmost circumspection, may be ruined by an earthquake or an inundation. Accidents of the first kind, however, are perhaps still more rare, and still more contrary to the common course of things than those of the second; and it still remains true, that the practice of truth, justice, and humanity, is a certain and almost infallible method of acquiring what those virtues chiefly aim at, the confidence and love of those we live with. A person may be easily misrepresented with regard to a particular action; but it is scarce possible that he should be so with regard to the general tenor of his conduct. An innocent man may be believed to have done wrong: this, however, will rarely happen. On the contrary, the established opinion of the innocence of his manners will often lead us to absolve him where he has really been in the fault, notwithstanding very strong presumptions.'[5]

I perfectly coincide in opinion with this writer, for I verily believe that few of either sex were ever despised for certain vices without deserving to be despised. I speak not of the calumny of the moment, which hovers over a character, like one of the dense morning fogs of November, over this metropolis, till it gradually subsides before the common light of day, I only contend that the daily conduct of the majority prevails to stamp their character with the impression of truth. Quietly does the clear light, shining day after day, refute the ignorant surmise, or malicious tale, which has thrown dirt on a pure character. A false light distorted, for a short time, its shadow – reputation;

but it seldom fails to become just when the cloud is dispersed
that produced the mistake in vision.

Many people, undoubtedly, in several respects obtain a better
reputation than, strictly speaking, they deserve; for unremitting
industry will mostly reach its goal in all races. They who only
strive for this paltry prize, like the Pharisees, who prayed at the
corners of streets, to be seen of men,[6] verily obtain the reward
they seek; for the heart of man cannot be read by man! Still the
fair fame that is naturally reflected by good actions, when the
man is only employed to direct his steps aright, regardless of
the lookers-on, is, in general, not only more true, but more sure.

There are, it is true, trials when the good man must appeal to
God from the injustice of man; and amidst the whining candour
or hissings of envy, erect a pavilion in his own mind to retire to
till the rumour be overpast; nay, the darts of undeserved censure
may pierce an innocent tender bosom through with many sorrows; but these are all exceptions to general rules. And it is
according to common laws that human behaviour ought to be
regulated. The eccentric orbit of the comet never influences
astronomical calculations respecting the invariable order established in the motion of the principal bodies of the solar system.

I will then venture to affirm, that after a man is arrived at
maturity, the general outline of his character in the world is just,
allowing for the before-mentioned exceptions to the rule. I do
not say that a prudent, worldly-wise man, with only negative
virtues and qualities, may not sometimes obtain a smoother
reputation than a wiser or a better man. So far from it, that I
am apt to conclude from experience, that where the virtue of
two people is nearly equal, the most negative character will be
liked best by the world at large, whilst the other may have
more friends in private life. But the hills and dales, clouds and
sunshine, conspicuous in the virtues of great men, set off each
other; and though they afford envious weakness a fairer mark
to shoot at, the real character will still work its way to light,
though bespattered by weak affection, or ingenious malice.*

---

* I allude to various biographical writings, but particularly to Boswell's Life
of Johnson.[7]

With respect to that anxiety to preserve a reputation hardly earned, which leads sagacious people to analyze it, I shall not make the obvious comment; but I am afraid that morality is very insidiously undermined, in the female world, by the attention being turned to the shew instead of the substance. A simple thing is thus made strangely complicated; nay, sometimes virtue and its shadow are set at variance. We should never, perhaps, have heard of Lucretia,[8] had she died to preserve her chastity instead of her reputation. If we really deserve our own good opinion we shall commonly be respected in the world; but if we pant after higher improvement and higher attainments, it is not sufficient to view ourselves as we suppose that we are viewed by others, though this has been ingeniously argued, as the foundation of our moral sentiments.* Because each by-stander may have his own prejudices, beside the prejudices of his age or country. We should rather endeavour to view ourselves as we suppose that Being views us who seeth each thought ripen into action, and whose judgment never swerves from the eternal rule of right. Righteous are all his judgments – just as merciful!

The humble mind that seeketh to find favour in His sight, and calmly examines its conduct when only His presence is felt, will seldom form a very erroneous opinion of its own virtues. During the still hour of self-collection the angry brow of offended justice will be fearfully deprecrated, or the tie which draws man to the Deity will be recognized in the pure sentiment of reverential adoration, that swells the heart without exciting any tumultuous emotions. In these solemn moments man discovers the germ of those vices, which like the Java tree[9] shed a pestiferous vapour around – death is in the shade! and he perceives them without abhorrence, because he feels himself drawn by some cord of love to all his fellow-creatures, for whose follies he is anxious to find every extenuation in their nature – in himself. If I, he may thus argue, who exercise my own mind, and have been refined by tribulation, find the serpent's egg[10] in some fold of my heart, and crush it with difficulty, shall not I pity those who have stamped with less vigour, or who have heedlessly nurtured

* Smith.[11]

the insidious reptile till it poisoned the vital stream it sucked? Can I, conscious of my secret sins, throw off my fellow-creatures, and calmly see them drop into the chasm of perdition, that yawns to receive them. – No! no! The agonized heart will cry with suffocating impatience – I too am a man! and have vices, hid, perhaps, from human eye, that bend me to the dust before God, and loudly tell me, when all is mute, that we are formed of the same earth, and breathe the same element. Humanity thus rises naturally out of humility, and twists the cords of love that in various convolutions entangle the heart.

This sympathy extends still further, till a man well pleased observes force in arguments that do not carry conviction to his own bosom, and he gladly places in the fairest light, to himself, the shews of reason that have led others astray, rejoiced to find some reason in all the errors of man; though before convinced that he who rules the day makes his sun to shine on all. Yet, shaking hands thus as it were with corruption, one foot on earth, the other with bold stride mounts to heaven, and claims kindred with superiour natures. Virtues, unobserved by man, drop their balmy fragrance at this cool hour, and the thirsty land, refreshed by the pure streams of comfort that suddenly gush out, is crowned with smiling verdure; this is the living green on which that eye may look with complacency that is too pure to behold iniquity!

But my spirits flag; and I must silently indulge the reverie these reflections lead to, unable to describe the sentiments, that have calmed my soul, when watching the rising sun, a soft shower drizzling through the leaves of neighbouring trees, seemed to fall on my languid, yet tranquil spirits, to cool the heart that had been heated by the passions which reason laboured to tame.

The leading principles which run through all my disquisitions, would render it unnecessary to enlarge on this subject, if a constant attention to keep the varnish of the character fresh, and in good condition, were not often inculcated as the sum total of female duty; if rules to regulate the behaviour, and to preserve the reputation, did not too frequently supersede moral obligations. But, with respect to reputation, the attention is confined to a single virtue – chastity. If the honour of a woman, as it is absurdly called, be safe, she may neglect every social duty; nay, ruin her family by gaming and extravagance; yet still present a shameless front – for truly she is an honourable woman!

Mrs Macaulay has justly observed, that 'there is but one fault which a woman of honour may not commit with impunity.' She then justly and humanely adds – 'This has given rise to the trite and foolish observation, that the first fault against chastity in woman has a radical power to deprave the character. But no such frail beings come out of the hands of nature. The human mind is built of nobler materials than to be easily corrupted; and with all their disadvantages of situation and education, women seldom become entirely abandoned till they are thrown into a state of desperation, by the venomous rancour of their own sex.'[12]

But, in proportion as this regard for the reputation of chastity is prized by women, it is despised by men: and the two extremes are equally destructive to morality.

Men are certainly more under the influence of their appetites than women; and their appetites are more depraved by unbridled indulgence and the fastidious contrivances of satiety. Luxury has introduced a refinement in eating, that destroys the constitution; and, a degree of gluttony which is so beastly, that a perception of seemliness of behaviour must be worn out before one being could eat immoderately in the presence of another, and afterwards complain of the oppression that his intemperance naturally produced. Some women, particularly French women, have also lost a sense of decency in this respect; for they will talk very calmly of an indigestion. It were to be wished that idleness was not allowed to generate, on the rank soil of wealth, those swarms of summer insects that feed on putrefaction, we should not then be disgusted by the sight of such brutal excesses.

There is one rule relative to behaviour that, I think, ought to regulate every other; and it is simply to cherish such an habitual respect for mankind as may prevent us from disgusting a fellow-creature for the sake of a present indulgence. The shameful indolence of many married women, and others a little advanced in life, frequently leads them to sin against delicacy. For, though convinced that the person is the band of union between the sexes, yet, how often do they from sheer indolence, or, to enjoy some trifling indulgence, disgust?

The depravity of the appetite which brings the sexes together, has had a still more fatal effect. Nature must ever be the standard of taste, the gauge of appetite – yet how grossly is nature insulted by the voluptuary. Leaving the refinements of love out of the question; nature, by making the gratification of an appetite, in this respect, as well as every other, a natural and imperious law to preserve the species, exalts the appetite, and mixes a little mind and affection with a sensual gust. The feelings of a parent mingling with an instinct merely animal, give it dignity; and the man and woman often meeting on account of the child, a mutual interest and affection is excited by the exercise of a common sympathy. Women then having necessarily some duty to fulfil, more noble than to adorn their persons, would not contentedly be the slaves of casual lust; which is now the situation of a very considerable number who are, literally speaking, standing dishes to which every glutton may have access.

I may be told that great as this enormity is, it only affects a devoted part of the sex – devoted for the salvation of the rest. But, false as every assertion might easily be proved, that recommends the sanctioning a small evil to produce a greater good; the mischief does not stop here, for the moral character, and peace of mind, of the chaster part of the sex, is undermined by the conduct of the very women to whom they allow no refuge from guilt: whom they inexorably consign to the exercise of arts that lure their husbands from them, debauch their sons, and force them, let not modest women start, to assume, in some degree, the same character themselves. For I will venture to assert, that all the causes of female weakness, as well as depravity, which I have already enlarged on, branch out of one grand cause – want of chastity in men.

This intemperance, so prevalent, depraves the appetite to such a degree, that a wanton stimulus is necessary to rouse it; but the parental design of nature is forgotten, and the mere person, and that for a moment, alone engrosses the thoughts. So voluptuous, indeed, often grows the lustful prowler, that he refines on female softness. Something more soft than woman[13] is then sought for;

till, in Italy and Portugal, men attend the levees of equivocal beings, to sigh for more than female languor.

To satisfy this genus of men, women are made systematically voluptuous, and though they may not all carry their libertinism to the same height, yet this heartless intercourse with the sex, which they allow themselves, depraves both sexes, because the taste of men is vitiated; and women, of all classes, naturally square their behaviour to gratify the taste by which they obtain pleasure and power. Women becoming, consequently, weaker, in mind and body, than they ought to be, were one of the grand ends of their being taken into the account, that of bearing and nursing children, have not sufficient strength to discharge the first duty of a mother; and sacrificing to lasciviousness the parental affection, that ennobles instinct, either destroy the embryo in the womb, or cast it off when born. Nature in every thing demands respect, and those who violate her laws seldom violate them with impunity. The weak enervated women who particularly catch the attention of libertines, are unfit to be mothers, though they may conceive; so that the rich sensualist, who has rioted among women, spreading depravity and misery, when he wishes to perpetuate his name, receives from his wife only an half-formed being that inherits both its father's and mother's weakness.

Contrasting the humanity of the present age with the barbarism of antiquity, great stress has been laid on the savage custom of exposing the children whom their parents could not maintain;[14] whilst the man of sensibility, who thus, perhaps, complains, by his promiscuous amours produces a most destructive barrenness and contagious flagitiousness of manners. Surely nature never intended that women, by satisfying an appetite, should frustrate the very purpose for which it was implanted?

I have before observed, that men ought to maintain the women whom they have seduced; this would be one means of reforming female manners, and stopping an abuse that has an equally fatal effect on population and morals. Another, no less obvious, would be to turn the attention of woman to the real virtue of chastity; for to little respect has that woman a claim, on the score of modesty, though her reputation may be white as the driven snow, who smiles on the libertine whilst she spurns the victims of his lawless appetites and their own folly.

Besides, she has a taint of the same folly, pure as she esteems herself, when she studiously adorns her person only to be seen by men, to excite respectful sighs, and all the idle homage of what is called innocent gallantry. Did women really respect virtue for its own sake, they would not seek for a compensation in vanity, for the self-denial which they are obliged to practise to preserve their reputation, nor would they associate with men who set reputation at defiance.

The two sexes mutually corrupt and improve each other. This I believe to be an indisputable truth, extending it to every virtue. Chastity, modesty, public spirit, and all the noble train of virtues, on which social virtue and happiness are built, should be understood and cultivated by all mankind, or they will be cultivated to little effect. And, instead of furnishing the vicious or idle with a pretext for violating some sacred duty, by terming it a sexual one, it would be wiser to shew that nature has not made any difference, for that the unchaste man doubly defeats the purpose of nature, by rendering women barren, and destroying his own constitution, though he avoids the shame that pursues the crime in the other sex. These are the physical consequences, the moral are still more alarming; for virtue is only a nominal distinction when the duties of citizens, husbands, wives, fathers, mothers, and directors of families, become merely the selfish ties of convenience.

Why then do philosophers look for public spirit? Public spirit must be nurtured by private virtue, or it will resemble the factitious sentiment which makes women careful to preserve their reputation, and men their honour. A sentiment that often exists unsupported by virtue, unsupported by that sublime morality which makes the habitual breach of one duty a breach of the whole moral law.

CHAP. IX

OF THE PERNICIOUS EFFECTS WHICH ARISE FROM THE UNNATURAL DISTINCTIONS ESTABLISHED IN SOCIETY

From the respect paid to property flow, as from a poisoned fountain, most of the evils and vices which render this world such a dreary scene to the contemplative mind. For it is in the most polished society that noisome reptiles and venomous serpents lurk under the rank herbage; and there is voluptuousness pampered by the still sultry air, which relaxes every good disposition before it ripens into virtue.

One class presses on another; for all are aiming to procure respect on account of their property: and property, once gained, will procure the respect due only to talents and virtue. Men neglect the duties incumbent on man, yet are treated like demi-gods; religion is also separated from morality by a ceremonial veil, yet men wonder that the world is almost, literally speaking, a den of sharpers or oppressors.

There is a homely proverb, which speaks a shrewd truth, that whoever the devil finds idle he will employ. And what but habitual idleness can hereditary wealth and titles produce? For man is so constituted that he can only attain a proper use of his faculties by exercising them, and will not exercise them unless necessity, of some kind, first set the wheels in motion. Virtue likewise can only be acquired by the discharge of relative duties; but the importance of these sacred duties will scarcely be felt by the being who is cajoled out of his humanity by the flattery of sycophants. There must be more equality established in society, or morality will never gain ground, and this virtuous equality will not rest firmly even when founded on a rock, if one half of mankind be chained to its bottom by fate, for they will be continually undermining it through ignorance or pride.

It is vain to expect virtue from women till they are, in some degree, independent of men; nay, it is vain to expect that strength of natural affection, which would make them good wives and mothers. Whilst they are absolutely dependent on their husbands they will be cunning, mean, and selfish, and the men who can be gratified by the fawning fondness of spaniel-like affection, have not much delicacy, for love is not to be bought, in any sense of the words, its silken wings are instantly shrivelled up when any thing beside a return in kind is sought. Yet whilst wealth enervates men; and women live, as it were, by their personal charms, how can we expect them to discharge those ennobling duties which equally require exertion and self-denial. Hereditary property sophisticates the mind, and the unfortunate victims to it, if I may so express myself, swathed from their birth, seldom exert the locomotive faculty of body or mind, and, thus viewing every thing through one medium, and that a false one, they are unable to discern in what true merit and happiness consist. False, indeed, must be the light when the drapery of situation hides the man, and makes him stalk in masquerade, dragging from one scene of dissipation to another the nerveless limbs that hang with stupid listlessness, and rolling round the vacant eye which plainly tells us that there is no mind at home.

I mean, therefore, to infer that the society is not properly organized which does not compel men and women to discharge their respective duties, by making it the only way to acquire that countenance from their fellow-creatures, which every human being wishes some way to attain. The respect, consequently, which is paid to wealth and mere personal charms, is a true north-east blast, that blights the tender blossoms of affection and virtue. Nature has wisely attached affections to duties, to sweeten toil, and to give that vigour to the exertions of reason which only the heart can give. But, the affection which is put on merely because it is the appropriated insignia of a certain character, when its duties are not fulfilled, is one of the empty compliments which vice and folly are obliged to pay to virtue and the real nature of things.

To illustrate my opinion, I need only observe, that when a woman is admired for her beauty, and suffers herself to be so far intoxicated by the admiration she receives, as to neglect to discharge the indispensable duty of a mother, she sins against herself by neglecting to cultivate an affection that would equally tend to make her useful and happy. True happiness, I mean all the contentment, and virtuous satisfaction, that can be snatched in this imperfect state, must arise from well-regulated affections; and an affection includes a duty. Men are not aware of the misery they cause, and the vicious weakness they cherish, by only inciting women to render themselves pleasing; they do not consider that they thus make natural and artificial duties clash, by sacrificing the comfort and respectability of a woman's life to voluptuous notions of beauty, when in nature they all harmonize.

Cold would be the heart of a husband, were he not rendered unnatural by early debauchery, who did not feel more delight at seeing his child suckled by its mother,[1] than the most artful wanton tricks could ever raise; yet this natural way of cementing the matrimonial tie, and twisting esteem with fonder recollections, wealth leads women to spurn. To preserve their beauty, and wear the flowery crown of the day, which gives them a kind of right to reign for a short time over the sex, they neglect to stamp impressions on their husbands' hearts, that would be remembered with more tenderness when the snow on the head began to chill the bosom, than even their virgin charms. The maternal solicitude of a reasonable affectionate woman is very interesting, and the chastened dignity with which a mother returns the caresses that she and her child receive from a father who has been fulfilling the serious duties of his station, is not only a respectable, but a beautiful sight. So singular, indeed, are my feelings, and I have endeavoured not to catch factitious ones, that after having been fatigued with the sight of insipid grandeur and the slavish ceremonies that with cumberous pomp supplied the place of domestic affections, I have turned to some other scene to relieve my eye by resting it on the refreshing green every where scattered by nature. I have then viewed with pleasure a woman nursing her children, and discharging the duties of her station with, perhaps, merely a servant maid to take off her hands the servile part of the household business. I have seen her prepare herself and children, with only the luxury of cleanliness, to receive her husband, who returning weary home in the evening found smiling babes and a clean hearth. My heart has loitered in the midst of the group, and has even throbbed with sympathetic emotion, when the scraping of the well known foot has raised a pleasing tumult.

Whilst my benevolence has been gratified by contemplating this artless picture, I have thought that a couple of this description, equally necessary and independent of each other, because each fulfilled the respective duties of their station, possessed all that life could give. – Raised sufficiently above abject poverty not to be obliged to weigh the consequence of every farthing they spend, and having sufficient to prevent their attending to a frigid system of œconomy, which narrows both heart and mind. I declare, so vulgar are my conceptions, that I know not what is wanted to render this the happiest as well as the most respectable situation in the world, but a taste for literature, to throw a little variety and interest into social converse, and some superfluous money to give to the needy and to buy books. For it is not pleasant when the heart is opened by compassion and the head active in arranging plans of usefulness, to have a prim urchin continually twitching back the elbow to prevent the hand from drawing out an almost empty purse, whispering at the same time some prudential maxim about the priority of justice.

Destructive, however, as riches and inherited honours are to the human character, women are more debased and cramped, if possible, by them, than men, because men may still, in some degree, unfold their faculties by becoming soldiers and statesmen.

As soldiers, I grant, they can now only gather, for the most part, vain glorious laurels, whilst they adjust to a hair the European balance, taking especial care that no bleak northern nook or sound incline the beam. But the days of true heroism are over, when a citizen fought for his country like a Fabricius or a Washington, and then returned to his farm[2] to let his virtuous fervour run in a more placid, but not a less salutary, stream. No, our British heroes are oftener sent from the gaming table than from the plow; and their passions have been rather inflamed by hanging with dumb suspense on the turn of a die, than sublimated by panting after the adventurous march of virtue in the historic page.

The statesman, it is true, might with more propriety quit the Faro Bank,[3] or card-table, to guide the helm, for he has still but to shuffle and trick. The whole system of British politics, if system it may courteously be called, consisting in multiplying dependents and contriving taxes which grind the poor to pamper the rich; thus a war, or any wild goose chace, is, as the vulgar use the phrase, a lucky turn-up of patronage for the minister, whose chief merit is the art of keeping himself in place. It is not necessary then that he should have bowels[4] for the poor, so he can secure for his family the odd trick. Or should some shew of respect, for what is termed with ignorant ostentation an Englishman's birth-right, be expedient to bubble the gruff mastiff that he has to lead by the nose, he can make an empty shew, very safely, by giving his single voice, and suffering his light squadron to file off to the other side. And when a question of humanity is agitated he may dip a sop in the milk of human kindness, to silence Cerberus,[5] and talk of the interest which his heart takes in an attempt to make the earth no longer cry for vengeance as it sucks in its children's blood, though his cold hand may at the very moment rivet their chains, by sanctioning the abominable traffick. A minister is no longer a minister, than while he can carry a point, which he is determined to carry. – Yet it is not necessary that a minister should feel like a man, when a bold push might shake his seat.

But, to have done with these episodical observations, let me return to the more specious slavery which chains the very soul of woman, keeping her for ever under the bondage of ignorance.

The preposterous distinctions of rank, which render civilization a curse, by dividing the world between voluptuous tyrants, and cunning envious dependents, corrupt, almost equally, every class of people, because respectability is not attached to the discharge of the relative duties of life, but to the station, and when the duties are not fulfilled the affections cannot gain sufficient strength to fortify the virtue of which they are the natural reward. Still there are some loop-holes out of which a man may creep, and dare to think and act for himself; but for a

woman it is an herculean task, because she has difficulties peculiar to her sex to overcome, which require almost superhuman
powers.

A truly benevolent legislator always endeavours to make it
the interest of each individual to be virtuous; and thus private
virtue becoming the cement of public happiness, an orderly
whole is consolidated by the tendency of all the parts towards a
common centre. But, the private or public virtue of woman is
very problematical; for Rousseau, and a numerous list of male
writers, insist that she should all her life be subjected to a severe
restraint, that of propriety. Why subject her to propriety – blind
propriety, if she be capable of acting from a nobler spring, if she
be an heir of immortality? Is sugar always to be produced by
vital blood? Is one half of the human species, like the poor
African slaves,[6] to be subject to prejudices that brutalize them,
when principles would be a surer guard, only to sweeten the cup
of man? Is not this indirectly to deny woman reason? for a gift
is a mockery, if it be unfit for use.

Women are, in common with men, rendered weak and luxurious by the relaxing pleasures which wealth procures; but added
to this they are made slaves to their persons, and must render
them alluring that man may lend them his reason to guide their
tottering steps aright. Or should they be ambitious, they must
govern their tyrants by sinister tricks, for without rights there
cannot be any incumbent duties. The laws respecting woman,
which I mean to discuss in a future part, make an absurd unit
of a man and his wife; and then, by the easy transition of only
considering him as responsible, she is reduced to a mere cypher.[7]

The being who discharges the duties of its station is independent; and, speaking of women at large, their first duty is to
themselves as rational creatures, and the next, in point of importance, as citizens, is that, which includes so many, of a mother.
The rank in life which dispenses with their fulfilling this duty,
necessarily degrades them by making them mere dolls. Or,
should they turn to something more important than merely
fitting drapery upon a smooth block, their minds are only
occupied by some soft platonic attachment; or, the actual
management of an intrigue may keep their thoughts in motion;

for when they neglect domestic duties, they have it not in their power to take the field and march and counter-march like soldiers, or wrangle in the senate to keep their faculties from rusting.

I know that, as a proof of the inferiority of the sex, Rousseau has exultingly exclaimed, How can they leave the nursery for the camp![8] – And the camp has by some moralists been termed the school of the most heroic virtues; though, I think, it would puzzle a keen casuist to prove the reasonableness of the greater number of wars that have dubbed heroes. I do not mean to consider this question critically; because, having frequently viewed these freaks of ambition as the first natural mode of civilization, when the ground must be torn up, and the woods cleared by fire and sword, I do not choose to call them pests; but surely the present system of war has little connection with virtue of any denomination, being rather the school of *finesse* and effeminacy, than of fortitude.

Yet, if defensive war, the only justifiable war, in the present advanced state of society, where virtue can shew its face and ripen amidst the rigours which purify the air on the mountain's top, were alone to be adopted as just and glorious, the true heroism of antiquity might again animate female bosoms. – But fair and softly, gentle reader, male or female, do not alarm thyself, for though I have compared the character of a modern soldier with that of a civilized woman, I am not going to advise them to turn their distaff into a musket, though I sincerely wish to see the bayonet converted into a pruning-hook.[9] I only recreated an imagination, fatigued by contemplating the vices and follies which all proceed from a feculent stream of wealth that has muddied the pure rills of natural affection, by supposing that society will some time or other be so constituted, that man must necessarily fulfil the duties of a citizen, or be despised, and that while he was employed in any of the departments of civil life, his wife, also an active citizen, should be equally intent to manage her family, educate her children, and assist her neighbours.

But, to render her really virtuous and useful, she must not, if she discharge her civil duties, want, individually, the protection

of civil laws; she must not be dependent on her husband's bounty
for her subsistence during his life, or support after his death –
for how can a being be generous who has nothing of its own?
or, virtuous, who is not free? The wife, in the present state of
things, who is faithful to her husband, and neither suckles nor
educates her children, scarcely deserves the name of a wife, and
has no right to that of a citizen. But take away natural rights,
and duties become null.

Women then must be considered as only the wanton solace
of men, when they become so weak in mind and body, that they
cannot exert themselves, unless to pursue some frothy pleasure,
or to invent some frivolous fashion. What can be a more melancholy sight to a thinking mind, than to look into the numerous
carriages that drive helter-skelter about this metropolis in a
morning full of pale-faced creatures who are flying from themselves. I have often wished, with Dr Johnson, to place some of
them in a little shop with half a dozen children looking up to
their languid countenances for support. I am much mistaken, if
some latent vigour would not soon give health and spirit to their
eyes, and some lines drawn by the exercise of reason on the
blank cheeks, which before were only undulated by dimples,
might restore lost dignity to the character, or rather enable it to
attain the true dignity of its nature. Virtue is not to be acquired
even by speculation, much less by the negative supineness that
wealth naturally generates.

Besides, when poverty is more disgraceful than even vice, is
not morality cut to the quick? Still to avoid misconstruction,
though I consider that women in the common walks of life are
called to fulfil the duties of wives and mothers, by religion and
reason, I cannot help lamenting that women of a superiour cast
have not a road open by which they can pursue more extensive
plans of usefulness and independence. I may excite laughter, by
dropping an hint, which I mean to pursue, some future time, for
I really think that women ought to have representatives, instead
of being arbitrarily governed without having any direct share
allowed them in the deliberations of government.

But, as the whole system of representation is now,[10] in this
country, only a convenient handle for despotism, they need not

complain, for they are as well represented as a numerous class of hard working mechanics, who pay for the support of royalty when they can scarcely stop their children's mouths with bread. How are they represented whose very sweat supports the splendid stud of an heir apparent, or varnishes the chariot of some female favourite who looks down on shame? Taxes on the very necessaries of life, enable an endless tribe of idle princes and princesses to pass with stupid pomp before a gaping crowd, who almost worship the very parade which costs them so dear. This is mere gothic grandeur, something like the barbarous useless parade of having sentinels on horseback at Whitehall,[11] which I could never view without a mixture of contempt and indignation.

How strangely must the mind be sophisticated when this sort of state impresses it! But, till these monuments of folly are levelled by virtue, similar follies will leaven the whole mass. For the same character, in some degree, will prevail in the aggregate of society: and the refinements of luxury, or the vicious repinings of envious poverty, will equally banish virtue from society, considered as the characteristic of that society, or only allow it to appear as one of the stripes of the harlequin coat, worn by the civilized man.

In the superiour ranks of life, every duty is done by deputies, as if duties could ever be waved, and the vain pleasures which consequent idleness forces the rich to pursue, appear so enticing to the next rank, that the numerous scramblers for wealth sacrifice every thing to tread on their heels. The most sacred trusts are then considered as sinecures, because they were procured by interest, and only sought to enable a man to keep *good company*. Women, in particular, all want to be ladies. Which is simply to have nothing to do, but listlessly to go they scarcely care where, for they cannot tell what.

But what have women to do in society? I may be asked, but to loiter with easy grace; surely you would not condemn them all to suckle fools and chronicle small beer![12] No. Women might certainly study the art of healing, and be physicians as well as nurses. And midwifery, decency seems to allot to them, though I am afraid the word midwife, in our dictionaries, will soon give place to *accoucheur*,[13] and one proof of the former delicacy of the sex be effaced from the language.

They might, also, study politics, and settle their benevolence on the broadest basis; for the reading of history will scarcely be more useful than the perusal of romances, if read as mere biography; if the character of the times, the political improvements, arts, &c. be not observed. In short, if it be not considered as the history of man; and not of particular men, who filled a niche in the temple of fame, and dropped into the black rolling stream of time, that silently sweeps all before it, into the shapeless void called – eternity. – For shape, can it be called, 'that shape hath none?'[14]

Business of various kinds, they might likewise pursue, if they were educated in a more orderly manner, which might save many from common and legal prostitution. Women would not then marry for a support, as men accept of places under government, and neglect the implied duties; nor would an attempt to earn their own subsistence, a most laudable one! sink them almost to the level of those poor abandoned creatures who live by prostitution. For are not milliners and mantua-makers[15] reckoned the next class? The few employments open to women, so far from being liberal, are menial; and when a superiour education enables them to take charge of the education of children as governesses, they are not treated like the tutors of sons, though even clerical tutors are not always treated in a manner calculated to render them respectable in the eyes of their pupils, to say nothing of the private comfort of the individual. But as women educated like gentlewomen, are never designed for the humiliating situation which necessity sometimes forces them to fill;[16] these situations are considered in the light of a degradation; and they know little of the human heart, who need to be told, that nothing so painfully sharpens sensibility as such a fall in life.

Some of these women might be restrained from marrying by a proper spirit or delicacy, and others may not have had it in their power to escape in this pitiful way from servitude; is not that government then very defective, and very unmindful of the happiness of one half of its members, that does not provide for honest, independent women, by encouraging them to fill respectable stations? But in order to render their private virtue a public benefit, they must have a civil existence in the state, married or single; else we shall continually see some worthy woman, whose sensibility has been rendered painfully acute by undeserved contempt, droop like 'the lily broken down by a plow-share.'[17]

It is a melancholy truth; yet such is the blessed effect of civilization! the most respectable women are the most oppressed; and, unless they have understandings far superiour to the common run of understandings, taking in both sexes, they must, from being treated like contemptible beings, become contemptible. How many women thus waste life away the prey of discontent, who might have practised as physicians, regulated a farm, managed a shop, and stood erect, supported by their own industry, instead of hanging their heads surcharged with the dew of sensibility, that consumes the beauty to which it at first gave lustre; nay, I doubt whether pity and love are so near akin as poets feign, for I have seldom seen much compassion excited by the helplessness of females, unless they were fair; then, perhaps, pity was the soft handmaid of love, or the harbinger of lust.

How much more respectable is the woman who earns her own bread by fulfilling any duty, than the most accomplished beauty! – beauty did I say? – so sensible am I of the beauty of moral loveliness, or the harmonious propriety that attunes the passions of a well-regulated mind, that I blush at making the comparison; yet I sigh to think how few women aim at attaining this respectability by withdrawing from the giddy whirl of pleasure, or the indolent calm that stupifies the good sort of women it sucks in.

Proud of their weakness, however, they must always be protected, guarded from care, and all the rough toils that dignify the mind. – If this be the fiat of fate, if they will make themselves insignificant and contemptible, sweetly to waste 'life away,' let them not expect to be valued when their beauty fades, for it is the fate of the fairest flowers to be admired and pulled to pieces by the careless hand that plucked them. In how many ways do I wish, from the purest benevolence, to impress this truth on my sex; yet I fear that they will not listen to a truth that dear bought experience has brought home to many an agitated bosom, nor willingly resign the privileges of rank and sex for the privileges of humanity, to which those have no claim who do not discharge its duties.

Those writers are particularly useful, in my opinion, who make man feel for man, independent of the station he fills, or the drapery of factitious sentiments. I then would fain convince reasonable men of the importance of some of my remarks; and prevail on them to weigh dispassionately the whole tenor of my observations. – I appeal to their understandings; and, as a fellow-creature, claim, in the name of my sex, some interest in their hearts. I entreat them to assist to emancipate their companion, to make her a *help meet* for them!

Would men but generously snap our chains, and be content with rational fellowship instead of slavish obedience, they would find us more observant daughters, more affectionate sisters, more faithful wives, more reasonable mothers – in a word, better citizens. We should then love them with true affection, because we should learn to respect ourselves; and the peace of mind of a worthy man would not be interrupted by the idle vanity of his wife, nor the babes sent to nestle in a strange bosom, having never found a home in their mother's.

CHAP. X

PARENTAL AFFECTION

Parental affection is, perhaps, the blindest modification of perverse self-love; for we have not, like the French,* two terms to distinguish the pursuit of a natural and reasonable desire, from the ignorant calculations of weakness. Parents often love their children in the most brutal manner, and sacrifice every relative duty to promote their advancement in the world. – To promote, such is the perversity of unprincipled prejudices, the future welfare of the very beings whose present existence they imbitter by the most despotic stretch of power. Power, in fact, is ever true to its vital principle, for in every shape it would reign without controul or inquiry. Its throne is built across a dark abyss, which no eye must dare to explore, lest the baseless fabric should totter under investigation. Obedience, unconditional obedience, is the catch-word of tyrants of every description, and to render 'assurance doubly sure,'[1] one kind of despotism supports another. Tyrants would have cause to tremble if reason were to become the rule of duty in any of the relations of life, for the light might spread till perfect day appeared. And when it did appear, how would men smile at the sight of the bugbears at which they started during the night of ignorance, or the twilight of timid inquiry.

Parental affection, indeed, in many minds, is but a pretext to tyrannize where it can be done with impunity, for only good and wise men are content with the respect that will bear discussion. Convinced that they have a right to what they insist on, they do not fear reason, or dread the sifting of subjects that recur to

* *L'amour propre. L'amour de soi même.*[2]

natural justice: because they firmly believe that the more enlightened the human mind becomes the deeper root will just and
simple principles take. They do not rest in expedients, or grant
that what is metaphysically true can be practically false; but
disdaining the shifts of the moment they calmly wait till time,
sanctioning innovation, silences the hiss of selfishness or envy.

If the power of reflecting on the past, and darting the keen
eye of contemplation into futurity, be the grand privilege of
man, it must be granted that some people enjoy this prerogative
in a very limited degree. Every thing new appears to them wrong;
and not able to distinguish the possible from the monstrous,
they fear where no fear should find a place, running from the
light of reason, as if it were a firebrand; yet the limits of the
possible have never been defined to stop the sturdy innovator's
hand.

Woman, however, a slave in every situation to prejudice,
seldom exerts enlightened maternal affection; for she either
neglects her children, or spoils them by improper indulgence.
Besides, the affection of some women for their children is, as I
have before termed it, frequently very brutish: for it eradicates
every spark of humanity. Justice, truth, every thing is sacrificed
by these Rebekah's,[3] and for the sake of their *own* children
they violate the most sacred duties, forgetting the common
relationship that binds the whole family on earth together. Yet,
reason seems to say, that they who suffer one duty, or affection,
to swallow up the rest, have not sufficient heart or mind to fulfil
that one conscientiously. It then loses the venerable aspect of a
duty, and assumes the fantastic form of a whim.

As the care of children in their infancy is one of the grand
duties annexed to the female character by nature, this duty
would afford many forcible arguments for strengthening the
female understanding, if it were properly considered.

The formation of the mind must be begun very early, and the
temper, in particular, requires the most judicious attention – an
attention which women cannot pay who only love their children
because they are their children, and seek no further for the
foundation of their duty, than in the feelings of the moment. It
is this want of reason in their affections which makes women so

often run into extremes, and either be the most fond or most careless and unnatural mothers.

To be a good mother – a woman must have sense, and that independence of mind which few women possess who are taught to depend entirely on their husbands. Meek wives are, in general, foolish mothers; wanting their children to love them best, and take their part, in secret, against the father, who is held up as a scarecrow. When chastisement is necessary, though they have offended the mother, the father must inflict the punishment; he must be the judge in all disputes: but I shall more fully discuss this subject when I treat of private education, I now only mean to insist, that unless the understanding of woman be enlarged, and her character rendered more firm, by being allowed to govern her own conduct, she will never have sufficient sense or command of temper to manage her children properly. Her parental affection, indeed, scarcely deserves the name, when it does not lead her to suckle her children, because the discharge of this duty is equally calculated to inspire maternal and filial affection: and it is the indispensable duty of men and women to fulfil the duties which give birth to affections that are the surest preservatives against vice. Natural affection, as it is termed, I believe to be a very faint tie, affections must grow out of the habitual exercise of a mutual sympathy; and what sympathy does a mother exercise who sends her babe to a nurse, and only takes it from a nurse to send it to a school?

In the exercise of their maternal feelings providence has furnished women with a natural substitute for love, when the lover becomes only a friend, and mutual confidence takes place of overstrained admiration – a child then gently twists the relaxing cord, and a mutual care produces a new mutual sympathy. – But a child, though a pledge of affection, will not enliven it, if both father and mother be content to transfer the charge to hirelings; for they who do their duty by proxy should not murmur if they miss the reward of duty – parental affection produces filial duty.

CHAP. XI

DUTY TO PARENTS

There seems to be an indolent propensity in man to make prescription always take place of reason, and to place every duty on an arbitrary foundation. The rights of kings are deduced in a direct line from the King of kings; and that of parents from our first parent.

Why do we thus go back for principles that should always rest on the same base, and have the same weight to-day that they had a thousand years ago – and not a jot more? If parents discharge their duty they have a strong hold and sacred claim on the gratitude of their children; but few parents are willing to receive the respectful affection of their offspring on such terms. They demand blind obedience, because they do not merit a reasonable service: and to render these demands of weakness and ignorance more binding, a mysterious sanctity is spread round the most arbitrary principle; for what other name can be given to the blind duty of obeying vicious or weak beings merely because they obeyed a powerful instinct?

The simple definition of the reciprocal duty, which naturally subsists between parent and child, may be given in a few words. The parent who pays proper attention to helpless infancy has a right to require the same attention when the feebleness of age comes upon him. But to subjugate a rational being to the mere will of another, after he is of age to answer to society for his own conduct, is a most cruel and undue stretch of power; and, perhaps, as injurious to morality as those religious systems which do not allow right and wrong to have any existence, but in the Divine will.

I never knew a parent who had paid more than common

attention to his children, disregarded;* on the contrary, the early habit of relying almost implicitly on the opinion of a respected parent is not easily shook, even when matured reason convinces the child that his father is not the wisest man in the world. This weakness, for a weakness it is, though the epithet amiable may be tacked to it, a reasonable man must steel himself against; for the absurd duty, too often inculcated, of obeying a parent only on account of his being a parent, shackles the mind, and prepares it for a slavish submission to any power but reason.

I distinguish between the natural and accidental duty due to parents.

The parent who sedulously endeavours to form the heart and enlarge the understanding of his child, has given that dignity to the discharge of a duty, common to the whole animal world, that only reason can give. This is the parental affection of humanity, and leaves instinctive natural affection far behind. Such a parent acquires all the rights of the most sacred friendship, and his advice, even when his child is advanced in life, demands serious consideration.

With respect to marriage, though after one and twenty a parent seems to have no right to withhold his consent on any account; yet twenty years of solicitude call for a return, and the son ought, at least, to promise not to marry for two or three years, should the object of his choice not entirely meet with the approbation of his first friend.

But, respect for parents is, generally speaking, a much more debasing principle; it is only a selfish respect for property. The father who is blindly obeyed, is obeyed from sheer weakness, or from motives that degrade the human character.

A great proportion of the misery that wanders, in hideous forms, around the world, is allowed to rise from the negligence of parents; and still these are the people who are most tenacious of what they term a natural right, though it be subversive of the birth-right of man, the right of acting according to the direction of his own reason.

I have already very frequently had occasion to observe, that

* Dr Johnson makes the same observation.[1]

vicious or indolent people are always eager to profit by enforcing arbitrary privileges; and, generally, in the same proportion as they neglect the discharge of the duties which alone render the privileges reasonable. This is at the bottom a dictate of common sense, or the instinct of self-defence, peculiar to ignorant weakness; resembling that instinct, which makes a fish muddy the water it swims in to elude its enemy, instead of boldly facing it in the clear stream.

From the clear stream of argument, indeed, the supporters of prescription, of every denomination, fly; and, taking refuge in the darkness, which, in the language of sublime poetry, has been supposed to surround the throne of Omnipotence, they dare to demand that implicit respect which is only due to His unsearchable ways. But, let me not be thought presumptuous, the darkness which hides our God from us, only respects speculative truths – it never obscures moral ones, they shine clearly, for God is light, and never, by the constitution of our nature, requires the discharge of a duty, the reasonableness of which does not beam on us when we open our eyes.

The indolent parent of high rank may, it is true, extort a shew of respect from his child, and females on the continent are particularly subject to the views of their families, who never think of consulting their inclination, or providing for the comfort of the poor victims of their pride. The consequence is notorious; these dutiful daughters become adulteresses, and neglect the education of their children, from whom they, in their turn, exact the same kind of obedience.

Females, it is true, in all countries, are too much under the dominion of their parents; and few parents think of addressing their children in the following manner, though it is in this reasonable way that Heaven seems to command the whole human race. It is your interest to obey me till you can judge for yourself; and the Almighty Father of all has implanted an affection in me to serve as a guard to you whilst your reason is unfolding; but when your mind arrives at maturity, you must only obey me, or rather respect my opinions, so far as they coincide with the light that is breaking in on your own mind.

A slavish bondage to parents cramps every faculty of the

mind; and Mr Locke very judiciously observes, that 'if the mind be curbed and humbled too much in children; if their spirits be abased and broken much by too strict an hand over them; they lose all their vigour and industry.'[2] This strict hand may in some degree account for the weakness of women; for girls, from various causes, are more kept down by their parents,[3] in every sense of the word, than boys. The duty expected from them is, like all the duties arbitrarily imposed on women, more from a sense of propriety, more out of respect for decorum, than reason; and thus taught slavishly to submit to their parents, they are prepared for the slavery of marriage. I may be told that a number of women are not slaves in the marriage state. True, but they then become tyrants; for it is not rational freedom, but a lawless kind of power resembling the authority exercised by the favourites of absolute monarchs, which they obtain by debasing means. I do not, likewise, dream of insinuating that either boys or girls are always slaves, I only insist that when they are obliged to submit to authority blindly, their faculties are weakened, and their tempers rendered imperious or abject. I also lament that parents, indolently availing themselves of a supposed privilege, damp the first faint glimmering of reason, rendering at the same time the duty, which they are so anxious to enforce, an empty name; because they will not let it rest on the only basis on which a duty can rest securely: for unless it be founded on knowledge, it cannot gain sufficient strength to resist the squalls of passion, or the silent sapping of self-love. But it is not the parents who have given the surest proof of their affection for their children, or, to speak more properly, who by fulfilling their duty, have allowed a natural parental affection to take root in their hearts, the child of exercised sympathy and reason, and not the overweening offspring of selfish pride, who most vehemently insist on their children submitting to their will merely because it is their will. On the contrary, the parent, who sets a good example, patiently lets that example work; and it seldom fails to produce its natural effect – filial reverence.

Children cannot be taught too early to submit to reason, the true definition of that necessity, which Rousseau insisted on, without defining it; for to submit to reason is to submit to the nature of things, and to that God, who formed them so, to promote our real interest.

Why should the minds of children be warped as they just begin to expand, only to favour the indolence of parents, who insist on a privilege without being willing to pay the price fixed by nature? I have before had occasion to observe, that a right always includes a duty, and I think it may, likewise, fairly be inferred, that they forfeit the right, who do not fulfil the duty.

It is easier, I grant, to command than reason; but it does not follow from hence that children cannot comprehend the reason why they are made to do certain things habitually: for, from a steady adherence to a few simple principles of conduct flows that salutary power which a judicious parent gradually gains over a child's mind. And this power becomes strong indeed, if tempered by an even display of affection brought home to the child's heart. For, I believe, as a general rule, it must be allowed that the affection which we inspire always resembles that we cultivate; so that natural affections, which have been supposed almost distinct from reason, may be found more nearly connected with judgment than is commonly allowed. Nay, as another proof of the necessity of cultivating the female understanding, it is but just to observe, that the affections seem to have a kind of animal capriciousness when they merely reside in the heart.

It is the irregular exercise of parental authority that first injures the mind, and to these irregularities girls are more subject than boys. The will of those who never allow their will to be disputed, unless they happen to be in a good humour, when they relax proportionally, is almost always unreasonable. To elude this arbitrary authority girls very early learn the lessons which they afterwards practise on their husbands; for I have frequently seen a little sharp-faced miss rule a whole family, excepting that now and then mamma's angry will burst out of some accidental cloud; – either her hair was ill dressed,* or she had lost more money at cards, the night before, than she was

---

* I myself heard a little girl once say to a servant, 'My mamma has been scolding me finely this morning, because her hair was not dressed to please her.' Though this remark was pert, it was just. And what respect could a girl acquire for such a parent without doing violence to reason?

willing to own to her husband; or some such moral cause of anger.

After observing sallies of this kind, I have been led into a melancholy train of reflection respecting females, concluding that when their first affection must lead them astray, or make their duties clash till they rest on mere whims and customs, little can be expected from them as they advance in life. How indeed can an instructor remedy this evil? for to teach them virtue on any solid principle is to teach them to despise their parents. Children cannot, ought not, to be taught to make allowance for the faults of their parents, because every such allowance weakens the force of reason in their minds, and makes them still more indulgent to their own. It is one of the most sublime virtues of maturity that leads us to be severe with respect to ourselves, and forbearing to others; but children should only be taught the simple virtues, for if they begin too early to make allowance for human passions and manners, they wear off the fine edge of the criterion by which they should regulate their own, and become unjust in the same proportion as they grow indulgent.

The affections of children, and weak people, are always selfish; they love their relatives, because they are beloved by them, and not on account of their virtues. Yet, till esteem and love are blended together in the first affection, and reason made the foundation of the first duty, morality will stumble at the threshold. But, till society is very differently constituted, parents, I fear, will still insist on being obeyed, because they will be obeyed, and constantly endeavour to settle that power on a Divine right which will not bear the investigation of reason.

CHAP. XII

ON NATIONAL EDUCATION

The good effects resulting from attention to private education will ever be very confined, and the parent who really puts his own hand to the plow, will always, in some degree, be disappointed, till education becomes a grand national concern. A man cannot retire into a desert with his child, and if he did he could not bring himself back to childhood, and become the proper friend and play-fellow of an infant or youth. And when children are confined to the society of men and women, they very soon acquire that kind of premature manhood which stops the growth of every vigorous power of mind or body. In order to open their faculties they should be excited to think for themselves; and this can only be done by mixing a number of children together, and making them jointly pursue the same objects.

A child very soon contracts a benumbing indolence of mind, which he has seldom sufficient vigour afterwards to shake off, when he only asks a question instead of seeking for information, and then relies implicitly on the answer he receives. With his equals in age this could never be the case, and the subjects of inquiry, though they might be influenced, would not be entirely under the direction of men, who frequently damp, if not destroy, abilities, by bringing them forward too hastily: and too hastily they will infallibly be brought forward, if the child be confined to the society of a man, however sagacious that man may be.

Besides, in youth the seeds of every affection should be sown, and the respectful regard, which is felt for a parent, is very different from the social affections that are to constitute the happiness of life as it advances. Of these equality is the basis, and an intercourse of sentiments unclogged by that observant seriousness which prevents disputation, though it may not inforce submission. Let a child have ever such an affection for his parent, he will always languish to play and prattle with children; and the very respect he feels, for filial esteem always has a dash of fear mixed with it, will, if it do not teach him cunning, at least prevent him from pouring out the little secrets which first open the heart to friendship and confidence, gradually leading to more expansive benevolence. Added to this, he will never acquire that frank ingenuousness of behaviour, which young people can only attain by being frequently in society where they dare to speak what they think; neither afraid of being reproved for their presumption, nor laughed at for their folly.

Forcibly impressed by the reflections which the sight of schools, as they are at present conducted, naturally suggested, I have formerly delivered my opinion rather warmly in favour of a private education; but further experience has led me to view the subject in a different light. I still, however, think schools, as they are now regulated, the hot-beds of vice and folly, and the knowledge of human nature, supposed to be attained there, merely cunning selfishness.

At school boys become gluttons and slovens, and, instead of cultivating domestic affections, very early rush into the libertinism which destroys the constitution before it is formed; hardening the heart as it weakens the understanding.

I should, in fact, be averse to boarding-schools, if it were for no other reason than the unsettled state of mind which the expectation of the vacations produce. On these the children's thoughts are fixed with eager anticipating hopes, for, at least, to speak with moderation, half of the time, and when they arrive they are spent in total dissipation and beastly indulgence.

But, on the contrary, when they are brought up at home, though they may pursue a plan of study in a more orderly manner than can be adopted when near a fourth part of the year is actually spent in idleness, and as much more in regret and anticipation; yet they there acquire too high an opinion of their own importance, from being allowed to tyrannize over servants, and from the anxiety expressed by most mothers, on the score of manners, who, eager to teach the accomplishments of a gentleman, stifle, in their birth, the virtues of a man. Thus brought into company when they ought to be seriously employed, and treated like men when they are still boys, they become vain and effeminate.

The only way to avoid two extremes equally injurious to morality, would be to contrive some way of combining a public and private education. Thus to make men citizens two natural steps might be taken, which seem directly to lead to the desired point; for the domestic affections, that first open the heart to the various modifications of humanity, would be cultivated, whilst the children were nevertheless allowed to spend great part of their time, on terms of equality, with other children.

I still recollect, with pleasure, the country day school; where a boy trudged in the morning, wet or dry, carrying his books, and his dinner, if it were at a considerable distance; a servant did not then lead master by the hand, for, when he had once put on coat and breeches, he was allowed to shift for himself, and return alone in the evening to recount the feats of the day close at the parental knee. His father's house was his home, and was ever after fondly remembered; nay, I appeal to many superiour men, who were educated in this manner, whether the recollection of some shady lane where they conned their lesson; or, of some stile, where they sat making a kite, or mending a bat, has not endeared their country to them?

But, what boy ever recollected with pleasure the years he spent in close confinement, at an academy near London? unless, indeed, he should, by chance, remember the poor scare-crow of an usher,[1] whom he tormented; or, the tartman, from whom he caught a cake, to devour it with a cattish appetite of selfishness. At boarding-schools of every description, the relaxation of the junior boys is mischief; and of the senior, vice. Besides, in great schools, what can be more prejudicial to the moral character than the system of tyranny and abject slavery which is established amongst the boys, to say nothing of the slavery to forms, which makes religion worse than a farce? For what good can be expected from the youth who receives the sacrament of the Lord's supper, to avoid forfeiting half a guinea, which he probably afterwards spends in some sensual manner? Half the employment of the youths is to elude the necessity of attending public worship; and well they may, for such a constant repetition of the same thing must be a very irksome restraint on their natural vivacity. As these ceremonies have the most fatal effect on their morals, and as a ritual performed by the lips, when the heart and mind are far away, is not now stored up by our church as a bank to draw on for the fees of the poor souls in purgatory, why should they not be abolished?

But the fear of innovation, in this country, extends to every thing. – This is only a covert fear, the apprehensive timidity of indolent slugs, who guard, by sliming it over, the snug place, which they consider in the light of an hereditary estate; and eat, drink, and enjoy themselves, instead of fulfilling the duties, excepting a few empty forms, for which it was endowed. These are the people who most strenuously insist on the will of the founder being observed, crying out against all reformation, as if it were a violation of justice. I am now alluding particularly to the relicks of popery retained in our colleges, when the protestant members seem to be such sticklers for the established church; but their zeal never makes them lose sight of the spoil of ignorance, which rapacious priests of superstitious memory have scraped together. No, wise in their generation, they venerate the prescriptive right of possession, as a strong hold, and still let the sluggish bell tinkle to prayers, as during the days when the elevation of the host was supposed to atone for the sins of the people, lest one reformation should lead to another, and the spirit kill the letter. These Romish customs have the most baneful effect on the morals of our clergy; for the idle vermin who two or three times a day perform in the most slovenly manner a service which they think useless, but call their duty, soon lose a sense of duty. At college, forced to attend or evade public worship, they acquire an habitual contempt for the very service, the performance of which is to enable them to live in idleness. It is mumbled over as an affair of business, as a stupid boy repeats his talk, and frequently the college cant escapes from the preacher the moment after he has left the pulpit, and even whilst he is eating the dinner which he earned in such a dishonest manner.

Nothing, indeed, can be more irreverent than the cathedral service as it is now performed in this country, neither does it contain a set of weaker men than those who are the slaves of this childish routine. A disgusting skeleton of the former state is still exhibited; but all the solemnity that interested the imagination, if it did not purify the heart, is stripped off. The performance of high mass on the continent must impress every mind, where a spark of fancy glows, with that awful melancholy, that sublime tenderness, so near akin to devotion. I do not say that these devotional feelings are of more use, in a moral sense, than any other emotion of taste; but I contend that the theatrical pomp which gratifies our senses, is to be preferred to the cold parade that insults the understanding without reaching the heart.

Amongst remarks on national education, such observations cannot be misplaced, especially as the supporters of these establishments, degenerated into puerilities, affect to be the champions of religion. – Religion, pure source of comfort in this vale of tears! how has thy clear stream been muddied by the dabblers, who have presumptuously endeavoured to confine in one narrow channel, the living waters that ever flow towards God – the sublime ocean of existence! What would life be without that peace which the love of God, when built on humanity, alone can impart? Every earthly affection turns back, at intervals, to prey upon the heart that feeds it; and the purest effusions of benevolence, often rudely damped by man, must mount as a free-will offering to Him who gave them birth, whose bright image they faintly reflect.

In public schools, however, religion, confounded with irksome ceremonies and unreasonable restraints, assumes the most ungracious aspect: not the sober austere one that commands respect whilst it inspires fear; but a ludicrous cast, that serves to point a pun. For, in fact, most of the good stories and smart things which enliven the spirits that have been concentrated at whist, are manufactured out of the incidents to which the very men labour to give a droll turn who countenance the abuse to live on the spoil.

There is not, perhaps, in the kingdom, a more dogmatical, or luxurious set of men, than the pedantic tyrants who reside in colleges and preside at public schools. The vacations are equally injurious to the morals of the masters and pupils, and the intercourse, which the former keep up with the nobility, introduces the same vanity and extravagance into their families, which banish domestic duties and comforts from the lordly mansion, whose state is awkwardly aped. The boys, who live at a great expence with the masters and assistants, are never domesticated, though placed there for that purpose; for, after a silent dinner, they swallow a hasty glass of wine, and retire to plan some mischievous trick, or to ridicule the person or manners of the very people they have just been cringing to, and whom they ought to consider as the representatives of their parents.

Can it then be a matter of surprise that boys become selfish and vicious who are thus shut out from social converse? or that a mitre often graces the brow of one of these diligent pastors?

The desire of living in the same style, as the rank just above them, infects each individual and every class of people, and meanness is the concomitant of this ignoble ambition; but those professions are most debasing whose ladder is patronage; yet, out of one of these professions the tutors of youth are, in general, chosen. But, can they be expected to inspire independent sentiments, whose conduct must be regulated by the cautious prudence that is ever on the watch for preferment?

So far, however, from thinking of the morals of boys, I have heard several masters of schools argue, that they only undertook to teach Latin and Greek; and that they had fulfilled their duty, by sending some good scholars to college.

A few good scholars, I grant, may have been formed by emulation and discipline; but, to bring forward these clever boys, the health and morals of a number have been sacrificed. The sons of our gentry and wealthy commoners are mostly educated at these seminaries, and will any one pretend to assert that the majority, making every allowance, come under the description of tolerable scholars?

It is not for the benefit of society that a few brilliant men should be brought forward at the expence of the multitude. It is true, that great men seem to start up, as great revolutions occur, at proper intervals, to restore order, and to blow aside the clouds that thicken over the face of truth; but let more reason and virtue prevail in society, and these strong winds would not be necessary. Public education, of every denomination, should be directed to form citizens; but if you wish to make good citizens, you must first exercise the affections of a son and a brother. This is the only way to expand the heart; for public affections, as well as public virtues, must ever grow out of the private character, or they are merely meteors that shoot athwart a dark sky, and disappear as they are gazed at and admired.

Few, I believe, have had much affection for mankind, who did not first love their parents, their brothers, sisters, and even the domestic brutes, whom they first played with. The exercise of youthful sympathies forms the moral temperature; and it is the recollection of these first affections and pursuits that gives life to those that are afterwards more under the direction of reason. In youth, the fondest friendships are formed, the genial juices mounting at the same time, kindly mix; or, rather the heart, tempered for the reception of friendship, is accustomed to seek for pleasure in something more noble than the churlish gratification of appetite.

In order then to inspire a love of home and domestic pleasures, children ought to be educated at home, for riotous holidays only make them fond of home for their own sakes. Yet, the vacations, which do not foster domestic affections, continually disturb the course of study, and render any plan of improvement abortive which includes temperance; still, were they abolished, children would be entirely separated from their parents, and I question whether they would become better citizens by sacrificing the preparatory affections, by destroying the force of relationships that render the marriage state as necessary as respectable. But, if a private education produce self-importance, or insulate a man in his family, the evil is only shifted, not remedied.

This train of reasoning brings me back to a subject, on which I mean to dwell, the necessity of establishing proper day-schools.

But, these should be national establishments, for whilst school-masters are dependent on the caprice of parents, little exertion can be expected from them, more than is necessary to please ignorant people. Indeed, the necessity of a master's giving the parents some sample of the boy's abilities, which during the vacation is shewn to every visitor,* is productive of more mischief than would at first be supposed. For it is seldom done entirely, to speak with moderation, by the child itself; thus the master countenances falsehood, or winds the poor machine up to some extraordinary exertion, that injures the wheels, and stops the progress of gradual improvement. The memory is loaded with unintelligible words, to make a shew of, without the understanding's acquiring any distinct ideas: but only that education deserves emphatically to be termed cultivation of mind, which teaches young people how to begin to think. The imagination should not be allowed to debauch the understanding before it gained strength, or vanity will become the forerunner of vice: for every way of exhibiting the acquirements of a child is injurious to its moral character.

How much time is lost in teaching them to recite what they do not understand? whilst, seated on benches, all in their best array, the mammas listen with astonishment to the parrot-like prattle, uttered in solemn cadences, with all the pomp of ignorance and folly. Such exhibitions only serve to strike the spreading fibres of vanity through the whole mind; for they neither teach children to speak fluently, nor behave gracefully. So far from it, that these frivolous pursuits might comprehensively be termed the study of affectation; for we now rarely see a simple, bashful boy, though few people of taste were ever disgusted by that awkward sheepishness so natural to the age, which schools and an early introduction into society, have changed into impudence and apish grimace.

Yet, how can these things be remedied whilst school-masters depend entirely on parents for a subsistence; and, when so many rival schools hang out their lures, to catch the attention of vain fathers and mothers, whose parental affection only leads them to wish that their children should outshine those of their neighbours?

---

* I now particularly allude to the numerous academies in and about London, and to the behaviour of the trading part of this great city.

Without great good luck, a sensible, conscientious man, would starve before he could raise a school, if he disdained to bubble weak parents by practising the secret tricks of the craft.

In the best regulated schools, however, where swarms are not crammed together, many bad habits must be acquired; but, at common schools, the body, heart, and understanding, are equally stunted, for parents are often only in quest of the cheapest school, and the master could not live, if he did not take a much greater number than he could manage himself; nor will the scanty pittance, allowed for each child, permit him to hire ushers sufficient to assist in the discharge of the mechanical part of the business. Besides, whatever appearance the house and garden may make, the children do not enjoy the comfort of either, for they are continually reminded by irksome restrictions that they are not at home, and the state-rooms, garden, &c. must be kept in order for the recreation of the parents; who, of a Sunday, visit the school, and are impressed by the very parade that renders the situation of their children uncomfortable.

With what disgust have I heard sensible women, for girls are more restrained and cowed than boys, speak of the wearisome confinement, which they endured at school. Not allowed, perhaps, to step out of one broad walk in a superb garden, and obliged to pace with steady deportment stupidly backwards and forwards, holding up their heads and turning out their toes, with shoulders braced back, instead of bounding, as nature directs to complete her own design, in the various attitudes so conducive to health.* The pure animal spirits, which make both

---

* I remember a circumstance that once came under my own observation, and raised my indignation. I went to visit a little boy at a school where young children were prepared for a larger one. The master took me into the school-room, &c. but whilst I walked down a broad gravel walk, I could not help observing that the grass grew very luxuriantly on each side of me. I immediately asked the child some questions, and found that the poor boys were not allowed to stir off the walk, and that the master sometimes permitted sheep to be turned in to crop the untrodden grass. The tyrant of this domain used to sit by a window that overlooked the prison yard, and one nook turning from it, where the unfortunate babes could sport freely, he enclosed, and planted it with potatoes. The wife likewise was equally anxious to keep the children in order, lest they should dirty or tear their clothes.

mind and body shoot out, and unfold the tender blossoms of hope, are turned sour, and vented in vain wishes or pert repinings, that contract the faculties and spoil the temper; else they mount to the brain, and sharpening the understanding before it gains proportionable strength, produce that pitiful cunning which disgracefully characterizes the female mind – and I fear will ever characterize it whilst women remain the slaves of power!

The little respect paid to chastity in the male world is, I am persuaded, the grand source of many of the physical and moral evils that torment mankind, as well as of the vices and follies that degrade and destroy women; yet at school, boys infallibly lose that decent bashfulness, which might have ripened into modesty, at home.

And what nasty indecent tricks do they not also learn from each other, when a number of them pig together in the same bedchamber, not to speak of the vices, which render the body weak, whilst they effectually prevent the acquisition of any delicacy of mind.[2] The little attention paid to the cultivation of modesty, amongst men, produces great depravity in all the relationships of society; for, not only love – love that ought to purify the heart, and first call forth all the youthful powers, to prepare the man to discharge the benevolent duties of life, is sacrificed to premature lust; but, all the social affections are deadened by the selfish gratifications, which very early pollute the mind, and dry up the generous juices of the heart. In what an unnatural manner is innocence often violated; and what serious consequences ensue to render private vices a public pest. Besides, an habit of personal order, which has more effect on the moral character, than is, in general, supposed, can only be acquired at home, where that respectable reserve is kept up which checks the familiarity, that sinking into beastliness, undermines the affection it insults.

I have already animadverted on the bad habits which females acquire when they are shut up together; and, I think, that the observation may fairly be extended to the other sex, till the natural inference is drawn which I have had in view throughout – that to improve both sexes they ought, not only in private families, but in public schools, to be educated together. If marriage be the cement of society, mankind should all be educated after the same model, or the intercourse of the sexes will never deserve the name of fellowship, nor will women ever fulfil the peculiar duties of their sex, till they become enlightened citizens, till they become free by being enabled to earn their own subsistence, independent of men; in the same manner, I mean, to prevent misconstruction, as one man is independent of another. Nay, marriage will never be held sacred till women, by being brought up with men, are prepared to be their companions rather than their mistresses; for the mean doublings of cunning will ever render them contemptible, whilst oppression renders them timid. So convinced am I of this truth, that I will venture to predict that virtue will never prevail in society till the virtues of both sexes are founded on reason; and, till the affections common to both are allowed to gain their due strength by the discharge of mutual duties.

Were boys and girls permitted to pursue the same studies together, those graceful decencies might early be inculcated which produce modesty without those sexual distinctions that taint the mind. Lessons of politeness, and that formulary of decorum, which treads on the heels of falsehood, would be rendered useless by habitual propriety of behaviour. Not, indeed, put on for visitors like the courtly robe of politeness, but the sober effect of cleanliness of mind. Would not this simple elegance of sincerity be a chaste homage paid to domestic affections, far surpassing the meretricious compliments that shine with false lustre in the heartless intercourse of fashionable life? But, till more understanding preponderates in society, there will ever be a want of heart and taste, and the harlot's *rouge* will supply the place of that celestial suffusion which only virtuous affections can give to the face. Gallantry, and what is called love, may subsist without simplicity of character; but the main pillars of friendship, are respect and confidence – esteem is never founded on it cannot tell what!

A taste for the fine arts requires great cultivation; but not more than a taste for the virtuous affections; and both suppose that enlargement of mind which opens so many sources of mental pleasure. Why do people hurry to noisy scenes, and crowded circles? I should answer, because they want activity of mind, because they have not cherished the virtues of the heart. They only, therefore, see and feel in the gross, and continually pine after variety, finding every thing that is simple insipid.

This argument may be carried further than philosophers are aware of, for if nature destined woman, in particular, for the discharge of domestic duties, she made her susceptible of the attached affections in a great degree. Now women are notoriously fond of pleasure; and, naturally must be so according to my definition, because they cannot enter into the minutiæ of domestic taste; lacking judgment, the foundation of all taste. For the understanding, in spite of sensual cavillers, reserves to itself the privilege of conveying pure joy to the heart.

With what a languid yawn have I seen an admirable poem thrown down, that a man of true taste returns to, again and again with rapture; and, whilst melody has almost suspended respiration, a lady has asked me where I bought my gown. I have seen also an eye glanced coldly over a most exquisite picture, rest, sparkling with pleasure, on a caricature rudely sketched; and whilst some terrific feature in nature has spread a sublime stillness through my soul, I have been desired to observe the pretty tricks of a lap-dog, that my perverse fate forced me to travel with. Is it surprising that such a tasteless being should rather caress this dog than her children? Or, that she should prefer the rant of flattery to the simple accents of sincerity?

To illustrate this remark I must be allowed to observe, that men of the first genius, and most cultivated minds, have appeared to have the highest relish for the simple beauties of nature; and they must have forcibly felt, what they have so well described, the charm which natural affections, and unsophisticated feelings spread round the human character. It is this power of looking into the heart, and responsively vibrating with each emotion, that enables the poet to personify each passion, and the painter to sketch with a pencil of fire.

True taste is ever the work of the understanding employed in observing natural effects; and till women have more understanding, it is vain to expect them to possess domestic taste. Their lively senses will ever be at work to harden their hearts, and the emotions struck out of them will continue to be vivid and transitory, unless a proper education store their mind with knowledge.

It is the want of domestic taste, and not the acquirement of knowledge, that takes women out of their families, and tears the smiling babe from the breast that ought to afford it nourishment. Women have been allowed to remain in ignorance, and slavish dependence, many, very many years, and still we hear of nothing but their fondness of pleasure and sway, their preference of rakes and soldiers, their childish attachment to toys, and the vanity that makes them value accomplishments more than virtues.

History brings forward a fearful catalogue of the crimes which their cunning has produced, when the weak slaves have had sufficient address to over-reach their masters. In France, and in how many other countries, have men been the luxurious despots, and women the crafty ministers? – Does this prove that ignorance and dependence domesticate them? Is not their folly the by-word of the libertines, who relax in their society; and do not men of sense continually lament that an immoderate fondness for dress and dissipation carries the mother of a family for ever from home? Their hearts have not been debauched by knowledge, or their minds led astray by scientific pursuits; yet, they do not fulfil the peculiar duties which as women they are called upon by nature to fulfil. On the contrary, the state of warfare which subsists between the sexes, makes them employ those wiles, that often frustrate the more open designs of force.

When, therefore, I call women slaves, I mean in a political and civil sense; for, indirectly they obtain too much power, and are debased by their exertions to obtain illicit sway.

Let an enlightened nation* then try what effect reason would have to bring them back to nature, and their duty; and allowing them to share the advantages of education and government with man, see whether they will become better, as they grow wiser

* France.[3]

and become free. They cannot be injured by the experiment; for it is not in the power of man to render them more insignificant than they are at present.

To render this practicable, day schools, for particular ages, should be established by government, in which boys and girls might be educated together. The school for the younger children, from five to nine years of age, ought to be absolutely free and open to all classes.* A sufficient number of masters should also be chosen by a select committee, in each parish, to whom any complaint of negligence, &c. might be made, if signed by six of the children's parents.

Ushers would then be unnecessary; for I believe experience will ever prove that this kind of subordinate authority is particularly injurious to the morals of youth. What, indeed, can tend to deprave the character more than outward submission and inward contempt? Yet how can boys be expected to treat an usher with respect, when the master seems to consider him in the light of a servant, and almost to countenance the ridicule which becomes the chief amusement of the boys during the play hours?

But nothing of this kind could occur in an elementary day-school, where boys and girls, the rich and poor, should meet together. And to prevent any of the distinctions of vanity, they should be dressed alike, and all obliged to submit to the same discipline, or leave the school. The school-room ought to be surrounded by a large piece of ground, in which the children might be usefully exercised, for at this age they should not be confined to any sedentary employment for more than an hour at a time. But these relaxations might all be rendered a part of elementary education, for many things improve and amuse the senses, when introduced as a kind of show, to the principles of which, dryly laid down, children would turn a deaf ear. For instance, botany, mechanics, and astronomy. Reading, writing, arithmetic, natural history, and some simple experiments in natural philosophy, might fill up the day; but these pursuits

---

* Treating this part of the subject, I have borrowed some hints from a very sensible pamphlet, written by the late Bishop of Autun[4] on Public Education.

should never encroach on gymnastic plays in the open air. The elements of religion, history, the history of man, and politics, might also be taught by conversations, in the socratic form.

After the age of nine, girls and boys, intended for domestic employments, or mechanical trades, ought to be removed to other schools, and receive instruction, in some measure appropriated to the destination of each individual, the two sexes being still together in the morning; but in the afternoon, the girls should attend a school, where plain-work, mantua-making, millinery, &c. would be their employment.

The young people of superior abilities, or fortune, might now be taught, in another school, the dead and living languages, the elements of science, and continue the study of history and politics, on a more extensive scale, which would not exclude polite literature.

Girls and boys still together? I hear some readers ask: yes. And I should not fear any other consequence than that some early attachment might take place; which, whilst it had the best effect on the moral character of the young people, might not perfectly agree with the views of the parents, for it will be a long time, I fear, before the world will be so far enlightened that parents, only anxious to render their children virtuous, shall allow them to choose companions for life themselves.

Besides, this would be a sure way to promote early marriages, and from early marriages the most salutary physical and moral effects naturally flow. What a different character does a married citizen assume from the selfish coxcomb,[5] who lives, but for himself, and who is often afraid to marry lest he should not be able to live in a certain style. Great emergencies excepted, which would rarely occur in a society of which equality was the basis, a man can only be prepared to discharge the duties of public life, by the habitual practice of those inferiour ones which form the man.

In this plan of education the constitution of boys would not be ruined by the early debaucheries, which now make men so selfish, or girls rendered weak and vain, by indolence, and frivolous pursuits. But, I presuppose, that such a degree of equality should be established between the sexes as would shut out gallantry and coquetry, yet allow friendship and love to temper the heart for the discharge of higher duties.

These would be schools of morality – and the happiness of man, allowed to flow from the pure springs of duty and affection, what advances might not the human mind make? Society can only be happy and free in proportion as it is virtuous; but the present distinctions, established in society, corrode all private, and blast all public virtue.

I have already inveighed against the custom of confining girls to their needle, and shutting them out from all political and civil employments; for by thus narrowing their minds they are rendered unfit to fulfil the peculiar duties which nature has assigned them.

Only employed about the little incidents of the day, they necessarily grow up cunning. My very soul has often sickened at observing the sly tricks practised by women to gain some foolish thing on which their silly hearts were set. Not allowed to dispose of money, or call any thing their own, they learn to turn the market penny; or, should a husband offend, by staying from home, or give rise to some emotions of jealousy – a new gown, or any pretty bawble, smooths Juno's angry brow.[6]

But these *littlenesses* would not degrade their character, if women were led to respect themselves, if political and moral subjects were opened to them; and, I will venture to affirm, that this is the only way to make them properly attentive to their domestic duties. – An active mind embraces the whole circle of its duties, and finds time enough for all. It is not, I assert, a bold attempt to emulate masculine virtues; it is not the enchantment of literary pursuits, or the steady investigation of scientific subjects, that leads women astray from duty. No, it is indolence and vanity – the love of pleasure and the love of sway, that will reign paramount in an empty mind. I say empty emphatically, because the education which women now receive scarcely deserves the name. For the little knowledge that they are led to acquire, during the important years of youth, is merely relative to accomplishments; and accomplishments without a bottom, for unless the understanding be cultivated, superficial and monotonous is every grace. Like the charms of a made up face, they only strike the senses in a crowd; but at home, wanting mind, they want variety. The consequence is obvious; in gay scenes of dissipation we meet the artificial mind and face, for those who fly from solitude dread, next to solitude, the domestic circle; not having it in their power to amuse or interest, they feel their own insignificance, or find nothing to amuse or interest themselves.

Besides, what can be more indelicate than a girl's *coming out* in the fashionable world? Which, in other words, is to bring to market a marriageable miss, whose person is taken from one public place to another, richly caparisoned. Yet, mixing in the giddy circle under restraint, these butterflies long to flutter at large, for the first affection of their souls is their own persons, to which their attention has been called with the most sedulous care whilst they were preparing for the period that decides their fate for life. Instead of pursuing this idle routine, sighing for tasteless shew, and heartless state, with what dignity would the youths of both sexes form attachments in the schools that I have cursorily pointed out; in which, as life advanced, dancing, music, and drawing, might be admitted as relaxations, for at these schools young people of fortune ought to remain, more or less, till they were of age. Those, who were designed for particular professions, might attend, three or four mornings in the week, the schools appropriated for their immediate instruction.

I only drop these observations at present, as hints; rather, indeed, as an outline of the plan I mean, than a digested one; but I must add, that I highly approve of one regulation mentioned in the pamphlet* already alluded to, that of making the children and youths independent of the masters respecting punishments. They should be tried by their peers, which would be an admirable method of fixing sound principles of justice in the mind, and might have the happiest effect on the temper, which is very early soured or irritated by tyranny, till it becomes peevishly cunning, or ferociously overbearing.

My imagination darts forward with benevolent fervour to greet these amiable and respectable groups, in spite of the sneering of cold hearts, who are at liberty to utter, with frigid self-

* The Bishop of Autun's.

importance, the damning epithet – romantic; the force of which
I shall endeavour to blunt by repeating the words of an eloquent
moralist. – 'I know not whether the allusions of a truly humane
heart, whose zeal renders every thing easy, be not preferable
to that rough and repulsing reason, which always finds an
indifference for the public good, the first obstacle to whatever
would promote it.'

I know that libertines will also exclaim, that woman would
be unsexed by acquiring strength of body and mind, and that
beauty, soft bewitching beauty! would no longer adorn the
daughters of men. I am of a very different opinion, for I think
that, on the contrary, we should then see dignified beauty, and
true grace; to produce which, many powerful physical and moral
causes would concur. – Not relaxed beauty, it is true, or the
graces of helplessness; but such as appears to make us respect the
human body as a majestic pile fit to receive a noble inhabitant, in
the relics of antiquity.

I do not forget the popular opinion that the Grecian statues
were not modelled after nature. I mean, not according to the
proportions of a particular man; but that beautiful limbs and
features were selected from various bodies to form an harmonious whole. This might, in some degree, be true. The fine ideal
picture of an exalted imagination might be superiour to the
materials which the statuary found in nature, and thus it might
with propriety be termed rather the model of mankind than of
a man. It was not, however, the mechanical selection of limbs
and features; but the ebullition of an heated fancy that burst
forth, and the fine senses and enlarged understanding of the
artist selected the solid matter, which he drew into this glowing
focus.

I observed that it was not mechanical, because a whole was
produced – a model of that grand simplicity, of those concurring
energies, which arrest our attention and command our reverence. For only insipid lifeless beauty is produced by a servile
copy of even beautiful nature. Yet, independent of these observations, I believe that the human form must have been far more
beautiful than it is at present, because extreme indolence, barbarous ligatures, and many causes, which forcibly act on it, in

our luxurious state of society, did not retard its expansion, or render it deformed. Exercise and cleanliness appear to be not only the surest means of preserving health, but of promoting beauty, the physical causes only considered; yet, this is not sufficient, moral ones must concur, or beauty will be merely of that rustic kind which blooms on the innocent, wholesome, countenances of some country people, whose minds have not been exercised. To render the person perfect, physical and moral beauty ought to be attained at the same time; each lending and receiving force by the combination. Judgment must reside on the brow, affection and fancy beam in the eye, and humanity curve the cheek, or vain is the sparkling of the finest eye or the elegantly turned finish of the fairest features: whilst in every motion that displays the active limbs and well-knit joints, grace and modesty should appear. But this fair assemblage is not to be brought together by chance; it is the reward of exertions calculated to support each other; for judgment can only be acquired by reflection, affection by the discharge of duties, and humanity by the exercise of compassion to every living creature.

Humanity to animals should be particularly inculcated as a part of national education, for it is not at present one of our national virtues. Tenderness for their humble dumb domestics, amongst the lower class, is oftener to be found in a savage than a civilized state. For civilization prevents that intercourse which creates affection in the rude hut, or mud hovel, and leads uncultivated minds who are only depraved by the refinements which prevail in the society, where they are trodden under foot by the rich, to domineer over them to revenge the insults that they are obliged to bear from their superiours.

This habitual cruelty is first caught at school, where it is one of the rare sports of the boys to torment the miserable brutes that fall in their way. The transition, as they grow up, from barbarity to brutes to domestic tyranny over wives, children, and servants, is very easy. Justice, or even benevolence, will not be a powerful spring of action unless it extend to the whole creation; nay, I believe that it may be delivered as an axiom, that those who can see pain, unmoved, will soon learn to inflict it.

The vulgar are swayed by present feelings, and the habits

which they have accidentally acquired; but on partial feelings much dependence cannot be placed, though they be just; for, when they are not invigorated by reflection, custom weakens them, till they are scarcely perceptible. The sympathies of our nature are strengthened by pondering cogitations, and deadened by thoughtless use. Macbeth's heart smote him more for one murder, the first, than for a hundred subsequent ones, which were necessary to back it.[7] But, when I used the epithet vulgar, I did not mean to confine my remark to the poor, for partial humanity, founded on present sensations, or whim, is quite as conspicuous, if not more so, amongst the rich.

The lady who sheds tears for the bird starved in a snare, and execrates the devils in the shape of men, who goad to madness the poor ox, or whip the patient ass, tottering under a burden above its strength, will, nevertheless, keep her coachman and horses whole hours waiting for her, when the sharp frost bites, or the rain beats against the well-closed windows which do not admit a breath of air to tell her how roughly the wind blows without. And she who takes her dogs to bed, and nurses them with a parade of sensibility, when sick, will suffer her babes to grow up crooked in a nursery.[8] This illustration of my argument is drawn from a matter of fact. The woman whom I allude to was handsome, reckoned very handsome, by those who do not miss the mind when the face is plump and fair; but her understanding had not been led from female duties by literature, nor her innocence debauched by knowledge. No, she was quite feminine, according to the masculine acceptation of the word; and, so far from loving these spoiled brutes that filled the place which her children ought to have occupied, she only lisped out a pretty mixture of French and English nonsense, to please the men who flocked round her. The wife, mother, and human creature, were all swallowed up by the factitious character which an improper education and the selfish vanity of beauty had produced.

I do not like to make a distinction without a difference, and I own that I have been as much disgusted by the fine lady who took her lap-dog to her bosom instead of her child; as by the ferocity of a man, who, beating his horse, declared, that he knew as well when he did wrong, as a Christian.

This brood of folly shews how mistaken they are who, if they allow women to leave their harams, do not cultivate their understandings, in order to plant virtues in their hearts. For had they sense, they might acquire that domestic taste which would lead them to love with reasonable subordination their whole family, from their husband to the house-dog; nor would they ever insult humanity in the person of the most menial servant by paying more attention to the comfort of a brute, than to that of a fellow-creature.

My observations on national education are obviously hints; but I principally wish to enforce the necessity of educating the sexes together to perfect both, and of making children sleep at home that they may learn to love home; yet to make private support, instead of smothering, public affections, they should be sent to school to mix with a number of equals, for only by the jostlings of equality can we form a just opinion of ourselves.

To render mankind more virtuous, and happier of course, both sexes must act from the same principle; but how can that be expected when only one is allowed to see the reasonableness of it? To render also the social compact truly equitable, and in order to spread those enlightening principles, which alone can meliorate the fate of man, women must be allowed to found their virtue on knowledge, which is scarcely possible unless they be educated by the same pursuits as men. For they are now made so inferiour by ignorance and low desires, as not to deserve to be ranked with them; or, by the serpentine wrigglings of cunning they mount the tree of knowledge, and only acquire sufficient to lead men astray.

It is plain from the history of all nations, that women cannot be confined to merely domestic pursuits, for they will not fulfil family duties, unless their minds take a wider range, and whilst they are kept in ignorance they become in the same proportion the slaves of pleasure as they are the slaves of man. Nor can they be shut out of great enterprises, though the narrowness of their minds often make them mar, what they are unable to comprehend.

The libertinism, and even the virtues of superiour men, will always give women, of some description, great power over them;

and these weak women, under the influence of childish passions and selfish vanity, will throw a false light over the objects which the very men view with their eyes, who ought to enlighten their judgment. Men of fancy, and those sanguine characters who mostly hold the helm of human affairs, in general, relax in the society of women; and surely I need not cite to the most superficial reader of history the numerous examples of vice and oppression which the private intrigues of female favourites have produced; not to dwell on the mischief that naturally arises from the blundering interposition of well-meaning folly. For in the transactions of business it is much better to have to deal with a knave than a fool, because a knave adheres to some plan; and any plan of reason may be seen through much sooner than a sudden flight of folly. The power which vile and foolish women have had over wise men, who possessed sensibility, is notorious; I shall only mention one instance.

Who ever drew a more exalted female character than Rousseau? though in the lump he constantly endeavoured to degrade the sex. And why was he thus anxious? Truly to justify to himself the affection which weakness and virtue had made him cherish for that fool Theresa. He could not raise her to the common level of her sex; and therefore he laboured to bring woman down to hers. He found her a convenient humble companion, and pride made him determine to find some superiour virtues in the being whom he chose to live with; but did not her conduct during his life, and after his death, clearly shew how grossly he was mistaken who called her a celestial innocent. Nay, in the bitterness of his heart, he himself laments, that when his bodily infirmities made him no longer treat her like a woman, she ceased to have an affection for him.[9] And it was very natural that she should, for having so few sentiments in common, when the sexual tie was broken, what was to hold her? To hold her affection whose sensibility was confined to one sex, nay, to one man, it requires sense to turn sensibility into the broad channel of humanity; many women have not mind enough to have an affection for a woman, or a friendship for a man. But the sexual weakness that makes woman depend on man for a subsistence, produces a kind of cattish affection which leads a wife to purr about her husband as she would about any man who fed and caressed her.

Men are, however, often gratified by this kind of fondness, which is confined in a beastly manner to themselves; but should they ever become more virtuous, they will wish to converse at their fire-side with a friend, after they cease to play with a mistress.

Besides, understanding is necessary to give variety and interest to sensual enjoyments, for low, indeed, in the intellectual scale, is the mind that can continue to love when neither virtue nor sense give a human appearance to an animal appetite. But sense will always preponderate; and if women be not, in general, brought more on a level with men, some superiour women, like the Greek courtezans,[10] will assemble the men of abilities around them, and draw from their families many citizens, who would have stayed at home had their wives had more sense, or the graces which result from the exercise of the understanding and fancy, the legitimate parents of taste. A woman of talents, if she be not absolutely ugly, will always obtain great power, raised by the weakness of her sex; and in proportion as men acquire virtue and delicacy, by the exertion of reason, they will look for both in women, but they can only acquire them in the same way that men do.

In France or Italy, have the women confined themselves to domestic life? though they have not hitherto had a political existence, yet, have they not illicitly had great sway? corrupting themselves and the men with whose passions they played. In short, in whatever light I view the subject, reason and experience convince me that the only method of leading women to fulfil their peculiar duties, is to free them from all restraint by allowing them to participate the inherent rights of mankind.

Make them free, and they will quickly become wise and virtuous, as men become more so; for the improvement must be mutual, or the injustice which one half of the human race are obliged to submit to, retorting on their oppressors, the virtue of man will be worm-eaten by the insect whom he keeps under his feet.

Let men take their choice, man and woman were made for

each other, though not to become one being; and if they will not improve women, they will deprave them!

I speak of the improvement and emancipation of the whole sex, for I know that the behaviour of a few women, who, by accident, or following a strong bent of nature, have acquired a portion of knowledge superiour to that of the rest of their sex, has often been overbearing; but there have been instances of women who, attaining knowledge, have not discarded modesty, nor have they always pedantically appeared to despise the ignorance which they laboured to disperse in their own minds. The exclamations then which any advice respecting female learning, commonly produces, especially from pretty women, often arise from envy. When they chance to see that even the lustre of their eyes, and the flippant sportiveness of refined coquetry will not always secure them attention, during a whole evening, should a woman of a more cultivated understanding endeavour to give a rational turn to the conversation, the common source of consolation is, that such women seldom get husbands. What arts have I not seen silly women use to interrupt by *flirtation*, a very significant word to describe such a manœuvre, a rational conversation which made the men forget that they were pretty women.

But, allowing what is very natural to man, that the possession of rare abilities is really calculated to excite over-weening pride, disgusting in both men and women – in what a state of inferiority must the female faculties have rusted when such a small portion of knowledge as those women attained, who have sneeringly been termed learned women, could be singular? – Sufficiently so to puff up the possessor, and excite envy in her contemporaries, and some of the other sex. Nay, has not a little rationality exposed many women to the severest censure? I advert to well known facts, for I have frequently heard women ridiculed, and every little weakness exposed, only because they adopted the advice of some medical men, and deviated from the beaten track in their mode of treating their infants.[11] I have actually heard this barbarous aversion to innovation carried still further, and a sensible woman stigmatized as an unnatural mother, who has thus been wisely solicitous to preserve the health of her children, when in the midst of her care she has lost one by some of the casualties of infancy, which no prudence can ward off. Her acquaintance have observed, that this was the consequence of new-fangled notions – the new-fangled notions of ease and cleanliness. And those who pretending to experience, though they have long adhered to prejudices that have, according to the opinion of the most sagacious physicians, thinned the human race, almost rejoiced at the disaster that gave a kind of sanction to prescription.

Indeed, if it were only on this account, the national education of women is of the utmost consequence, for what a number of human sacrifices are made to that moloch prejudice![12] And in how many ways are children destroyed by the lasciviousness of man? The want of natural affection, in many women, who are drawn from their duty by the admiration of men, and the ignorance of others, render the infancy of man a much more perilous state than that of brutes; yet men are unwilling to place women in situations proper to enable them to acquire sufficient understanding to know how even to nurse their babes.

So forcibly does this truth strike me, that I would rest the whole tendency of my reasoning upon it, for whatever tends to incapacitate the maternal character, takes woman out of her sphere.

But it is vain to expect the present race of weak mothers either to take that reasonable care of a child's body, which is necessary to lay the foundation of a good constitution, supposing that it do not suffer for the sins of its fathers;[13] or, to manage its temper so judiciously that the child will not have, as it grows up, to throw off all that its mother, its first instructor, directly or indirectly taught; and unless the mind have uncommon vigour, womanish follies will stick to the character throughout life. The weakness of the mother will be visited on the children! And whilst women are educated to rely on their husbands for judgment, this must ever be the consequence, for there is no improving an understanding by halves, nor can any being act wisely from imitation, because in every circumstance of life there is a kind of individuality, which requires an exertion of judgment to modify general rules. The being who can think justly in one track, will soon extend its intellectual empire; and she who has sufficient judgment to manage her children, will not submit, right or wrong, to her husband, or patiently to the social laws which make a nonentity of a wife.

In public schools women, to guard against the errors of ignorance, should be taught the elements of anatomy and medicine, not only to enable them to take proper care of their own health, but to make them rational nurses of their infants, parents, and husbands; for the bills of mortality[14] are swelled by the blunders of self-willed old women, who give nostrums of their own without knowing any thing of the human frame. It is likewise proper only in a domestic view, to make women acquainted with the anatomy of the mind, by allowing the sexes to associate together in every pursuit; and by leading them to observe the progress of the human understanding in the improvement of the sciences and arts; never forgetting the science of morality, or the study of the political history of mankind.

A man has been termed a microcosm; and every family might also be called a state. States, it is true, have mostly been governed by arts that disgrace the character of man; and the want of a just constitution, and equal laws, have so perplexed the notions of the worldly wise, that they more than question the reasonableness of contending for the rights of humanity. Thus morality, polluted in the national reservoir, sends off streams of vice to corrupt the constituent parts of the body politic; but should more noble, or rather, more just principles regulate the laws, which ought to be the government of society, and not those who execute them, duty might become the rule of private conduct.

Besides, by the exercise of their bodies and minds women would acquire that mental activity so necessary in the maternal character, united with the fortitude that distinguishes steadiness of conduct from the obstinate perverseness of weakness. For it is dangerous to advise the indolent to be steady, because they instantly become rigorous, and to save themselves trouble, punish with severity faults that the patient fortitude of reason might have prevented.

But fortitude presupposes strength of mind; and is strength of mind to be acquired by indolent acquiescence? by asking advice instead of exerting the judgment? by obeying through fear, instead of practising the forbearance, which we all stand in need of ourselves? – The conclusion which I wish to draw, is obvious; make women rational creatures, and free citizens, and they will quickly become good wives, and mothers; that is – if men do not neglect the duties of husbands and fathers.

Discussing the advantages which a public and private education combined, as I have sketched, might rationally be expected to produce, I have dwelt most on such as are particularly relative to the female world, because I think the female world oppressed; yet the gangrene, which the vices engendered by oppression have produced, is not confined to the morbid part, but pervades society at large: so that when I wish to see my sex become more like moral agents, my heart bounds with the anticipation of the general diffusion of that sublime contentment which only morality can diffuse.

CHAP. XIII

SOME INSTANCES OF THE FOLLY WHICH THE
IGNORANCE OF WOMEN GENERATES; WITH
CONCLUDING REFLECTIONS ON THE MORAL
IMPROVEMENT THAT A REVOLUTION IN
FEMALE MANNERS MIGHT NATURALLY BE
EXPECTED TO PRODUCE

There are many follies, in some degree, peculiar to women: sins against reason of commission as well as of omission; but all flowing from ignorance or prejudice, I shall only point out such as appear to be particularly injurious to their moral character. And in animadverting on them, I wish especially to prove, that the weakness of mind and body, which men have endeavoured, impelled by various motives, to perpetuate, prevents their discharging the peculiar duty of their sex: for when weakness of body will not permit them to suckle their children, and weakness of mind makes them spoil their tempers – is woman in a natural state?

SECT. I

One glaring instance of the weakness which proceeds from ignorance, first claims attention, and calls for severe reproof.

In this metropolis a number of lurking leeches infamously gain a subsistence by practising on the credulity of women, pretending to cast nativities,[1] to use the technical phrase; and many females who, proud of their rank and fortune, look down on the vulgar with sovereign contempt, shew by this credulity, that the distinction is arbitrary, and that they have not sufficiently cultivated their minds to rise above vulgar prejudices. Women, because they have not been led to consider the knowledge of their duty as the one thing necessary to know, or, to live in the present moment by the discharge of it, are very anxious to peep into futurity, to learn what they have to expect to render life interesting, and to break the vacuum of ignorance.

I must be allowed to expostulate seriously with the ladies who follow these idle inventions; for ladies, mistresses of families, are not ashamed to drive in their own carriages to the door of the cunning man.* And if any of them should peruse this work, I entreat them to answer to their own hearts the following questions, not forgetting that they are in the presence of God.

Do you believe that there is but one God, and that he is powerful, wise, and good?

Do you believe that all things were created by him, and that all beings are dependent on him?

Do you rely on his wisdom, so conspicuous in his works, and in your own frame, and are you convinced that he has ordered all things which do not come under the cognizance of your senses, in the same perfect harmony, to fulfil his designs?

Do you acknowledge that the power of looking into futurity, and seeing things that are not, as if they were, is an attribute of the Creator? And should he, by an impression on the minds of his creatures, think fit to impart to them some event hid in the shades of time yet unborn, to whom would the secret be revealed by immediate inspiration? The opinion of ages will answer this question – to reverend old men, to people distinguished for eminent piety.

The oracles of old were thus delivered by priests dedicated to the service of the God who was supposed to inspire them. The glare of worldly pomp which surrounded these impostors, and the respect paid to them by artful politicians, who knew how to avail themselves of this useful engine to bend the necks of the strong under the dominion of the cunning, spread a sacred mysterious veil of sanctity over their lies and abominations. Impressed by such solemn devotional parade, a Greek, or Roman lady might be excused, if she inquired of the oracle, when she was anxious to pry into futurity, or inquire about some dubious event: and her inquiries, however contrary to

---

* I once lived in the neighbourhood of one of these men, a *handsome* man, and saw with surprise and indignation, women, whose appearance and attendance bespoke that rank in which females are supposed to receive a superiour education, flock to his door.

reason, could not be reckoned impious. – But, can the professors of Christianity ward off that imputation? Can a Christian suppose that the favourites of the most High, the highly favoured, would be obliged to lurk in disguise, and practise the most dishonest tricks to cheat silly women out of the money – which the poor cry for in vain?

Say not that such questions are an insult to common sense – for it is your own conduct, O ye foolish women! which throws an odium on your sex! And these reflections should make you shudder at your thoughtlessness, and irrational devotion. – For I do not suppose that all of you laid aside your religion, such as it is, when you entered those mysterious dwellings. Yet, as I have throughout supposed myself talking to ignorant women, for ignorant ye are in the most emphatical sense of the word, it would be absurd to reason with you on the egregious folly of desiring to know what the Supreme Wisdom has concealed.

Probably you would not understand me, were I to attempt to shew you that it would be absolutely inconsistent with the grand purpose of life, that of rendering human creatures wise and virtuous: and that, were it sanctioned by God, it would disturb the order established in creation; and if it be not sanctioned by God, do you expect to hear truth? Can events be foretold, events which have not yet assumed a body to become subject to mortal inspection, can they be foreseen by a vicious worldling, who pampers his appetites by preying on the foolish ones?

Perhaps, however, you devoutly believe in the devil, and imagine, to shift the question, that he may assist his votaries; but, if really respecting the power of such a being, an enemy to goodness and to God, can you go to church after having been under such an obligation to him?

From these delusions to those still more fashionable deceptions, practised by the whole tribe of magnetisers,[2] the transition is very natural. With respect to them, it is equally proper to ask women a few questions.

Do you know any thing of the construction of the human frame? If not, it is proper that you should be told what every child ought to know, that when its admirable œconomy has been disturbed by intemperance or indolence, I speak not of violent disorders, but of chronical diseases, it must be brought into a healthy state again, by slow degrees, and if the functions of life have not been materially injured, regimen,[3] another word for temperance, air, exercise, and a few medicines, prescribed by persons who have studied the human body, are the only human means, yet discovered, of recovering that inestimable blessing health, that will bear investigation.

Do you then believe that these magnetisers, who, by hocus pocus tricks, pretend to work a miracle, are delegated by God, or assisted by the solver of all these kind of difficulties – the devil?

Do they, when they put to flight, as it is said, disorders that have baffled the powers of medicine, work in conformity to the light of reason? or, do they effect these wonderful cures by supernatural aid?

By a communication, an adept may answer, with the world of spirits. A noble privilege, it must be allowed. Some of the ancients mention familiar dæmons, who guarded them from danger by kindly intimating, we cannot guess in what manner, when any danger was nigh; or, pointed out what they ought to undertake. Yet the men who laid claim to this privilege, out of the order of nature, insisted that it was the reward, or conse- quence, of superiour temperance and piety. But the present workers of wonders are not raised above their fellows by superi- our temperance or sanctity. They do not cure for the love of God, but money. These are the priests of quackery, though it is true they have not the convenient expedient of selling masses for souls in purgatory, or churches where they can display crutches, and models of limbs made sound by a touch or a word.

I am not conversant with the technical terms, or initiated into the arcana, therefore, I may speak improperly; but it is clear that men who will not conform to the law of reason, and earn a subsistence in an honest way, by degrees, are very fortunate in becoming acquainted with such obliging spirits. We cannot, indeed, give them credit for either great sagacity or goodness, else they would have chosen more noble instruments, when they wished to shew themselves the benevolent friends of man.

It is, however, little short of blasphemy to pretend to such powers!

From the whole tenour of the dispensations of Providence, it appears evident to sober reason, that certain vices produce certain effects; and can any one so grossly insult the wisdom of God, as to suppose that a miracle will be allowed to disturb his general laws, to restore to health the intemperate and vicious, merely to enable them to pursue the same course with impunity? Be whole, and sin no more,[4] said Jesus. And, are greater miracles to be performed by those who do not follow his footsteps, who healed the body to reach the mind?

The mentioning of the name of Christ, after such vile impostors, may displease some of my readers – I respect their warmth; but let them not forget that the followers of these delusions bear his name, and profess to be the disciples of him, who said, by their works we should know who were the children of God or the servants of sin. I allow that it is easier to touch the body of a saint, or to be magnetised, than to restrain our appetites or govern our passions; but health of body or mind can only be recovered by these means, or we make the Supreme Judge partial and revengeful.

Is he a man that he should change, or punish out of resentment? He – the common father, wounds but to heal, says reason, and our irregularities producing certain consequences, we are forcibly shewn the nature of vice; that thus learning to know good from evil, by experience, we may hate one and love the other, in proportion to the wisdom which we attain. The poison contains the antidote; and we either reform our evil habits and cease to sin against our own bodies, to use the forcible language of scripture, or a premature death, the punishment of sin, snaps the thread of life.

Here an awful stop is put to our inquiries. – But, why should I conceal my sentiments? Considering the attributes of God, I believe that whatever punishment may follow, will tend, like the anguish of disease, to shew the malignity of vice, for the purpose of reformation. Positive punishment appears so contrary to the nature of God, discoverable in all his works, and in our own reason, that I could sooner believe that the Deity paid no attention to the conduct of men, than that he punished without the benevolent design of reforming.

To suppose only that an all-wise and powerful Being, as good as he is great, should create a being foreseeing, that after fifty or sixty years of feverish existence, it would be plunged into never ending woe – is blasphemy. On what will the worm feed that is never to die? On folly, on ignorance, say ye – I should blush indignantly at drawing the natural conclusion could I insert it, and wish to withdraw myself from the wing of my God! On such a supposition, I speak with reverence, he would be a consuming fire. We should wish, though vainly, to fly from his presence when fear absorbed love, and darkness involved all his counsels!

I know that many devout people boast of submitting to the Will of God blindly, as to an arbitrary sceptre or rod, on the same principle as the Indians worship the devil.[5] In other words, like people in the common concerns of life, they do homage to power, and cringe under the foot that can crush them. Rational religion, on the contrary, is a submission to the will of a being so perfectly wise, that all he wills must be directed by the proper motive – must be reasonable.

And, if thus we respect God, can we give credit to the mysterious insinuations, which insult his laws? can we believe, though it should stare us in the face, that he would work a miracle to authorize confusion by sanctioning an error? Yet we must either allow these impious conclusions, or treat with contempt every promise to restore health to a diseased body by supernatural means, or to foretell the incidents that can only be foreseen by God.

SECT. II

Another instance of that feminine weakness of character, often produced by a confined education, is a romantic twist of the mind, which has been very properly termed *sentimental*.

Women subjected by ignorance to their sensations, and only taught to look for happiness in love, refine on sensual feelings, and adopt metaphysical notions respecting that passion, which lead them shamefully to neglect the duties of life, and frequently in the midst of these sublime refinements they plump into actual vice.

These are the women who are amused by the reveries of the stupid novelists,[6] who, knowing little of human nature, work up stale tales, and describe meretricious scenes, all retailed in a sentimental jargon, which equally tend to corrupt the taste, and draw the heart aside from its daily duties. I do not mention the understanding, because never having been exercised, its slumbering energies rest inactive, like the lurking particles of fire which are supposed universally to pervade matter.

Females, in fact, denied all political privileges, and not allowed, as married women, excepting in criminal cases, a civil existence, have their attention naturally drawn from the interest of the whole community to that of the minute parts, though the private duty of any member of society must be very imperfectly performed when not connected with the general good. The mighty business of female life is to please, and restrained from entering into more important concerns by political and civil oppression, sentiments become events, and reflection deepens what it should, and would have effaced, if the understanding had been allowed to take a wider range.

But, confined to trifling employments, they naturally imbibe opinions which the only kind of reading calculated to interest an innocent frivolous mind, inspires. Unable to grasp any thing great, is it surprising that they find the reading of history a very dry task, and disquisitions addressed to the understanding intolerably tedious, and almost unintelligible? Thus are they necessarily dependent on the novelist for amusement. Yet, when I exclaim against novels, I mean when contrasted with those works which exercise the understanding and regulate the imagination. – For any kind of reading I think better than leaving a blank still a blank, because the mind must receive a degree of enlargement and obtain a little strength by a slight exertion of its thinking powers; besides, even the productions that are only addressed to the imagination, raise the reader a little above the gross gratification of appetites, to which the mind has not given a shade of delicacy.

This observation is the result of experience; for I have known several notable women, and one in particular, who was a very good woman – as good as such a narrow mind would allow her to be, who took care that her daughters (three in number) should never see a novel. As she was a woman of fortune and fashion, they had various masters to attend them, and a sort of menial governess to watch their footsteps. From their masters they learned how tables, chairs, &c. were called in French and Italian; but as the few books thrown in their way were far above their capacities, or devotional, they neither acquired ideas nor sentiments, and passed their time, when not compelled to repeat *words*, in dressing, quarrelling with each other, or conversing with their maids by stealth, till they were brought into company as marriageable.

Their mother, a widow, was busy in the mean time in keeping up her connections, as she termed a numerous acquaintance, lest her girls should want a proper introduction into the great world. And these young ladies, with minds vulgar in every sense of the word, and spoiled tempers, entered life puffed up with notions of their own consequence, and looking down with contempt on those who could not vie with them in dress and parade.

With respect to love, nature, or their nurses, had taken care to teach them the physical meaning of the word; and, as they had few topics of conversation, and fewer refinements of senti- ment, they expressed their gross wishes not in very delicate phrases, when they spoke freely, talking of matrimony.

Could these girls have been injured by the perusal of novels? I almost forgot a shade in the character of one of them; she affected a simplicity bordering on folly, and with a simper would utter the most immodest remarks and questions, the full meaning of which she had learned whilst secluded from the world, and afraid to speak in her mother's presence, who gov- erned with a high hand: they were all educated, as she prided herself, in a most exemplary manner; and read their chapters and psalms before breakfast, never touching a silly novel.

This is only one instance; but I recollect many other women who, not led by degrees to proper studies, and not permitted to choose for themselves, have indeed been overgrown children; or have obtained, by mixing in the world, a little of what is termed common sense: that is, a distinct manner of seeing common occurrences, as they stand detached: but what deserves the name of intellect, the power of gaining general or abstract ideas, or even intermediate ones, was out of the question. Their minds were quiescent, and when they were not roused by sensible objects and employments of that kind, they were low-spirited, would cry, or go to sleep.

When, therefore, I advise my sex not to read such flimsy works, it is to induce them to read something superiour; for I coincide in opinion with a sagacious man, who, having a daughter and niece under his care, pursued a very different plan with each.

The niece, who had considerable abilities, had, before she was left to his guardianship, been indulged in desultory reading. Her he endeavoured to lead, and did lead to history and moral essays; but his daughter, whom a fond weak mother had indulged, and who consequently was averse to every thing like application, he allowed to read novels: and used to justify his conduct by saying, that if she ever attained a relish for reading them, he should have some foundation to work upon; and that erroneous opinions were better than none at all.

In fact the female mind has been so totally neglected, that knowledge was only to be acquired from this muddy source, till from reading novels some women of superiour talents learned to despise them.

The best method, I believe, that can be adopted to correct a fondness for novels is to ridicule them: not indiscriminately, for then it would have little effect; but, if a judicious person, with some turn for humour, would read several to a young girl, and point out both by tones, and apt comparisons with pathetic incidents and heroic characters in history, how foolishly and ridiculously they caricatured human nature, just opinions might be substituted instead of romantic sentiments.

In one respect, however, the majority of both sexes resemble, and equally shew a want of taste and modesty. Ignorant women, forced to be chaste to preserve their reputation, allow their imagination to revel in the unnatural and meretricious scenes sketched by the novel writers of the day, slighting as insipid the sober dignity, and matron graces of history,* whilst men carry the same vitiated taste into life, and fly for amusement to the wanton, from the unsophisticated charms of virtue, and the grave respectability of sense.

Besides, the reading of novels makes women, and particularly ladies of fashion, very fond of using strong expressions and superlatives in conversation; and, though the dissipated artificial life which they lead prevents their cherishing any strong legitimate passion, the language of passion in affected tones slips for ever from their glib tongues, and every trifle produces those phosphoric bursts which only mimick in the dark the flame of passion.

SECT. III

Ignorance and the mistaken cunning that nature sharpens in weak heads as a principle of self-preservation, render women very fond of dress, and produce all the vanity which such a fondness may naturally be expected to generate, to the exclusion of emulation and magnanimity.

I agree with Rousseau that the physical part of the art of pleasing consists in ornaments,[7] and for that very reason I should guard girls against the contagious fondness for dress so common to weak women, that they may not rest in the physical part. Yet, weak are the women who imagine that they can long please without the aid of the mind, or, in other words, without the moral art of pleasing. But the moral art, if it be not a profanation to use the word art, when alluding to the grace which is an effect of virtue, and not the motive of action, is never to be found with ignorance; the sportiveness of innocence, so pleasing to refined libertines of both sexes, is widely different in its essence from this superiour gracefulness.

---

* I am not now alluding to that superiority of mind which leads to the creation of ideal beauty, when he, surveyed with a penetrating eye, appears a tragi-comedy, in which little can be seen to satisfy the heart without the help of fancy.

A strong inclination for external ornaments ever appears in barbarous states, only the men not the women adorn themselves; for where women are allowed to be so far on a level with men, society has advanced, at least, one step in civilization.

The attention to dress, therefore, which has been thought a sexual propensity, I think natural to mankind. But I ought to express myself with more precision. When the mind is not sufficiently opened to take pleasure in reflection, the body will be adorned with sedulous care; and ambition will appear in tattooing or painting it.

So far is this first inclination carried, that even the hellish yoke of slavery cannot stifle the savage desire of admiration which the black heroes inherit from both their parents, for all the hardly earned savings of a slave are commonly expended in a little tawdry finery. And I have seldom known a good male or female servant that was not particularly fond of dress. Their clothes were their riches; and, I argue from analogy, that the fondness for dress, so extravagant in females, arises from the same cause – want of cultivation of mind. When men meet they converse about business, politics, or literature; but, says Swift, 'how naturally do women apply their hands to each other's lappets and ruffles.'[8] And very natural is it – for they have not any business to interest them, have not a taste for literature, and they find politics dry, because they have not acquired a love for mankind by turning their thoughts to the grand pursuits that exalt the human race, and promote general happiness.

Besides, various are the paths to power and fame which by accident or choice men pursue, and though they jostle against each other, for men of the same profession are seldom friends, yet there is a much greater number of their fellow-creatures with whom they never clash. But women are very differently situated with respect to each other – for they are all rivals.

Before marriage it is their business to please men; and after, with a few exceptions, they follow the same scent with all the persevering pertinacity of instinct. Even virtuous women never forget their sex in company, for they are for ever trying to make themselves *agreeable*. A female beauty, and a male wit, appear to be equally anxious to draw the attention of the company to themselves; and the animosity of contemporary wits is proverbial.

Is it then surprising that when the sole ambition of woman centres in beauty, and interest gives vanity additional force, perpetual rivalships should ensue? They are all running the same race, and would rise above the virtue of mortals, if they did not view each other with a suspicious and even envious eye.

An immoderate fondness for dress, for pleasure, and for sway, are the passions of savages; the passions that occupy those uncivilized beings who have not yet extended the dominion of the mind, or even learned to think with the energy necessary to concatenate that abstract train of thought which produces principles. And that women from their education and the present state of civilized life, are in the same condition, cannot, I think, be controverted. To laugh at them then, or satirize the follies of a being who is never to be allowed to act freely from the light of her own reason, is as absurd as cruel; for, that they who are taught blindly to obey authority, will endeavour cunningly to elude it, is most natural and certain.

Yet let it be proved that they ought to obey man implicitly, and I shall immediately agree that it is woman's duty to cultivate a fondness for dress, in order to please, and a propensity to cunning for her own preservation.

The virtues, however, which are supported by ignorance must ever be wavering – the house built on sand could not endure a storm. It is almost unnecessary to draw the inference. – If women are to be made virtuous by authority, which is a contradiction in terms, let them be immured in seraglios and watched with a jealous eye. – Fear not that the iron will enter into their souls – for the souls that can bear such treatment are made of yielding materials, just animated enough to give life to the body.

> 'Matter too soft a lasting mark to bear,
> And best distinguish'd by black, brown, or fair.'[9]

The most cruel wounds will of course soon heal, and they may still people the world, and dress to please man – all the purposes

which certain celebrated writers have allowed that they were
created to fulfil.

SECT. IV

Women are supposed to possess more sensibility, and even
humanity, than men, and their strong attachments and instantaneous emotions of compassion are given as proofs; but the
clinging affection of ignorance has seldom any thing noble in it,
and may mostly be resolved into selfishness, as well as the
affection of children and brutes. I have known many weak
women whose sensibility was entirely engrossed by their husbands; and as for their humanity, it was very faint indeed, or
rather it was only a transient emotion of compassion. Humanity
does not consist 'in a squeamish ear,' says an eminent orator.
'It belongs to the mind as well as the nerves.'

  But this kind of exclusive affection, though it degrades the
individual, should not be brought forward as a proof of the
inferiority of the sex, because it is the natural consequence of
confined views: for even women of superior sense, having their
attention turned to little employments, and private plans, rarely
rise to heroism, unless when spurred on by love! and love, as an
heroic passion, like genius, appears but once in an age. I therefore agree with the moralist who asserts, 'that women have
seldom so much generosity as men;'[10] and that their narrow
affections, to which justice and humanity are often sacrificed,
render the sex apparently inferior, especially, as they are commonly inspired by men; but I contend that the heart would
expand as the understanding gained strength, if women were
not depressed from their cradles.

  I know that a little sensibility, and great weakness, will produce a strong sexual attachment, and that reason must cement
friendship; consequently, I allow that more friendship is to be
found in the male than the female world, and that men have a
higher sense of justice. The exclusive affections of women seem
indeed to resemble Cato's most unjust love for his country.[11] He
wished to crush Carthage, not to save Rome, but to promote its

vain-glory; and, in general, it is to similar principles that humanity is sacrificed, for genuine duties support each other.

Besides, how can women be just or generous, when they are
the slaves of injustice?

SECT. V

As the rearing of children, that is, the laying a foundation of
sound health both of body and mind in the rising generation,
has justly been insisted on as the peculiar destination of woman,
the ignorance that incapacitates them must be contrary to the
order of things. And I contend that their minds can take in much
more, and ought to do so, or they will never become sensible
mothers. Many men attend to the breeding of horses, and overlook the management of the stable, who would, strange want
of sense and feeling! think themselves degraded by paying any
attention to the nursery; yet, how many children are absolutely
murdered by the ignorance of women! But when they escape,
and are destroyed neither by unnatural negligence nor blind
fondness, how few are managed properly with respect to the
infant mind! So that to break the spirit, allowed to become
vicious at home, a child is sent to school; and the methods taken
there, which must be taken to keep a number of children in
order, scatter the seeds of almost every vice in the soil thus
forcibly torn up.

I have sometimes compared the struggles of these poor children, who ought never to have felt restraint, nor would, had
they been always held in with an even hand, to the despairing
plunges of a spirited filly, which I have seen breaking on a
strand: its feet sinking deeper and deeper in the sand every time
it endeavoured to throw its rider, till at last it sullenly submitted.

I have always found horses, animals I am attached to, very
tractable when treated with humanity and steadiness, so that I
doubt whether the violent methods taken to break them, do not
essentially injure them; I am, however, certain that a child should
never be thus forcibly tamed after it has injudiciously been
allowed to run wild; for every violation of justice and reason, in

the treatment of children, weakens their reason. And, so early do they catch a character, that the base of the moral character, experience leads me to infer, is fixed before their seventh year, the period during which women are allowed the sole management of children. Afterwards it too often happens that half the business of education is to correct, and very imperfectly is it done, if done hastily, the faults, which they would never have acquired if their mothers had had more understanding.

One striking instance of the folly of women must not be omitted. – The manner in which they treat servants in the presence of children, permitting them to suppose that they ought to wait on them, and bear their humours. A child should always be made to receive assistance from a man or woman as a favour; and, as the first lesson of independence, they should practically be taught, by the example of their mother, not to require that personal attendance, which it is an insult to humanity to require, when in health; and instead of being led to assume airs of consequence, a sense of their own weakness should first make them feel the natural equality of man. Yet, how frequently have I indignantly heard servants imperiously called to put children to bed, and sent away again and again, because master or miss hung about mamma, to stay a little longer. Thus made slavishly to attend the little idol, all those most disgusting humours were exhibited which characterize a spoiled child.

In short, speaking of the majority of mothers, they leave their children entirely to the care of servants; or, because they are their children, treat them as if they were little demi-gods, though I have always observed, that the women who thus idolize their children, seldom shew common humanity to servants, or feel the least tenderness for any children but their own.

It is, however, these exclusive affections, and an individual manner of seeing things, produced by ignorance, which keep women for ever at a stand, with respect to improvement, and make many of them dedicate their lives to their children only to weaken their bodies and spoil their tempers, frustrating also any plan of education that a more rational father may adopt; for unless a mother concur, the father who restrains will ever be considered as a tyrant.

But, fulfilling the duties of a mother, a woman with a sound constitution, may still keep her person scrupulously neat, and assist to maintain her family, if necessary, or by reading and conversations with both sexes, indiscriminately, improve her mind. For nature has so wisely ordered things, that did women suckle their children, they would preserve their own health, and there would be such an interval between the birth of each child, that we should seldom see a houseful of babes.[12] And did they pursue a plan of conduct, and not waste their time in following the fashionable vagaries of dress, the management of their household and children need not shut them out from literature, or prevent their attaching themselves to a science, with that steady eye which strengthens the mind, or practising one of the fine arts that cultivate the taste.

But, visiting to display finery, card-playing, and balls, not to mention the idle bustle of morning trifling, draw women from their duty to render them insignificant, to render them pleasing, according to the present acceptation of the word, to every man, but their husband. For a round of pleasures in which the affections are not exercised, cannot be said to improve the understanding, though it be erroneously called seeing the world; yet the heart is rendered cold and averse to duty, by such a senseless intercourse, which becomes necessary from habit even when it has ceased to amuse.

But, we shall not see women affectionate till more equality be established in society, till ranks are confounded and women freed, neither shall we see that dignified domestic happiness, the simple grandeur of which cannot be relished by ignorant or vitiated minds; nor will the important task of education ever be properly begun till the person of a woman is no longer preferred to her mind. For it would be as wise to expect corn from tares, or figs from thistles, as that a foolish ignorant woman should be a good mother.

SECT. VI

It is not necessary to inform the sagacious reader, now I enter on my concluding reflections, that the discussion of this subject merely consists in opening a few simple principles, and clearing away the rubbish which obscured them. But, as all readers are not sagacious, I must be allowed to add some explanatory remarks to bring the subject home to reason – to that sluggish reason, which supinely takes opinions on trust, and obstinately supports them to spare itself the labour of thinking.

Moralists have unanimously agreed, that unless virtue be nursed by liberty, it will never attain due strength – and what they say of man I extend to mankind, insisting that in all cases morals must be fixed on immutable principles; and, that the being cannot be termed rational or virtuous, who obeys any authority, but that of reason.

To render women truly useful members of society, I argue that they should be led, by having their understandings cultivated on a large scale, to acquire a rational affection for their country, founded on knowledge, because it is obvious that we are little interested about what we do not understand. And to render this general knowledge of due importance, I have endeavoured to shew that private duties are never properly fulfilled unless the understanding enlarges the heart; and that public virtue is only an aggregate of private. But, the distinctions established in society undermine both, by beating out the solid gold of virtue, till it becomes only the tinsel-covering of vice; for whilst wealth renders a man more respectable than virtue, wealth will be sought before virtue; and, whilst women's persons are caressed, when a childish simper shews an absence of mind – the mind will lie fallow. Yet, true voluptuousness must proceed from the mind – for what can equal the sensations produced by mutual affection, supported by mutual respect? What are the cold, or feverish caresses of appetite, but sin embracing death, compared with the modest overflowings of a pure heart and exalted imagination? Yes, let me tell the libertine of fancy when he despises understanding in woman – that the mind, which he disregards, gives life to the enthusiastic affection from which rapture, short-lived as it is, alone can flow! And, that, without virtue, a sexual attachment must expire, like a tallow candle in the socket, creating intolerable disgust. To prove this, I need only observe, that men who have wasted great part of their lives with women, and with whom they have sought for pleasure with eager thirst, entertain the meanest opinion of the sex. – Virtue, true refiner of joy! – if foolish men were to fright thee from earth, in order to give loose to all their appetites without a check – some sensual weight of taste would scale the heavens to invite thee back, to give a zest to pleasure!

That women at present are by ignorance rendered foolish or vicious, is, I think, not to be disputed; and, that the most salutary effects tending to improve mankind might be expected from a REVOLUTION in female manners, appears, at least, with a face of probability, to rise out of the observation. For as marriage has been termed the parent of those endearing charities which draw man from the brutal herd, the corrupting intercourse that wealth, idleness, and folly, produce between the sexes, is more universally injurious to morality than all the other vices of mankind collectively considered. To adulterous lust the most sacred duties are sacrificed, because before marriage, men, by a promiscuous intimacy with women, learned to consider love as a selfish gratification – learned to separate it not only from esteem, but from the affection merely built on habit, which mixes a little humanity with it. Justice and friendship are also set at defiance, and that purity of taste is vitiated which would naturally lead a man to relish an artless display of affection rather than affected airs. But that noble simplicity of affection, which dares to appear unadorned, has few attractions for the libertine, though it be the charm, which by cementing the matrimonial tie, secures to the pledges of a warmer passion the necessary parental attention; for children will never be properly educated till friendship subsists between parents. Virtue flies from a house divided against itself – and a whole legion of devils take up their residence there.

The affection of husbands and wives cannot be pure when they have so few sentiments in common, and when so little confidence is established at home, as must be the case when their pursuits are so different. That intimacy from which tenderness should flow, will not, cannot subsist between the vicious.

Contending, therefore, that the sexual distinction which men have so warmly insisted upon, is arbitrary, I have dwelt on an observation, that several sensible men, with whom I have conversed on the subject, allowed to be well founded; and it is simply this, that the little chastity to be found amongst men, and consequent disregard of modesty, tend to degrade both sexes; and further, that the modesty of women, characterized as such, will often be only the artful veil of wantonness instead of being the natural reflection of purity, till modesty be universally respected.

From the tyranny of man, I firmly believe, the greater number of female follies proceed; and the cunning, which I allow makes at present a part of their character, I likewise have repeatedly endeavoured to prove, is produced by oppression.

Were not dissenters,[13] for instance, a class of people, with strict truth, characterized as cunning? And may I not lay some stress on this fact to prove, that when any power but reason curbs the free spirit of man, dissimulation is practised, and the various shifts of art are naturally called forth? Great attention to decorum, which was carried to a degree of scrupulosity, and all that puerile bustle about trifles and consequential solemnity, which Butler's caricature[14] of a dissenter, brings before the imagination, shaped their persons as well as their minds in the mould of prim littleness. I speak collectively, for I know how many ornaments to human nature have been enrolled amongst sectaries; yet, I assert, that the same narrow prejudice for their sect, which women have for their families, prevailed in the dissenting part of the community, however worthy in other respects; and also that the same timid prudence, or headstrong efforts, often disgraced the exertions of both. Oppression thus formed many of the features of their character perfectly to coincide with that of the oppressed half of mankind; for is it not notorious that dissenters were, like women, fond of deliberating together, and asking advice of each other, till by a complication of little contrivances, some little end was brought about? A similar attention to preserve their reputation was conspicuous in the dissenting and female world, and was produced by a similar cause.

Asserting the rights which women in common with men ought to contend for, I have not attempted to extenuate their faults; but to prove them to be the natural consequence of their education and station in society. If so, it is reasonable to suppose that they will change their character, and correct their vices and follies, when they are allowed to be free in a physical, moral, and civil sense.*

Let woman share the rights and she will emulate the virtues of man; for she must grow more perfect when emancipated, or justify the authority that chains such a weak being to her duty. – If the latter, it will be expedient to open a fresh trade with Russia for whips; a present which a father should always make to his son-in-law on his wedding day, that a husband may keep his whole family in order by the same means; and without any violation of justice reign, wielding this sceptre, sole master of his house, because he is the only being in it who has reason: – the divine, indefeasible earthly sovereignty breathed into man by the Master of the universe. Allowing this position, women have not any inherent rights to claim; and, by the same rule, their duties vanish, for rights and duties are inseparable.

Be just then, O ye men of understanding! and mark not more severely what women do amiss, than the vicious tricks of the horse or the ass for whom ye provide provender – and allow her the privileges of ignorance, to whom ye deny the rights of reason, or ye will be worse than Egyptian task-masters, expecting virtue where nature has not given understanding!

END OF THE FIRST VOLUME.

---

* I had further enlarged on the advantages which might reasonably be expected to result from an improvement in female manners, towards the general reformation of society; but it appeared to me that such reflections would more properly close the last volume.

Notes

[DEDICATION]

1   *M. TALLEYRAND-PÉRIGORD*: Charles Maurice de Talleyrand-Périgord (1754–1838), French diplomat and statesman. As
Bishop of Autun (1789), Talleyrand recommended the formation
of a national constitution, a scheme for democratic local self-
government, abolition of significant feudal and class privileges
and a reform of the administration of justice system. Wollstonecraft met Talleyrand during his visit to London in 1792.

2   *dedicate this volume to you*: Wollstonecraft refers to Talleyrand's
ideas on national education, which he presented to the Constituent Assembly on 10 September 1791, advocating free, secular,
national education for both sexes leading up to university level.

In Wollstonecraft's most lengthy and significant revision for
the second edition, she deleted a long passage at this point from
her original dedicatory letter:

> – the first dedication that I have ever written, to induce you to read
> it with attention; and, because I think that you will understand me,
> which I do not suppose many pert witlings will, who may ridicule
> the arguments they are unable to answer. But, Sir, I carry my respect
> for your understanding still farther; so far, that I am confident you
> will not throw my work aside, and hastily conclude that I am in the
> wrong, because you did not view the subject in the same light
> yourself. – And, pardon my frankness, but I must observe, that you
> treated it in too cursory a manner, contented to consider it as it had
> been considered formerly, when the rights of man, not to advert to
> woman, were trampled on as chimerical – I call upon you, therefore,
> now to weigh

(The two versions are identical from 'what I have advanced' on.) By choosing to excise most of this paragraph, Wollstonecraft presented herself to the reader in her second edition less as a petitioner and more as the confident and acclaimed author she had notably become in the intervening months after publication of the first edition.

3   *The box of mischief*: According to the legend of Pandora's box, Zeus gave Pandora (meaning the 'all-giving') a jar containing all manner of evils to counteract the blessing of Prometheus' gift of fire to mortals. Made beautiful, seductive, flattering, and curious to ensure she would be welcomed among men, Pandora opened the jar despite warnings and allowed evils to scatter over the world.

4   *'wise in their generation'*: From Luke 16:8: '. . . the children of this world are in their generation wiser than the children of light' (all quotations are from the Authorized Version). See also p. 199.

ADVERTISEMENT

1   *a second volume*: Wollstonecraft did not publish one. See also footnote on p. 242.

INTRODUCTION

1   *Sandford and Merton*: (Published in 3 vols, 1783, 1787 and 1789.) It was one of the most widely read and admired books of children's stories from the 1780s to the mid-Victorian era. Its author, Thomas Day, was an English disciple of Jean-Jacques Rousseau, who echoed his educational maxims in stories about the poor and resourceful Sandford and the rich ne'er-do-well Merton.

2   *seraglio*: As understood in the eighteenth century, a seraglio was a harem or place of confinement in a Turkish palace in which women were secluded.

CHAP. I
THE RIGHTS AND INVOLVED DUTIES OF MANKIND CONSIDERED

1   *'must hide its diminished head'*: From John Milton (1608–74), *Paradise Lost* (1667), IV.34–5: '. . . at whose sight all the Stars/ Hide thir diminisht heads . . .'

2   *man was naturally a solitary animal*: In *A Discourse on the Origin*

of Inequality, Part I (1754), Rousseau describes a pre-political time when men lived in a state of nature inhabited by an amoral, solitary people preoccupied with self but no menace to others. (All references to *Discourses* are to New York: Everyman, 1950.)

In the next paragraph, Wollstonecraft misrepresents Rousseau. In fact, he does not imagine a return to the state of nature, but prefers a democratic self-governing ideal as outlined in *The Social Contract* (1762).

3   *a carnivorous animal . . . towards herding*: See Rousseau, *Discourse*, I, 94. Rousseau describes man in the state of nature as 'solitary' and not knowing 'even his own children' (*Discourse*, I, 206, 231).

4   *all will be right*: Alexander Pope (1688–1744) immortalized the Augustan optimism to which Wollstonecraft refers: 'And spite of Pride, in erring Reason's spite,/One truth is clear, Whatever IS, is RIGHT' ('An Essay on Man' (1732–4), I.293–4).

5   *Fabricius*: The Roman general Fabricius Gaius Luscinus was renowned for his integrity when he was commissioned to arrange for the ransom of prisoners after the defeat of the Roman army by Pyrrhus. See also p. 178.

6   *the brutal Spartans*: In *Discourse on the Moral Effects of the Arts and Sciences* (1750), Rousseau praises Sparta for its simple, virtuous and heroic ideals (I, 201).

7   *the citizen of Geneva*: Rousseau was born in the Republic of Geneva in 1712. The son of a watchmaker, he articulated egalitarian ideals (for men), revolutionary in their time. He died in 1778.

8   *regal power . . . noble stem*: Wollstonecraft's indictment of monarchy and the hereditary principle here echoes parts of Thomas Paine's *Common Sense* (1776). She admired Paine, whom she met in London at the time of writing *Vindication of the Rights of Woman*.

9   *an infant was made the organ of the detestable Dubois*: Cardinal Guillaume Dubois (1656–1723), French cardinal and statesman, tutor to the young duke of Chartres, later regent duke of Orleans. He was considered unscrupulous and ambitious, having encouraged his pupil in indulgences to win his favour.

10 *expect corn from tares, and figs from thistles*: See Matthew 7:16: 'Ye shall know them by their fruits. Do men gather grapes of thorns, or figs of thistles?' See also p. 238.

11 *A standing army*: Opposition to an army of professional soldiers, often paid mercenaries, was one of the defining features of republican sentiment in seventeenth- and eighteenth-century Britain.

Such sentiment held that only voluntary militias, manned by civic-spirited citizens, should defend a republic.

12   *Dr Price*: Richard Price (1723–91), Dissenting minister and moral theologian, liberal advocate of parliamentary reform, was a supporter of the American colonists during the Revolutionary era and good friend of Benjamin Franklin. It was his address praising the revolutionaries in France to an audience of Dissenters that provoked Edmund Burke to his famous *Reflections on the Revolution in France* (see p. 141 and Chap. V, note 64). Price was a member of the dissenting community at Stoke Newington where Wollstonecraft established a school. He supported and encouraged her in her political writings.

13   *pestiferous purple*: Purple is the traditional colour signifying ecclesiastical, imperial or monarchical rank.

14   *perfection of man in the establishment of true civilization*: In *Discourse on the Moral Effects of the Arts and Sciences*, Rousseau does criticize his fellow Enlightenment thinkers for their smug confidence in civilized superiority. Against their sophisticated salon manners, he praises the simplicity and innocence of the natural state.

CHAP. II
THE PREVAILING OPINION OF A SEXUAL CHARACTER DISCUSSED

1   *women are formed for softness and sweet attractive grace*: Milton, *Paradise Lost*, IV.297–9: 'For contemplation he and valor form'd/For softness she and sweet attractive grace/He for God only, she for God in him.'

2   *true Mahometan strain . . . deprive us of souls*: This misleading belief about Islam was widespread in medieval and early modern Christendom. There are certain Islamic sources depicting women in a negative light, but there are also positive sources. (See, for example, Koran 40:8.) The Koran does not regard Eve as responsible for humanity's downfall.

3   *'Certainly . . . ignoble creature'*: Francis Bacon (1561–1626), Renaissance author and father of deductive reasoning, *Essays* (1625), XVI, 'Of Atheism'.

4   *'To whom . . . her praise'*: Milton, *Paradise Lost*, IV.634–8 (emphases are Wollstonecraft's).

5   *'Hast thou . . . rational delight –'*: Milton, *Paradise Lost*, VIII.381–92 (emphases are Wollstonecraft's).

6   *exercise of its own reason . . . I extend it to women*: In his

work on education, *Émile* (1762), Rousseau writes: 'Consult the women's opinions in bodily matters, in all that concerns the senses; consult the men in matters of morality and all that concerns the understanding' (IV, 306). (All references to *Émile* are to London: Dent, 1911.)

7   *Dr Gregory*: John Gregory (1724–73), author of the popular and conventional *A Father's Legacy to his Daughters* (1774), in which he urged his daughters to acquire traditional feminine accomplishments and virtues.

8   *Why should women be censured . . . a passion for a scarlet coat*: On Augustan poet and satirist Jonathan Swift (1667–1745) in his poem 'The Furniture of a Woman's Mind' (1733), ll. 1–6, see Introduction, p. xxxvii; see also p. 146.

9   *Sophia . . . appears to me grossly unnatural*: Rousseau offers the training of 'Sophy' in *Émile*, a young girl raised to become Émile's companion: 'A woman's education must . . . be planned in relation to man. To be pleasing in his sight . . . to make his life pleasant and happy . . . this is what she should be taught while she is young' (V, 328).

10   *turned to hell for sublimer objects*: Many early Romantic contemporaries shared Wollstonecraft's preference for Milton's depiction of satanic rebellion in *Paradise Lost* over Edenic bliss. Burke's *A Philosophical Inquiry Into the Origin of Our Ideas of the Sublime and the Beautiful* (1756) described the aesthetic of the 'sublime', with its evocations of awesome power.

11   *a woman should never . . . relax himself*: Rousseau, *Émile*, V, 333.

12   *Moses's poetical story . . . one of Adam's ribs*: A widespread assumption in the eighteenth century was that Moses was the author of the first five books of the Bible. See Genesis 2:22: 'And the rib, which the Lord God had taken from man, made he a woman.' See also p. 101.

13   *'Yet ne'er . . . we hate'*: Pope, 'Epistle II. To a Lady: Of the Characters of Women' (1735), *Moral Essays*, II.51–2.

14   *out Quixote Cervantes*: Miguel de Cervantes (Saavedra) (1547–1616), Spanish novelist, playwright and poet. His masterwork *Don Quixote* (1605–15) parodies the extravagances of the chivalric romances of his time.

15   *the whole tendency of female education . . . render them pleasing*: Rousseau, *Émile*, V, 328.

16   *recommends dissimulation, and advises . . . she little thinks of*: Dr Gregory writes: 'I would have you to dance with spirit, but never allow yourselves to be so far transported with mirth, as to forget

the delicacy of your sex.' He warns that men recoil from women who boast of their good health (*A Father's Legacy*, pp. 57, 50–51).

17 *Out of the abundance of the heart . . . a wiser than Solomon . . . the heart should be made clean*: Respectively, Matthew 12:34: 'for out of the abundance of the heart the mouth speaketh' (see also p. 109). Legendary for his wisdom, Solomon was a king of Israel (tenth century BC). His predecessor as king was David, who writes in Psalm 24:4–5: 'He that hath clean hands, and a pure heart . . . He shall receive the blessing from the Lord.'

18 *advises a wife never . . . extent of her sensibility or affection*: Dr Gregory writes: 'If you love him, let me advise you never to discover to him the full extent of your love, no not although you marry him' (*A Father's Legacy*, pp. 87–8).

19 *the philosopher's stone*: As practised in the Middle Ages and the Renaissance, the search for the 'philosopher's stone', a substance that would turn metal into gold or silver.

20 *a shrewd satirist . . . still rarer*: Refers to La Rochefoucauld (François de Marsillac, duc de (1613–80)), the cynical observer of the court of Louis XIV (reigned 1643–1715), best known for his witty epigrams. This is number 473: 'Quelque rare que soit le veritable amour, il l'est encore moins que la veritable amitie' (*Maximes* (1665)).

21 *Eloisa, love St Preux*: Rousseau became celebrated in Europe in 1761 after the publication of *Julie*, a novel known afterwards as *La Nouvelle Héloïse*, reprising the famous romance between the French philosopher and theologian Peter Abelard (1079–1142) (Rousseau's St Preux) and his pupil Héloïse. Readers admired the virtue, sentiment and eloquence of Rousseau's 'Julie' – Wollstonecraft's 'Eloisa' and 'Heloisa' (p. 157). See also p. 217, Rousseau's 'exalted female character'. Abelard and Héloïse's correspondence survived and has been published and made the subject of poems and plays.

22 *delicacy of sentiment . . . determined to marry*: Gregory, *A Father's Legacy*, pp. 119–20.

23 *'submissive charms'*: Milton, *Paradise Lost*, IV.497–9: 'he in delight/Both of her Beauty and submissive charms/Smil'd with superior love'.

24 *neither marrying nor giving in marriage*: See Matthew 22:30: 'For in the resurrection they neither marry, nor are given in marriage, but are as the angels of God in heaven.' Wollstonecraft included the phrase in the conclusion to her novel *Mary, a Fiction* (1788): 'She thought she was hastening to that world *where there is neither*

marrying, nor giving in marriage' (emphasis is Wollstonecraft's) (ed. Gary Kelly (London: Oxford University Press, 1976), p. 68).

25 *Swedenborg*: Emanuel Swedenborg (1688–1772), Swedish scientist and mystic, believed that men and women were constituted by similar substances in a different organization. In women, reason is subordinated to feeling; in men, feeling is subordinated to reason. In their union a spiritual marriage between love and truth is effected. The first English congregation was founded in the 1780s.

26 *Newton*: Sir Isaac Newton (1642–1727), philosopher and mathematician, formulator of the law of gravitation (see Chap. V, note 22).

27 '*If weak women ... than they*': Matthew Prior (1664–1721), 'Hans Carvel' (1701), ll. 11–12: 'That, if weak Women went astray,/Their Stars were more in Fault than They.'

28 *China ... where a living man has been made a God*: Refers to the practice of ancient Chinese emperors' claiming they ruled by virtue of a mandate from heaven.

CHAP. III
THE SAME SUBJECT CONTINUED

1 *the sword's destroying the scabbard*: In his autobiographical *Confessions* (1782), Rousseau writes: 'The sword wears out its sheath, as is sometimes said. That is my story' (I.v, 209). (All references are to the Penguin 1953 edition.)

2 *Dr Priestley ... lived beyond forty-five*: Joseph Priestley, LLD (1733–1804), dissenting theologian, eminent scientist, 'discoverer' of oxygen, reform advocate, writes: '. . . men who have been famous have lived, one with another, fifty or sixty years a piece. It generally requires a good constitution, and a considerable age, either for great achievements in politics, or discoveries in science' (*A Description of a Chart of Biography*, 2nd edn (London, 1765), p. 30).

3 *the baseless fabric of a vision ... airy dagger ... led Satan far ... 'in a fine phrenzy'*: Respectively, William Shakespeare's *The Tempest* (1611), IV.1.151: 'Like the baseless fabric of this vision', and his *Macbeth* (1606), III.v.62–3: 'This is the air-drawn dagger which, you said, led you to Duncan.' In Milton's *Paradise Lost*, Book II, Satan leaves Hell to tempt Eve in the Garden of Eden, the fall leading to humanity's redemption in the sacrifice of Jesus Christ. Shakespeare's *A Midsummer Night's Dream* (1595–6), V.1.12: 'the poet's eye, in a fine frenzy rolling . . .'

4 *Turkish bashaws*: 'Bashaw' is an earlier form of the Turkish term

'pasha' and is generally used to indicate an official in the Turkish hierarchy, a man of wealth and eminence.

5   'Researches into abstract . . . Emilius: Rousseau, Émile, V, 349–50.

6   the divine right of kings: The traditional medieval view was that power had been given by God to kings to rule in the secular realm. It was this 'divine right' that the seventeenth-century Stuart monarchs James I and Charles I called upon unsuccessfully in their confrontation with the Republican forces during the English civil wars.

7   Chinese bands: Until the practice was ended by the Communist Revolution in twentieth-century China, the feet of young girls were bound to prevent them from normal growth and thus to conform them to an aesthetic preference for tiny feet.

8   A respectable old man . . . Vol. III: From Day's Sandford and Merton, 'The Conclusion of the Story of Sophron and Ticrones'.

9   a fondness for dolls: Rousseau, Émile, V, 331. He argues that girls have from birth a fondness for dressing dolls. Ultimately they become their own 'doll'.

10 a girl is naturally a coquette: Rousseau, Émile, V, 329: 'Woman is a coquette by profession, but her coquetry varies with her aims; let these aims be in accordance with those of nature, and a woman will receive a fitting education.'

11 the soul: Rousseau describes reason's natural apprehension of the presence of God in his discussion of Émile's religious education in Book IV of Émile.

12 inflammable senses: Wollstonecraft's belief that Rousseau's sensual life blinded him to a clearer understanding of human nature reflects his own self-assessment in Confessions: 'My passions have made me live, and my passions have killed me . . . my soul was always disturbed. I was devoured alternatively by desires and by fears' (I.v,209–10). See also p. 115.

13 the learned pig: The fantastic achievements of such 'learned' pigs, exhibited at festivals alongside other curiosities, were a staple of English popular culture in the eighteenth century.

14 a girl . . . always be a romp: Wollstonecraft was the oldest of three sisters and reminisced as an adult about her own childhood when 'she sported in the open air' in the Yorkshire country market-town of Beverley. See Godwin's Memoirs (London, 1798).

15 'I once knew . . . Emilius: Rousseau, Émile, V, 332.

16 I once knew a weak woman of fashion: Wollstonecraft's closest acquaintance with titled and wealthy people had been during her year as a governess in Ireland. Caroline, Lady Kingsborough, her employer, served her as a model of female vanity and dereliction

of duty. (See, for example, in *The Collected Letters of Mary Wollstonecraft*, ed. Janet Todd (London: Penguin 2003), letters to Everina Wollstonecraft, nos. 43, 52, 59.)

17   *Sybarites*: Natives of Sybaris, an ancient Greek city in southern Italy noted for decadence and indulgence.

18   *that destructive blast which desolates Turkey . . . unfruitful*: The hot and desolate sand-laden wind called the 'Simoom' blows across Turkey from the desert. Wollstonecraft also alludes to the decadence of the Ottoman Empire, which, she suggests, causes sterility in men.

19   *seeking whom he should devour*: From 1 Peter 5:8: 'Be sober, be vigilant; because your adversary the devil, as a roaring lion, walketh about, seeking whom he may devour.'

20   *a fair defect . . . justify the ways of Providence*: See Milton, *Paradise Lost*, X. 891–2: 'this novelty on Earth, this fair defect/ of Nature . . .' (see also pp. 72, 84); and I.25–6: 'I may assert Eternal Providence/And justify the ways of God to men.'

21   *religion . . . a matter of sentiment or taste*: Gregory writes: 'Religion is rather a matter of sentiment than reasoning' (*A Father's Legacy*, p. 13).

22   *'be pure . . . is pure'*: See Matthew 5:48: 'Be ye therefore perfect, even as your Father which is in heaven is perfect.'

23   *'thus far shalt thou go . . . be stayed'*: From Job 38:11: 'Hitherto shalt thou come, but no further: and here shall thy proud waves be stayed.'

24   *The serpent's tooth*: See Shakespeare, *King Lear* (1604–5), I.iv. 271–2: 'How sharper than a serpent's tooth it is/To have a thankless child!'

25   *'In the union . . . Emilius*: Rousseau, *Émile*, V, 322.

26   *her tythe of mint and cummin*: See Matthew 23:23: 'Woe unto you, scribes and Pharisees, hypocrites! for ye pay tithe of mint and anise and cummin, and have omitted the weightier matters of the law, judgement, mercy, and faith.' Biblical herbalists used plants like these for flavouring food and for healing. As such they were a currency that could be tithed.

27   *'O how lovely . . . Emilius*: Rousseau, *Émile*, V, 373.

28   *thou gavest me a talent – and here are five talents*: Refers to the parable of the talents in Matthew 25:14–30. The 'talent' was an ancient Hebrew monetary unit, which in the parable represents a power of mind or body given by God to a person for use and improvement.

CHAP. IV

OBSERVATIONS ON THE STATE OF DEGRADATION
TO WHICH WOMAN IS REDUCED

1   *asserting their birthright . . . to-morrow we die*: See Hebrews
    12:16: 'Lest there be any fornicator, or profane person, as Esau,
    who for one morsel of meat sold his birthright' (see also p. 188
    and note); and 1 Corinthians 15:32: '. . . what advantageth it me,
    if the dead rise not? let us eat and drink; for to morrow we die.'

2   *'absolute in loveliness'*: See Milton, *Paradise Lost*, VIII.545–7:
    '. . . yet when I approach/ Her loveliness, so absolute she seems/
    And in herself complete . . .'

3   *'The brutes . . . upon them'*: James Burnet, Lord Monboddo
    (1714–99), Scottish judge, man of letters and author of *Origin
    and Progress of Language* (Edinburgh, 1774). Wollstonecraft
    misrepresents his opinion about the capabilities of animals, whose
    skills, he believed, could be 'very much improved by use and
    instruction, by which they may be made to do things that are
    really wonderful . . .' (I.1.x, 137).

4   *'that with honour he may love' . . . Milton*: See *Paradise Lost*,
    VIII.58–9: 'O when meet now/Such pairs, in Love and Mutual
    Honor join'd?'

5   *The power of generalizing ideas, of drawing comprehensive con-
    clusions from individual observations*: Refers to *Essay on Human
    Understanding* (1689), by John Locke (1632–1704). It was the
    eighteenth-century's canonical text on the workings of the
    human mind. He wrote that sensory observations register on a
    'tabula rasa', a blank tablet, to be formed into generalizations
    through the associational creativity of the mind. See also Chap.
    VI, note 3.

6   *Mrs Barbauld*: Anna Letitia Barbauld (1743–1825) was a dis-
    senting essayist, poet, bluestocking and writer of children's
    stories. The two lines are from 'To Mrs P—, With some Drawings
    of Birds and Insects', *Poems*, by Anna Laetitia Aikin, 3rd edn
    (London, 1773), p. 47; *'inferior* kind' refers to birds. 'To a Lady,
    with some painted flowers', pp. 95–7, is given in full by Woll-
    stonecraft (emphasis is hers).

7   *Mr Hume's*: David Hume (1711–76) was a Scottish philosopher,
    moralist and political writer. The quotation is from his 'A Dia-
    logue', in *Enquiries Concerning Human Understanding and Con-
    cerning the Principles of Morals* (1777), ed. L. A. Selby-Bigge,
    3rd edn (Oxford: Clarendon Press, 1975), p. 332.

8   *Saturnalia*: The festival of Saturn was celebrated with revelry in
     the classical world.

9   *provided with . . . raiment, for which they neither toil nor spin*:
     See Matthew 6:28: 'And why take ye thought for raiment? Con-
     sider the lilies of the field, how they grow; they toil not, neither
     do they spin.'

10   *'In beauty's empire . . . not ador'd'*: Barbauld, 'Song V', ll. 16–18,
     Poems, p. 78.

11   *'I have endeavoured . . . fig for'*: Philip Dormer Stanhope, fourth
     Earl of Chesterfield (1694–1773), politician and wit, dispensed
     worldly wisdom and advice about social decorum to his natural
     son. The work achieved wide popularity after Chesterfield's death.
     In *Letters Written by the . . . Earl of Chesterfield to His Son* (1774),
     Letter CCXCIV, Chesterfield writes: 'I will own to you, under the
     secrecy of confession, that my vanity has very often made me take
     great pains to make a woman in love with me, if I could, for whose
     person I would not have given a pinch of snuff.' See also p. 132.

12   *Dr Smith's Theory of Moral Sentiments*: Adam Smith (1723–90),
     political economist and professor of moral philosophy, was the
     author of *The Theory of Moral Sentiments* (1759). His *Wealth
     of Nations* (1776) would forever shape the capitalist future, but
     he was known in his own time more as a moral theorist.

13   *his historian*: Voltaire (1694–1778), French satirist, novelist, his-
     torian, poet, etc. Smith's translation is from *Le Siècle de Louis
     XIV* (1751).

14   *'Do the great seem insensible . . . before them'*: Smith, *The Theory
     of Moral Sentiments*, I.III.ii, 81–3. (All references are to the 6th
     edn (Dublin, 1777).)

15   *Woman also thus 'in herself complete' . . . her wait'*: From Milton,
     Paradise Lost, VIII.547–8: 'so absolute she seems/And in herself
     complete'; and VIII.549–54 (emphasis is Wollstonecraft's).

16   *'Fine by defect, and amiably weak'*: See Pope, 'Epistle II. To a
     Lady', II.44: 'Fine by defect, and delicately weak'.

17   *'Educate women . . . over us'*: Rousseau, *Émile*, IV, 326. He
     continues: 'and then men will be masters indeed'. Rousseau does
     not argue for equal education for both sexes, but does regret a
     girl's wasting her time on 'foolish trifles', which 'charm' men.

18   *'Quickness of sensation . . . Dr Johnson*: *A Dictionary of the
     English Language* (1755) by Samuel Johnson (1709–84), critical
     essayist, wit and lexicographer, was the first of its kind in English
     and his humorous definitions are still quoted.

19   *seventy times seven*: See Matthew 18:22 (on forgiveness): 'Jesus

saith unto him, I say not unto thee, Until seven times: but, Until seventy times seven.'

20 *'He that hath wife . . . childless men'*: In 'Of Marriage and Single Life', Bacon continues: '. . . which, both in affection and means, have married and endowed the public' (*Essays*, VIII (New York: Modern Library, 1955), p. 22).

21 *dependent on . . . the bounty of their brothers*: In Wollstonecraft's family, her younger sister Everina remained in their older brother's household after the death of their father. There was a good deal of enmity between the sisters and their brother.

22 *Cowley*: The poet Abraham Cowley (1618–67) was supposed to have been a prodigy, as were Milton and Pope.

23 *Forster's Account of the Isles of the South-Sea*: Johann Reinhold Forster (1729–98) was a traveller, naturalist and writer, and published a diary about accompanying Captain Cook on his second journey to the South Seas.

24 *Magdalens*: Hostelries for the reform of prostitutes.

25 *When Richardson makes Clarissa tell Lovelace*: Samuel Richardson (1689–1761), was the author of the sentimental novel *Clarissa* in four volumes (1747–8), which established his literary reputation. In this novel, the predatory voluptuary Lovelace rapes the virtuous Clarissa Harlowe.

26 *Leibnitz . . . other errors'*: Gottfried Wilhelm Leibniz (1646–1716), German philosopher, scientist, historian and diplomat, in *Preface to Theodicy*, writes: '. . . Even errors have their use at times, but generally as providing a remedy for other errors: and truth is unquestionably better' (*Theodicy*, ed. Austin Farrer, trans. E. M. Huggard (New Haven: Yale University Press, 1952), p. 56).

27 *Dr Young . . . the light of day*: In his play *Busiris, King of Egypt* (1719), Edward Young (1683–1765) writes: 'So black a story well might shun the day' (*British Theatre* (London, 1777), Vol. XVI, p. 11).

28 *A love of pleasure or sway seems to divide mankind*: See Pope, 'Epistle II. To a Lady': 'In men, we various Ruling Passions find/ In Women, two almost divide the kind;/Those, only fix'd, they first or last obey/The Love of Pleasure, and the Love of Sway' (II. 207–10). See also pp. 211, 234.

29 *'scale to heavenly'*: See Milton, *Paradise Lost*, VIII.589–92: '. . . love refines/The thoughts, and heart enlarges, hath his seat/ In reason, and is judicious, is the scale/By which to heav'nly Love thou may'st ascend.'

30 *young girls ought to dedicate . . . to needle-work*: Rousseau in

Émile writes that 'little girls . . . are always ready to learn to sew' and that 'cutting out, embroidery, lace-making' are tasks that naturally follow (V, 331).

31   *lappets, and knot ribands*: A 'lappet' is a small decorative fold or flap, especially of lace or muslin, in a garment or headdress. 'Ribands' were loosely-hanging parts of a garment or headdress, like decorative ribbons.

32   *'I take her body,' says Ranger*: Dr Benjamin Hoadly (1706–57), writer and reformer, in the play written with his brother, *The Suspicious Husband*, has Ranger, after a night of drink and debauchery, avow he only wants a mistress 'capable of love', and quotes 'Song' from the play *The Maid's Last Prayer* (c. 1693), attributed to William Congreve: 'I take their bodies, you their mind! which has the better bargain?' (*Modern Scottish Drama* (London, 1811), Vol. 4, p. 367).

33   *'Supposing that women . . . Knox's Essays*: Vicesimus Knox (1752–1821), education critic and reformer, *Essays, Moral and Literary* (1782), V, *Works* (1824), p. 24. Knox refers to those who are subjects to the tyranny of 'fashionable modes of thinking and living'.

34   *Sappho . . . Madame d'Eon*: One of the great Greek lyrists and few known female poets of the ancient world, Sappho was born in Lesbos between the sixth and seventh century BC; for Catherine Macaulay, see Chap. V, note 54; Catherine the Great (1729–96) was Empress of Russia; the Chevalier d'Eon (1728–1810) was a French secret agent disguised as a woman, whose sex was revealed posthumously.

CHAP. V
ANIMADVERSIONS ON SOME OF THE WRITERS
WHO HAVE RENDERED WOMEN OBJECTS OF PITY

1   *'Hence we deduce a third . . . it expedient'*: Rousseau, *Émile*, V, 323 (emphasis is Wollstonecraft's).

2   *'It being once demonstrated,' continues Rousseau . . . decorate themselves'*: Rousseau, *Émile*, V, 326–31.

3   *'Girls ought . . . caused us'*: Rousseau, *Émile*, V, 332.

4   *'The common . . . for obedience'*: Rousseau, *Émile*, V, 333.

5   *'For the same . . . than boys'*: Rousseau, *Émile*, V, 334.

6   *'There results . . . the superiority'*: Rousseau, *Émile*, V, 333.

7   *'Each sex . . . over him'*: Rousseau, *Émile*, V, 334.

8   *'Daughters should . . . Whatever is, is right'*: Rousseau, *Émile*, V, 334. Rousseau says: 'What is, is good, and no general law can be bad' (*Émile*, V, 334). As Wollstonecraft closes the quotation, the

sentiment echoes Pope's sanguine poetic couplet: see Chap. I, note 4.

9   *'The superiority ... cultivate both'*: Rousseau, *Émile*, V, 334–5.

10 *'Beauty cannot be acquired ... Eastern bashaw'*: Rousseau, *Émile*, V, 336, 337. 'Circassian' young women, originating in the central European region of Circassia, were thought frequently to have been sold into the harems of Turkish 'bashaws'.

11 *'The tongues of women are very ... an untruth'*: Rousseau, *Émile*, V, 339.

12 *'It is easy to be conceived ... to infidelity'*: Rousseau, *Émile*, V, 340 (emphasis is Wollstonecraft's). Wollstonecraft omits a paragraph from Rousseau's text, before the last paragraph, in which he claims that women are either too 'reckless' or too 'pious' in their faith, owing to their natural penchant for 'exaggeration' (V, 340).

13 *'Her dress ... the imagination'*: Rousseau, *Émile*, V, 356–7.

14 *'that with ... them neatly'*: Rousseau, *Émile*, V, 358 (emphasis is Wollstonecraft's).

15 *'Your husband ... good time'*: Rousseau, *Émile*, V, 359 (emphasis is Wollstonecraft's).

16 *Tully's offices*: The *De Officiis* of Marcus Tullius Cicero (106–43 BC) provided a canonical text on virtue for the eighteenth-century Enlightenment. Cicero was a favourite source for writers in the English and French republican tradition.

17 *'They who pass their whole ... or amiable'*: Rousseau, *Émile*, V, 371.

18 *'Sensual pleasures ... is ideal'*: Rousseau, *Émile*, V, 411.

19 *'Emilius, in becoming your husband ... of reason'*: Rousseau, *Émile*, V, 442–3.

20 *'And yet ... his children'*: Rousseau, *Émile*, V, 443.

21 *'The charm ... own breast'*: Smith, *The Theory of Moral Sentiments*, I.1.ii, 9.

22 *under the shade ... indulged contemplation*: Refers to the popular belief that Newton derived his theory of gravity after watching an apple fall to the ground.

23 *'Curs'd vassalage ... Dryden*: John Dryden (1631–1700), poet and dramatist, from his play *The State of Innocence: and Fall of Man* (1667), V.1.58–60. Eve foresees future misery for women, having urged Adam to eat from the tree of knowledge.

24 *created to flutter our hour out and die*: See *Macbeth*, V.v.23–6: '... out, out brief candle?/Life's but a walking shadow, a poor player/that struts and frets his hour upon the stage/And then is heard no more.'

25 *Telemachus*: Son of Odysseus and Penelope, he helped Odysseus

slay Penelope's suitors. Rousseau describes Sophy's love for the imaginary Telemachus, whom she encountered as a young girl reading François de Fénelon's adventures of *Télémaque* (1699) (*Émile*, V, 367).

26   *Dr Fordyce's sermons*: James Fordyce (1720–96) was a Scots Presbyterian minister, a poet and the author of *Sermons to Young Women* (1765) and *The Character and Conduct of the Female Sex* (1776), works which embodied traditional views of women.

27   *'Behold these . . . fiercest vengeance'*: Fordyce, Sermon III, *Sermons to Young Women*, 3rd edn, I.99–100.

28   *Hervey's Meditations*: James Hervey (1714–58), a devotional writer, and author of *Meditations and Contemplations* (1748).

29   *walk without leading-strings*: Refers to the practice of restraining young children with harnesses to prevent their falling or wandering.

30   *'Never, perhaps . . . kindred angels'*: Fordyce, *Sermons to Young Women*, Sermon XI, II.163.

31   *'As a small . . . have beauty'*: Fordyce, *Sermons to Young Women*, Sermon XIII, II.248.

32   *'Let it be . . . and gentle'*: Fordyce, *Sermons to Young Women*, Sermon XIII, II.224–5.

33   *'I am astonished . . . domestic bliss'*: Fordyce, *Sermons to Young Women*, Sermon XIV, II.264–5 (emphasis is Wollstonecraft's).

34   *'that they . . . no interest in deceiving them'*: Dr Gregory writes in *A Father's Legacy*: '. . . no interest in flattering or deceiving you'.

35   *In Portugal*: Wollstonecraft had a poor opinion of Portugal, which she had visited in 1786. In a review of William Costigan's *Sketches of Society and Manners in Portugal* (1787) for the *Analytical Journal*, she writes: 'Portugal may be termed the most savage part of Europe, where superstition still reigns triumphant' (I (August 1788), p. 451).

36   *'Be even . . . cultivated understanding'*: Gregory, *A Father's Legacy*, pp. 31–2.

37   *hide her talents under a bushel*: See Matthew 5:15: 'Neither do men light a candle, and put it under a bushel, but on a candlestick; and it giveth light unto all that are in the house' (see also Mark 4: 21 and Luke 11: 33).

38   *Seems! I . . . passeth show*: See *Hamlet*, I.ii.76, 85: 'Seems, madam! Nay, it is; I know not seems/ . . . But I have that within which passeth show'.

39   *'The men . . . aware of'*: Gregory, *A Father's Legacy*, pp. 36–7.

40   *'The sentiment . . . your sex'*: Gregory, *A Father's Legacy*, p. 44.

41   *'The power . . . she conceives'*: Gregory, *A Father's Legacy*, p. 42.

42 *'Wisdom is . . . hate knowledge'*: Proverbs 4:7 and 1:22.

43 *the mighty shoulders of a son of the earth*: Refers to ancient Indian
    mythology that depicts the earth being supported by elephants
    standing on the back of a giant tortoise. According to Greek
    myth, Atlas owned the pillars that supported the heavens and the
    earth. In ancient Greek art, he is frequently depicted bearing the
    weight of the earth on his shoulders.

44 *'which passeth understanding'*: From Philippians 4:7: 'And the
    peace of God, which passeth all understanding, shall keep your
    hearts and minds through Christ Jesus.'

45 *'He is . . . Cowper*: William Cowper (1731–1800), from his poem
    'The Winter Morning Walk', *The Task* (1785), V.733 (emphasis
    is Wollstonecraft's).

46 *Mrs Piozzi . . . Johnsonian periods . . . her husband'*: Hester Lynch
    Thrale Piozzi (1741–1821) was a friend of Dr Johnson's, a blue-
    stocking and a woman of letters. His much-admired prose style
    is notable for long sentences with phrases and clauses in balance.
    'Johnsonian periods' were regarded as the prose equivalent of the
    heroic couplet.
        The quotation is from Piozzi's *A Letter to a young Gentleman
    on his Marriage* (Hartford, Conn. 1806), p. 113.

47 *Medicean symmetry*: The marble statue of the *Venus de Medici*,
    acquired by the Medici family in Florence in the late sixteenth or
    early seventeenth century, figured prominently in the eighteenth-
    century mind as a representation of classical beauty.

48 *Baroness de Stael . . . to adoration'*: Anne-Louise-Germaine
    Necker, baronne de Staël-Holstein (or Mme de Staël) (1766–
    1817), a celebrated woman of letters, essayist and writer on the
    French Revolution, *Lettres sur les ecrits et le caractere de J J
    Rousseau, Oeuvres Completes* (Paris, 1814), pp. 168–9.

49 *'he admits the passion of love'*: de Staël, *Lettres*, pp. 168–9.

50 *'What signifies . . . devotedly theirs'*: de Staël, *Lettres*, pp. 168–9.

51 *Madame Genlis . . . Letters on Education*: Madame Genlis, Felic-
    ité, née Ducrest, comtesse de Genlis (1746–1830), a celebrated
    woman of letters and the author of *Adele et Théodore, ou lettres
    sur l'education* (1782).

52 *She tells a story . . . father's consent*: Recounted in Genlis' *Tales
    of the Castle* (1785), chapter III, 'Theophilus and Olympia'.

53 *Mrs Chapone's Letters*: Hester Chapone (1727–1801), essayist,
    bluestocking, author of *Letters on the Improvement of the Mind;
    addressed to a young lady* (1773).

54 *The very word respect brings Mrs Macaulay*: Catherine Macaulay

(1731–91), republican historian, essayist, parliamentary reformer and bluestocking, was subjected to mockery about her
personal appearance after the publication of the first volume of
her history of England. She was the object of more abuse when
at age 47 she married the 21-year-old William Graham some
years after the death of her first husband.

55 *For every thing . . . there is a season*: Ecclesiastes 3:1 continues:
'and a time to every purpose under the heaven'.

56 *He who . . . love God*: See 1 John 4:20: 'If a man say, I love God,
and hateth his brother, he is a liar: for he that loveth not his
brother whom he hath seen, how can he love God whom he hath
not seen.'

57 *ignis fatuus*: Literally means 'the foolish fire', so named for spec-
tral lights that according to legend deceived night-time travellers
or signified approaching death.

58 *all that is done under the sun is vanity*: Ecclesiastes 1:14: 'I have
seen all the works that are done under the sun; and, behold, all is
vanity and vexation of spirit.'

59 *an Inkle*: Sir Richard Steele, essayist and playwright (1672–
1729), tells the story of the adventurer Thomas Inkle, raised to
value material gain, in the *Spectator*, no. 11 (13 March 1711).
Inkle travels to America where he sells into slavery the Indian
maid who rescued him from death and fell in love with him.
Wollstonecraft reprinted the story in her anthology, *The Female
Reader* (1789; reprinted New York: Scholar, 1980), pp. 29–31.

60 *'I find . . . Sidney*: Sir Philip Sidney (1554–86), Renaissance poet,
from the first version of *Arcadia* (1581), I.18.

61 *'pursuing the bubble fame in the cannon's mouth'*: See Shakespeare's *As You Like It* (1599), II.vii.152–3: 'Seeking the bubble
reputation/Even in the cannon's mouth'.

62 *Pantaloon's*: Pantalone, a stock character in sixteenth-century
Italian *commedia dell'arte*, was a foolish, lascivious old Venetian
merchant, often the head of a household, the object of humour
as he is often deceived in the course of lovers' intrigues.

63 *Yahoos . . . Houyhnhnm*: In Book IV of Swift's *Gulliver's Travels*
(1726), the Yahoos are a bestial race of human beings without
reason, and the Houyhnhnms are a society of rational horses
without passion.

64 *Mr Burke*: Edmund Burke (1729–97), statesman, parliamentary
orator and political thinker. Wollstonecraft responds to this
observation in his *Reflections on the Revolution in France* (1790):
'. . . instead of casting away all our old prejudices, we cherish

them to a very considerable degree, and, to take more shame
to ourselves, we cherish them because they are prejudices . . .'
(Harmondsworth: Penguin, 1986), p. 183.

65   'Convince a man . . . opinion still': See Samuel Butler (1612–80),
     poet and satirist, in his mock heroic poem Hudibras (1678), III.iii.
     547–8: 'He that complies against his will/Is of his own opinion
     still'. See also p. 241 and note.

66   cannot serve God and mammon: See Matthew 6:24: 'No man
     can serve two masters: for either he will hate the one, and love
     the other; or else he will hold to the one, and despise the other.
     Ye cannot serve God and mammon.'

67   excellent essay . . . in Prose: Barbauld, 'Against Inconsistency in
     our Expectations', Miscellaneous Pieces in Prose (London, 1773),
     pp. 59–78.

CHAP. VI
THE EFFECT WHICH AN EARLY ASSOCIATION
OF IDEAS HAS UPON THE CHARACTER

1   an early association of ideas: Wollstonecraft is calling upon the
     philosophy of David Hartley (1705–57), physician and Christian
     philosopher, whose very influential Observations on Man, his
     Frame, his Duty, and his Expectations (1749) combined scientific
     perfectionism with religious certainty. Hartley's psychological
     theory of associationism argued that ideas originate in physical
     sensations compelled into association with each other by the
     brain.

2   grows 'with our growth': See Pope's Essay on Man, II.133–6: 'As
     Man, perhaps, the moment of his breath/Receives the lurking prin-
     ciple of death;/The young disease, that must subdue at length, /
     Grows with his growth, and strengthens with his strength.' Pope is
     referring to the passions, Wollstonecraft to the early development
     of ideas.

3   materialists: Philosophical followers of Locke's emphasis on sen-
     sationalism, such as Hartley and Priestley, were called 'material-
     ists' as opposed to the still-powerful influence of the earlier
     Cambridge Platonists, who were philosophical idealists.

4   Egyptian bondage: Refers to the slavery of the Jews in Egypt, as
     recounted in Exodus. See also p. 242.

5   'highest praise is to obey, unargued': Milton, Paradise Lost,
     IV.637–8: 'God is thy Law, thou mine: to know no more/Is
     woman's happiest knowledge and her praise'.

6   'that every woman is at heart a rake': Pope, 'Epistle II. To a Lady':

'Men some to Bus'ness, some to Pleasure take;/But ev'ry Woman
is at heart a Rake' (II.215–16).

7   'Where love . . . surly pride': Dryden, 'Palamon and Arcite', Fables
Ancient and Modern (1700), Book III, 230–32.

8   'Whose service is perfect freedom': From the Collect for the
Morning Prayer in the Anglican Book of Common Prayer. The
phrase refers to God, not reason: 'O God, who art the author of
peace and lover of concord, in knowledge of whom standeth our
eternal life, whose service is perfect freedom.'

CHAP. VII
MODESTY

1   General Washington . . . command of the American forces:
George Washington (1732–99) took command of the Continen-
tal Army in 1775. In the gruelling war that lasted 8½ years, he
proved a daring and courageous leader of poorly trained and
equipped troops.

2   Moses was humble, and Peter vain: In the biblical account of the
deliverance of the ancient Hebrews from bondage in Egypt, Moses
is fearful of undertaking God's command that he lead his people
to freedom, and protesting that he is not eloquent enough to
plead before Pharaoh, he says: 'O my Lord, send, I pray thee',
some other person (Exodus 4: 13). Wollstonecraft may be referring to the Anglican denial of the Roman Catholic teaching that
Peter, as first among the disciples, was given authority over the
established church (Matthew 16:18–19).

3   'Such is . . . Gay: John Gay (1685–1732), poet and dramatist,
Fable XIII, 'The Tame Stag' (London, 1727), ll. 27–36.

4   'The lady . . . They cannot': John Berkenhout, A Volume of
Letters from Doctor Berkenhout to his Son at the University
(1790). Wollstonecraft's objection echoes an unidentified
reviewer in the Analytical Review, to which she was often a
contributor (1 (January 1791), p. 160).

5   pharisaical cloak: Referring to strict religious observance of external forms with indifference to matters of the spirit. The 'Pharisees'
were a Jewish sect that flourished during the first century BC and
first century AD, and were opposed to the ministry of Jesus. See
also p. 168 and Chap. VIII, note 6.

6   'Can any . . . resisting temptation': Knox, Essays (Moral and
Literary), I, xxxiv. He says: 'it is not to be wondered at, if they
who know not how to be wives and mothers are soon degraded
to the rank of harlots' (p. 176).

7   *Essenes*: A Palestinian sect (second–third century BC) noted for celibacy and ascetism. Wollstonecraft probably refers to their careful adherence to rituals for washing.

8   *jokes and hoiden tricks ... in my youth*: Wollstonecraft spent her youth in the Yorkshire market-town of Beverley, where her father's position, although economically uncertain, would have accorded her the status of gentry. In her girlhood correspondence with Jane Arden, her sensitivity to the slights of friends, real and imagined, is painfully clear (*Collected Letters*, ed. Todd, 2003, nos. 4–6).

9   *Diana ... goddess of chastity*: Roman virgin goddess of the moon and hunt, protector of women.

10 *Temple of the living God*: From 2 Corinthians 6:16: '... what agreement hath the temple of God with idols? for ye are the temple of the living God.'

CHAP. VIII
MORALITY UNDERMINED BY SEXUAL NOTIONS OF THE IMPORTANCE OF A GOOD REPUTATION

1   *chameleon's food*: The chameleon is so sedentary in position, a commonplace sentiment believed he lived without nourishment.

2   *lull their Argus to sleep*: A giant with one hundred eyes, some of which were always awake, guarded Ito, loved by Zeus and transformed by him from a woman to a cow to conceal her from his wife's jealousy.

3   *equally faithless ... from heaven knows where*: Refers to the widespread concern that the frequent infidelity of an infant's parents, leading to sexual disease, might poison the baby in the womb. See also p. 173.

4   *'that reputation is no less ... among women'*: Rousseau, *Émile*, V, 325, 328.

5   *'That by some very extraordinary ... strong presumptions'*: Smith, *The Theory of Moral Sentiments*, III.i.iii, 215–16.

6   *Pharisees ... to be seen of men*: See Matthew 6:5: 'And when thou prayest, thou shalt not be as the hypocrites are: for they love to pray standing in the synagogues and in the corners of the streets, that they may be seen of men.'

7   *Boswell's Life of Johnson*: James Boswell's intimate record (1791) of his friendship with the renowned literary lion records Johnson's eccentricities and aversions, as well as his loyalty and kindness. Wollstonecraft was taken to meet the ageing Johnson while she

was a teacher at Newington Green, and he apparently encouraged her as a writer.

8   *Lucretia*: According to legend, the Roman matron Lucretia killed herself after obtaining the promise of her husband and father that they would avenge her rape by the son of King Sextus Tarquinius. Her suicide led to the expulsions of the Tarquins and the establishment of the Roman republic.

9   *Java tree*: The juice of the fruit of the java plum tree (*Eugenia jambolana*), a harmless diuretic and antidiabetic, had been considered poisonous in the eighteenth century.

10 *serpent's egg*: See Shakespeare, *Julius Caesar* (1599), II.i.32: 'And therefore think him as a serpent's egg, which, hatch'd, would, as his kind, grow mischievous.'

11 *Smith*: Smith, *The Theory of Moral Sentiments*, I.III.ii, 74.

12 *'there is but one fault . . . own sex'*: Catherine Macaulay, *Letters on Education* (London, 1790), pp. 210, 212.

13 *Something more soft than woman*: Refers to homosexuals.

14 *exposing the children whom their parents could not maintain*: In ancient Greek society, infanticide, particularly of female newborns, was widely practised; the decision to rear a baby was left to the male, who was also believed to be solely responsible for conception. In ancient Rome, a law attributed to Romulus required a father to raise all male children, but only the first-born female.

CHAP. IX

OF THE PERNICIOUS EFFECTS WHICH ARISE
FROM THE UNNATURAL DISTINCTIONS
ESTABLISHED IN SOCIETY

1   *his child suckled by its mother*: Wollstonecraft would have been influenced by Rousseau's advocacy of breastfeeding in *Émile*, I, 5–15. He angrily berates French women of fashion for using a wet nurse instead of nursing their own babies (see p. 219 and Chap. XII, note 11.

2   *Washington . . . returned to his farm*: After two terms as the first president of the United States, Washington returned in retirement to extensive landholdings in Virginia at his Mt Vernon plantation (where the ploughing was done by slaves).

3   *Faro Bank*: A popular eighteenth-century card game played on a board for money, the derivation of the name possibly from 'pharaoh', the designation of the king of hearts in the game.

4   *bowels*: Compassion.

5   *the milk of human kindness . . . Cerberus*: From *Macbeth*, I.v.17:
    '. . . yet I do fear thy nature/It is too full o' the milk of human
    kindness.' Cerberus is the guard dog at the entrance of Hades, a
    monster with three heads and a serpent's tail.

6   *the poor African slaves*: In the eighteenth century, the English
    were heavily involved in the African slave trade, which provoked
    the outrage of William Wilberforce (1759–1833) who succeeded
    in having the trade abolished in Britain and its colonies in
    1833.

7   *The laws . . . she is reduced to a mere cypher*: Refers to William
    Blackstone's (1723–80) *Commentaries* on English common law
    (1765–9) by which a woman's legal existence was suspended and
    subsumed by her husband. See also pp. 184, 229.

8   *leave the nursery for the camp*: Rousseau writes: '. . . can a woman
    suddenly change her way of life without danger? Can she be a
    nursing mother today and a soldier tomorrow?' (*Émile*, V, 325).

9   *the bayonet converted into a pruning-hook*: See Isaiah 2:4: 'and
    they shall beat their swords into plowshares, and their spears into
    pruninghooks'.

10 *the whole system of representation is now*: The suffrage in the
    1790s was severely restricted and biased in favour of the rural
    counties. Among the disenfranchised men were many middle-
    class professionals and merchants, most of whom would be
    enfranchised in the Great Reform Bill of 1832. Disenfranchised
    as well were craftsmen and labourers, most of whom received the
    vote in 1867. (Women in England won the right to vote in 1927.)

11 *Whitehall*: The symbolic centre of the English government, White-
    hall Palace was once the chief residence of English monarchs in
    London. It sits on the main thoroughfare between Trafalgar
    Square and the Houses of Parliament.

12 *to suckle fools and chronicle small beer*: Iago's ironic prophecy
    of the fate of deserving women (*Othello* (1604), II.i.160).

13 *accoucheur*: A man who assists at childbirth. Wollstonecraft's
    preference for a midwife was honoured by her husband William
    Godwin at the birth of their daughter Mary.

14 *'that shape hath none'*: From Milton, *Paradise Lost*, II.666–8:
    '. . . the other shape/If shape it might be call'd that shape had
    none/Distinguishable in member . . .'

15 *mantua-makers*: Dressmakers (a 'mantua' was a loose gown).

16 *the humiliating situation which necessity sometimes forces them
    to fill*: In letters to her sisters from Ireland, Wollstonecraft recorded

her unhappiness as a governness being subjected to the condescension and patronage of her employers (see, for example, letter to Everina Wollstonecraft, *Collected Letters*, ed. Todd, no. 52).

17   '*the lily broken down by a plow-share*': In Fénelon's *Télémaque*, to honour a vow made to the gods, Ideomenous is compelled to slay his own son: 'As a fair lily in the field, cut from the root by the keen trenchant plow, languishes . . .' (*Telemachus, Son of Ulysses*, ed. and trans. Patrick Riley (Cambridge: Cambridge University Press, 1994), Book V, p. 63).

CHAP. X
PARENTAL AFFECTION

1   '*assurance doubly sure*': See *Macbeth*, IV.i.83: 'But yet I'll make assurance double sure . . .'

2   *L'amour propre. L'amour de soi même*: See Rousseau's *Discourse on the Origin of Inequality*, p. 223, n. 2: 'Egoism ("amour de soi meme") must not be confused with self-respect ("amour propre") for they differ both in themselves and in their effects. Self-respect is a natural feeling which leads every animal to look to its own preservation and which, guided in man by reason and modified by compassion, creates humanity and virtue. Egoism is a purely relative and factitious feeling, which arises in the state of society, leads each individual to make more of himself than of any other, causes all the mutual damage men inflict one on another, and is the real source of the "sense of honour".'

3   *Rebekah's*: Rebekah, wife of the patriarch Isaac, helps her son Jacob attain his father's deathbed blessing by deceit, preventing the elder son Esau from receiving what was his by birthright (Genesis 27:1–30).

CHAP. XI
DUTY TO PARENTS

1   *Dr Johnson makes the same observation*: In the *Rambler*, 'The Cruelty of Parental Tyranny', essay no. 148 (17 August 1751), Johnson describes a natural reciprocity reinforcing affectionate ties between parents and offspring: 'We naturally endear to ourselves those to whom we impart any kind of pleasure, because we imagine their affection and esteem secured to us by the benefits which they receive.'

2   '*if the mind . . . and industry*': Locke, *Some Thoughts Concerning Education* (1690), XLVI. 2.

3   *girls . . . are more kept down by their parents*: In her autobio-

graphical fiction, Wollstonecraft recorded her resentment at the preference she believed her parents accorded her older brother Edward. See *The Wrongs of Woman or Maria, A Fragment* (1796), ed. Gary Kelly (London: Oxford University Press, 1976), I, 125.

CHAP. XII
ON NATIONAL EDUCATION

1   *usher*: A subordinate teacher, or assistant in a school. Wollstonecraft's impressions of English public school education were derived from her visit to Eton in 1786, and later shared by the biographer and critic Lytton Strachey (1880–1932). Writing in *Eminent Victorians* (1918) about Rugby School and its headmaster Dr Thomas Arnold, Strachey describes English elite education at the time Wollstonecraft wrote as 'virgin forests untouched by the hand of reform', 'a system of anarchy tempered by despotism' (London: Continuum, 2002), p. 186.

2   *vices . . . delicacy of mind*: Masturbation was widely believed to weaken body and mind.

3   *France*: Many late-eighteenth-century English intellectuals like Wollstonecraft regarded France as the home of 'enlightened ideas', i.e. that the light of reason would dispel the superstition and unreason of the Dark Ages.

4   *pamphlet, written by the late bishop of Autun*: Talleyrand, *Rapport sur l'instruction publique, fait au nom du Comite de constitution* (1791).

5   *coxcomb*: A foolish and pretentious dandy.

6   *market penny . . . Juno's angry brow*: An additional profit made by one person who buys for another. Juno, Roman goddess and wife of Jupiter, jealously exacted revenge upon the unfortunate mortals whom her husband loved.

7   *Macbeth's heart smote . . . necessary to back it*: After slaying Duncan the King, Macbeth is assailed by his own terrible guilt (II.i). He subsequently arranges the murder of Banquo and the wife, children and servants of Macduff.

8   *she who takes her dogs to bed . . . crooked in a nursery*: Wollstonecraft wrote dismissively of Lady Kingsborough to her sister Everina: 'I have not seen much of her as she is confined to her room by a sore thoart [*sic*] – but I have seen half dozen of her companions – I mean not her children, but her dogs' (*Collected Letters*, ed. Todd, no. 40).

9   *that fool Theresa . . . ceased to have an affection for him*: Rous-

seau's longtime mistress Thérèse Levasseur (1721–1801) had little education. Rousseau wrote in the *Confessions*: 'her mind is as Nature made it; culture and teaching have no effect on it' (II.vii, 311). He reported her disinclination: 'She persisted in her attachment to me, but it was out of duty, not out of love' (II.xii, 549).

10 *the Greek courtezans*: The Greek 'hetairai' or 'companions to men' were at the top of the social scale among prostitutes. Many had intellectual training and artistic talent.

11 *deviated . . . in their mode of treating their infants*: Refers to the practice of mothers' choosing to nurse their own infants: see also Chap. IX, note 1.

12 *that moloch prejudice*: Of uncertain origin, the worship of Moloch among ancient Israelites included the sacrifice of children. Wollstonecraft's usage suggests any object of worship that requires inordinate sacrifice.

13 *the sins of its fathers*: See Exodus 20:5: 'I the Lord thy God am a jealous God, visiting the iniquity of the fathers upon the children unto the third and fourth generation of them that hate me.' See also Chap. VIII, note 3.

14 *the bills of mortality*: Death notices published in every London parish.

CHAP. XIII
SOME INSTANCES OF THE FOLLY WHICH THE IGNORANCE OF WOMEN GENERATES

1 *to cast nativities*: Horoscopes read on the basis of a birthdate.

2 *magnetisers*: Dating back to ancient Greeks, practitioners used magnets to promote general healing. In the late 1700s the Viennese physician Franz Anton Mesmer (1733–1815) popularized a practice called 'animal magnetism' in which a patient swallowed a solution containing traces of iron, after which magnets were attached to the body stimulating an invisible electric energy or fluid in the body that was supposed to produce a cure.

3 *regimen*: A friend and physician to Samuel Richardson, Scottish physician Dr George Cheyne (1671–1743) popularized the idea of the treatment of diseases of nervous sensibility through a 'regimen' or a system of diet, exercise, purging and bodily management. See his *Essay on Health and Long Life* (1725).

4 *Be whole, and sin no more*: See John 5:14: 'Behold, thou art made whole: sin no more . . .'

5 *the Indians worship the devil*: Perhaps refers to the Hindu Great

Goddess Kali, usually represented with black skin, a protruding bright red tongue, and her many arms raised as if in constant motion. She wears a necklace of decapitated heads on her naked chest and a skirt of severed arms. Interpretation of Kali's worship suggests her regenerative and redemptive association with a death-defying female force.

6   *the stupid novelists*: Wollstonecraft draws upon a familiar criticism of the novel as light entertainment for women. In the course of the eighteenth century, popular romances and short novellas, made possible by widespread increases in literacy and the development of print culture, were thought to be consumed largely by women.

7   *the art of pleasing consists in ornaments*: 'Is it our fault,' asks Rousseau of women, 'if we love to see them prettily dressed, if we let them display at leisure the weapons by which we are subjugated?' (*Émile*, V, 327).

8   '*how naturally do women . . . ruffles*': Swift's 'A Letter to a very young Lady on her Marriage' (1722): 'And when you are among yourselves, how naturally, after the first Compliments, do you apply your Hands to each others Lappets and Ruffles . . .'

9   '*Matter too . . . or fair*': The preceding lines in Pope's 'Epistle II. To a Lady': 'Nothing so true as what you once let fall/"Most Women have no Characters at all"' (II.3–4).

10 '*that women have seldom so much generosity as men*': See Smith, *The Theory of Moral Sentiments*, IV.i.ii, 256: 'Humanity is the virtue of a woman, generosity of a man. The fair sex, who have commonly much more tenderness than ours, have seldom so much generosity.'

11 *Cato's most unjust love for his country*: Marcus Porcius Cato (Cato the elder) (234–149 BC), Roman statesman and spokesman for conservative Roman landholders during the early Republican period, believed that Rome must be safeguarded against the influence of Carthaginian luxury and indulgence. He ended his senate speeches with the familiar epigram 'Et memento – delenda est carthgo' ('And remember – Carthage must be destroyed').

12 *we should seldom see a houseful of babes*: Wollstonecraft passes on the commonplace and unreliable assumption that a nursing mother is rendered temporarily infertile.

13 *dissenters*: While only seven per cent of the population in late-eighteenth-century Britain, Dissenters (Presbyterians, Congregationalists, Baptists, Unitarians and Quakers) were at the forefront of scientific innovation and political reform. Wollstone-

craft met members of the dissenting community in Newington Green.

14   *Butler's caricature*: In *Hudibras*, the principal character is a Presbyterian knight so steeped in scholastic learning that he fails to understand commonplaces in everyday life.

THE STORY OF PENGUIN CLASSICS

Before 1946 . . . "Classics" are mainly the domain of academics and students; readable editions for everyone else are almost unheard of. This all changes when a little-known classicist, E. V. Rieu, presents Penguin founder Allen Lane with the translation of Homer's *Odyssey* that he has been working on in his spare time.

1946 Penguin Classics debuts with *The Odyssey*, which promptly sells three million copies. Suddenly, classics are no longer for the privileged few.

1950s Rieu, now series editor, turns to professional writers for the best modern, readable translations, including Dorothy L. Sayers's *Inferno* and Robert Graves's unexpurgated *Twelve Caesars*.

1960s The Classics are given the distinctive black covers that have remained a constant throughout the life of the series. Rieu retires in 1964, hailing the Penguin Classics list as "the greatest educative force of the twentieth century."

1970s A new generation of translators swells the Penguin Classics ranks, introducing readers of English to classics of world literature from more than twenty languages. The list grows to encompass more history, philosophy, science, religion, and politics.

1980s The Penguin American Library launches with titles such as *Uncle Tom's Cabin* and joins forces with Penguin Classics to provide the most comprehensive library of world literature available from any paperback publisher.

1990s The launch of Penguin Audiobooks brings the classics to a listening audience for the first time, and in 1999 the worldwide launch of the Penguin Classics Web site extends their reach to the global online community.

The 21st Century Penguin Classics are completely redesigned for the first time in nearly twenty years. This world-famous series now consists of more than 1,300 titles, making the widest range of the best books ever written available to millions—and constantly redefining what makes a "classic."

The Odyssey continues . . .

The best books ever written

PENGUIN (🐧) CLASSICS

SINCE 1946

Find out more at www.penguinclassics.com